Chasing Rainbows — The stolen
future of Caroline Ann Stuttle

Richard Stuttle

Chasing Rainbows — The stolen future of Caroline Ann Stuttle

Pegasus

PEGASUS PAPERBACK

© Copyright 2021
Richard Stuttle

ISBN-978 1 910903 54 4

Pegasus is an imprint of
Pegasus Elliot MacKenzie Publishers Ltd.
www.pegasuspublishers.com

First Published in 2021

Pegasus
Sheraton House Castle Park
Cambridge CB3 0AX England

Printed & Bound in Great Britain

Dedication

For my sister, Caroline, may you live forever in our hearts and minds.
All my love, Richard.

Contents

Introduction

In 2002, our family received the worst news possible. The headline in the newspaper read 'English backpacker thrown to her death in Australia'.

I used to start every adventure feeling excited and looking forward to what was going to happen. The murder of Caroline Ann Stuttle has made me completely rethink travel and what's important in life. I'm Caroline's brother, Richard, and over the years many people have said, 'I don't know how you go on; I don't think I could cope.' The truth is we had no choice.

If you had met Caroline, you would have undoubtedly been impressed. She was an intelligent and confident young lady who you could tell was going places. To engage in conversation could be dangerous as she was a powerhouse of chat, the speed her mind worked could sometimes leave you breathless. To fully tell Caroline's story, it's important to understand who she was as a person and her outlook on life. It's not her murder that defined her or the charity set up in her name, but the effect she had on people.

What happened just wasn't fair. At 19 my sister was just getting started in life. Some degenerated individual in Australia ended it, without a second thought as to the consequences of his actions. "Smashed off me face," he said to the police as he sat in an interview room.

On April 10th 2002 our lives completely changed forever, any aspirations we had before that day immediately evaporated into the ether. We found ourselves on a completely different road that no one could have predicted.

My hope is that readers are able to understand the impact Caroline's murder had on our family, her friends and people around the world.

Ultimately, I believe this is a positive story. It's a journey spanning 19 years highlighting how passion and love for one young lady inspired people to build something special for themselves and others from tragic foundations.

Chapter 1
The call that changed our world

It was the end of another amazing winter season in Meribel, my third in The Three Valleys. I'd first visited in 1999; it was now April 2002. I'd been working as a chef, alongside a host, and ski guide, running a chalet for eighteen guests. It was hard work and it felt like it had been a long season. The snow had turned, making it very wet and slushy; the lower runs were muddy and, in many places, unpassable. I had packed up my knives and we shut down the chalet. Our boss was happy, and we had all finally finished work.

I loved Meribel. It ticked all the boxes: stunning surroundings, wonderful snowboarding, like-minded people and cooking for a living. It was a completely different lifestyle to anything I had done before. My picturesque five-month escape from everything that was really happening in the world. The beauty of the French Alps was completely inspiring, and I enjoyed the instant connection between seasonaires (people working during the ski season). We all worked the winters out of choice, everyone had a deep-rooted passion for the mountains and a love for extreme winter sports.

This season was no exception. Some of my best days were spent riding around the mountain with friends and hitting the snowboard parks. Once we had our fix for the day, we would jump on the final lift of the day up to the top of the Saulire, which was one of the main summits in Meribel. We would ride down the short distance to a place we called The Hut; the views were breath-taking. We could see for miles in every direction, straight down the valley to Moutier or over towards Saint Martin and Les Menuires. To our left was Mont Vallon, with the peaks of Val Thorens far beyond. The Hut was a happy place for many seasonaires. We used to chat about the day and watch the last few people making their way down the piste, like ants following each other trying to find their way home. We'd enjoy the changing colours of the mountains as the sun slowly made its way towards the jagged

13

horizon. It felt like paradise. When we saw the ski patrol riding down, it was our cue to move. I always enjoyed the final run, before either heading back to get ready for work or calling in to the Rond Point, a bar just off the piste, for après-ski.

Though the season was over, I was in no rush to return to reality. I was looking forward to a few quiet days relaxing before driving down to the south of France, where landscape painting and time on the beach awaited. Painting was in my genes thanks to my father who is an artist. My watercolours and oil paints were ready and I was looking forward to painting the wonderful colours and landscapes of the Côte d'Azur.

I was craving the sea, especially after five months in the mountains, and I yearned for sand between my toes and the smell of fresh salty air. This love stems back to my childhood, family days out at the seaside and holidays abroad. My sister Caroline and I would spend many hours building sandcastles on the beach and splashing around in the sea. It was always a magical place for us. Every time I sank my feet into warm soft sand and closed my eyes something was triggered inside; it took me back to those special memories and put a smile on my face.

A lot of friends had already started to leave the resort, some going home, others onwards for their next adventure. It was exciting but at the same time sad to say goodbye, although I knew many of them would be back next year. Life was good and chefs were always in demand. It was one of the reasons why I got into hospitality, restaurants and hotels were always looking for decent chefs, I could get a job anywhere.

The end of the season was a time of contemplation, I was thinking a lot about what the rest of my twenties was going to bring: travel, different experiences and finding out what I actually wanted to do with my life.

It was 4:30 a.m. when my mobile rang. I was in bed, but answered. No one I recognised, their voice hesitant.

"Mr Stuttle?"

"Yes?" I replied, snapping out of my sleepy haze.

"I am from the police and I am afraid I have some bad news."

A thousand thoughts flooded through my mind in that split second, but even if I had another 614,962,476 seconds to guess what he was about to tell me, I would never have got it. At the time, my naive mind knew bad things happened in this world, but never to us or to people we knew.

"It's about your sister, Caroline." His voice was now solid and very serious.

Caroline was on a gap year in Australia with one of her best friends. What had the kid got herself into now? Probably arrested for something stupid or ran out of money.

The officer continued, "I'm so sorry to have to tell you this, but Caroline has been involved in an incident and she is dead."

I sat bolt upright. Surely, I wasn't understanding this correctly. "Are you joking? What the hell are you talking about?"

"There has been a serious situation in Australia, and I am so sorry to have to tell you. She has lost her life. I am here with your mother, Marjorie."

I could hear uncontrollable sobbing in the background, which sounded like my mother, but I had never heard anything like it before. In those few moments my whole world shattered, and our lives were changed forever.

"We are here at your home. Please don't worry, we will make sure we do everything we can for your mother. One of my colleagues is with your father in Scarborough."

"I don't understand. What's happened to Caroline in Australia?" I asked.

"I am afraid I don't have many details at the moment. All I know is that there has been an incident on a bridge, Caroline has gone over the railings and unfortunately lost her life. Her friend Sarah is safe and with the police in Bundaberg."

"OK, I will be home as soon as I can."

Hanging up the phone, I just stared at it. I had no idea what to do with myself, no idea what to think. I was stuck in a French ski resort and it was still the middle of the night. Absolutely nothing I could do until morning. I felt completely powerless.

After a few moments my mind caught up, still trying to process the conversation. There was no way this could be true. What the hell had just happened? I slumped down on the edge of the bed, numb and in complete disbelief. I couldn't feel anything. Looking down at my fingers, they had no sense of touch, nothing felt real. I couldn't comprehend what I had just heard. I felt lightheaded and burst into tears.

Just a few hours ago, before I went to bed, the last five months had been some of the best times of my life, but now they meant absolutely nothing.

A feeling of shock took over my body, I took some deep breaths and tried to steady myself. Standing up, I paced the room and kept repeating, "What the… has just happened? What was she doing on a bridge, how the hell has she gone over the railings? I can't believe this. Caroline is dead? She can't be dead."

Hands shaking, I rolled a cigarette and smoked it until it burnt my fingers. It sent my head spinning and my thoughts were immediately with Mum and Dad. What the hell were they going through? Surely none of this can be true. I had no idea what was going on, no details, no way of finding out any more information and no way of being with my family.

In those life-changing few moments, a piece of my heart had been ripped out and I knew could never be replaced. If you break a china pot, it's possible to piece it back together but you will always know it's been broken even if you can't see the joins.

At that time, I was relatively innocent to grief and loss, seeing but not truly understanding the cruelty and pain death can bring. Up until that point, 1985 had been the worst year of my life with both my grandfathers and my uncle dying. I was eight years old and took it very badly. I remember crying and being comforted by Mum as she tried to explain, they were old and had enjoyed a full life. Over time, I was able to come to terms with it, although I still felt that childhood sadness sometimes. This was completely different, something I knew instantly that I would never get over no matter how much time passed. Caroline was just a girl with her whole life ahead of her; she was my little sister.

I had no Internet access. I was completely cut off from the outside world; originally that had been part of the appeal. I stood on the balcony, looking out at the silhouette of the mountains. It was deadly quiet. There were still a couple of hours to go before the sun would break the horizon. I felt like nothing was real any more; I was in limbo with only time to think.

I just couldn't believe she was dead; how could she be? She was a strong and feisty young lady. How could she have been taken away from us?

I replayed the phone call in my head, "I'm so sorry to have to tell you this, but Caroline has been involved in an incident and she is dead." This couldn't be right, maybe the officer might have meant something else, he might have been mistaken? It could have been some other poor girl; deep down though, I knew it was true.

Chain-smoking cigarettes, I thought about our lives as brother and sister. I always believed we had been brought up the right way, loving parents, a traditional family with a normal life. Never wanting for much, we took pleasure in the simple things. We didn't deserve this happening to us. I now realised, just like in the rest of life, 'deserve' has nothing to do with it. I always thought of our childhood as special, we were lucky as a family. Living in Huntington, York, our primary and secondary schools were both within walking distance and many of our friends lived just around the corner.

Mum and Dad had always pushed us to be active; Caroline was a member of the local gymnastics club and I thought she was really good at it. Mum and I would go to pick her up and watch as she effortlessly jumped and span around the floor. We both loved swimming and would go to the pool a few times a week for training. When we went on holiday, we were water babies and loved snorkelling in the sea or splashing around in the pool. These memories all came flooding back like an incoherent movie playing in my mind at double speed. My emotions were all over the place. I didn't know what I should be feeling and couldn't work out what I was actually feeling.

I remembered our lives growing up. Dad was an artist by profession and loved showing us different animals and insects that lived in our garden. Butterflies were our favourite. The life cycle from caterpillar to chrysalis to butterfly was extraordinary and fascinated the pair of us. I remember Caroline and I being amazed by how this transformation took place and we desperately wanted to see a butterfly emerging from a chrysalis. Dad in all his years had never seen it happen. One day, Caroline came running into the kitchen. "Dad, Dad, I've seen it." We rushed outside and saw a red admiral butterfly sat flexing his wings on its empty chrysalis.

She was always the lucky one, so I just couldn't understand it. Why hadn't she been lucky this time? All the scrapes I had gotten into over the years and I was still here. It just wasn't fair.

She had such a caring nature which she got from Mum, who'd been a nanny in her early career. I had never met anyone who gave so much love so willingly to everyone she met. Sometimes we could both be very naughty, but for us it was of course always unconditional love, no matter what we did. Sometimes Caroline would go and see Grandma for dinner and chat incessantly about everything that happened at school and with her friends. They both loved spending time together and Grandma used to joke, "I love Caroline, but she has worn my ears out and I need a rest after every visit."

Sundays were always our family day. Mum used to cook the best Sunday roasts with all the trimmings, apart from the beef, which was always overcooked. I never realised at the time but when I trained as a chef I understood, medium rare and well rested. That's how beef should be cooked and that was the end of it. It became a long running family joke.

Grandma, Grandad, my aunties and uncle all lived locally. Dad would go to work in the morning but was always back in time for lunch. We would eat early afternoon and catch up with the week's news, Caroline always liked to be centre of attention and would tell us everything that she had been up to in excruciating detail. After lunch, and fully stuffed, the older family members would have a little rest and could be heard snoring in the living room. As Mum always managed to use every pan, bowl and plate in our kitchen, it always looked like a bombsite. It was mine and Caroline's job to wash up. A worthy trade as Mum's food was amazing, despite the beef. We would do it together, we were a team, and the kitchen would always be spotless after we had finished.

Still waiting for the sun to rise above the mountains, I remembered these times, it pulled on my stomach and made me feel physically sick. Of course, we weren't perfect and like most brothers and sisters when we were younger, we sometimes fought like cat and dog. Deep down we always loved each other dearly. My head was spinning, tears brought me back to reality as they streamed down my face. I needed another cigarette. There was still an hour to go before anyone would be awake.

Taking a long drag, I thought about how over the last few years we had become great friends. When I was in the UK, we would regularly meet in York for coffee and were never lost for conversation; we could talk to each other about anything. I would give her advice like a good big brother should. It was one of Caroline's big dreams to go travelling and I remember when she and Sarah were planning their Australian adventure. She was so excited and had been organising everything for months down to every last detail. When we discussed all the things she was going to do, her face would light up. She could hardly contain herself and looked so alive. Why didn't I talk more about staying safe instead of just making jokes about how the hell was she going to manage without her hair straighteners? I am sure I said, "Be careful, make sure you look after yourself and each other." I now felt it was nowhere near enough, but Australia was considered a safe place to visit.

I would have done anything to have had one more coffee with her. I loved her so much and kept getting flashes in my mind of the moments we shared. Once I accidentally trapped her fingers in the car door and never properly apologised. I was only a kid, but it haunted me now that I could never say sorry or apologise for anything I had ever done. She was gone. It hit me again like an avalanche, she was dead. We wouldn't share anything again in this world… ever.

Chapter 2
Going home

It seemed like an absolute eternity, but morning finally arrived and I was on the phone to my boss. I didn't really think about what I was going to say and just blurted out, "I need to go home now. I had a call in the night and my sister is dead. Can you please help me?"

I was booked on the earliest flight available, one of the senior staff had kindly offered to drive me to the airport. There was time to see a couple of friends and let them know what was happening, no one could believe it. I tried to stay strong but needed a hug.

I left my car in the resort, threw in my snowboard gear, paints and pictures, and stuffed the keys in my pocket. The season was well and truly over. The only thing that mattered now was getting home.

Driving down the twenty-one hairpin turns and past Moutier, I remember looking out at the mountains in desperation. Everything looked strangely different. I would never have thought five months ago, when I was so excited about the season, I would be leaving Meribel like this. My heart was breaking more with every mile; the closer we got to Geneva, the closer I felt to the reality of our situation. I thought of Mum and Dad, they wouldn't have slept either. Mum was still in our family home in York, Dad lived in Scarborough.

When we arrived, I headed straight to a public computer and typed in 'Caroline Stuttle', hitting return. I didn't really expect anything to come up but there it was: top story by *The Independent* and *Guardian,* they both led with, 'British Backpacker Thrown to her Death.'

York Press
York backpacker found murdered
A YORK teenager has been found murdered under a bridge in Queensland, Australia.

Former York College student Caroline Ann Stuttle, 19, who was on a backpacking holiday in the town of Bundaberg, may have been robbed and thrown from the structure, detectives said.

Caroline's mother, Marjorie, was today trying to come to terms with the news at her home in Huntington Road, York.

She was too upset, to talk about her daughter's death, but family friend David Marks told the Evening Press today: "She is very upset. She has got close friends and relatives comforting her at this time."

Caroline's father, Alan, runs an art gallery in York and lives in Scarborough. Queensland Police said Caroline had walked over a bridge from a caravan park in Bundaberg yesterday to telephone a friend in the UK from a public phone.

At 9.15pm, she called her travelling companion on a mobile phone to say she was on her way back to the site.

Police then received an anonymous call 15 minutes later reporting screams from the bridge.

Detective Oliphant said: "An examination of the scene found the victim's thongs (sandals) on the ground on the opposite side of the bridge to where Miss Stuttle was found."

Police in Australia are trying to trace three young men, who were believed to have been in the area at the time of the attack.

A spokeswoman for York College said everyone was "visibly shocked" by the news.

Caroline, who left the college last summer, studied psychology, English and History A-levels.

In the middle of Geneva airport, I felt my legs giving way as I became overwhelmed with emotion. The people around me were just white noise. There were so many questions going through my mind, it felt as though I was on another planet. It wasn't the same place where I had spent the last twenty-five years. What was Caroline doing? Who has done this to my sister? Why has this happened? I needed to take in the information properly and read the reports again. Wait a minute, family friend David Marks? Who the hell was this guy? I hadn't met him or even heard of him.

I was even more confused. I checked in and went through passport control. Before the flight I made a call home. The police answered and passed me over to Mum. I tried to reassure her, but I was talking through floods of tears and didn't know if she even heard me. "I am about to get on the plane and will be home soon. Love you."

Mum was in complete despair. There was nothing either of us could do, we were both utterly helpless. The police told me David Marks was coming to pick me up. They didn't know I had no idea who he was. As far as they were concerned, he was a close family friend. I didn't argue or even ask about the man who would later become my stepfather. It felt like the world was caving in around me and I had lost every shred of confidence. The wait seemed eternal and the flight took forever. In my head I kept repeating, 'My sister is gone. My sister is dead'. Deep down my heart knew the truth, but my head still couldn't comprehend it. I didn't want to imagine life without her. We were part of each other; our bond was unique and supposed to last a lifetime.

Stepping foot on UK soil normally felt so good. Not this time. Everything was heavier and each step took far more effort. I felt scared like never before, like a lost child not knowing which way to turn. Walking through the arrivals gate at John Lennon Airport in Liverpool, it felt like everyone was looking at me. I had no idea who I was looking for, so focused on different faces. They all looked through me, waiting in anticipation for their own loved ones to return.

I caught sight of a man walking towards me, as though he recognised me. He was stocky and well-dressed in a light-coloured suit and tie. This must be David. We greeted each other with a firm handshake. He offered his sympathies, saying he couldn't imagine what I was going through and would get me home as quickly as possible. We walked out together, he offered me a cigarette, which I took, and I thanked him for coming to pick me up. He drove a black Jaguar XKR. I had never been in a sports car before, and under normal circumstances I would have been excited, but not this time. I was still feeling completely disoriented.

David and I talked. It wasn't awkward, but it was an absolutely horrendous situation for us both to be in. I wanted to know everything and to find out how he knew our family. He told me he had been introduced to Mum by a mutual friend, Wendy, and that only yesterday they were sitting having lunch in York on their first meeting. Later we found out it was the exact same time Caroline had lost her life in Australia.

As soon as he heard the news this morning, he had gone around to our house to see if he could help. He offered to pick me up and speak to the media. We needed to make a statement and Mum wasn't in a fit state. I told him of my confusion reading his name on a computer screen in Geneva and pressed him for more information.

From my first meeting with David, I had the utmost respect for the man. He didn't have to drive over and pick me up, he didn't have to come around to our home and help our family, but he did. Months later, when Mum would talk about their meeting, she would say an angel was taken from our lives and one was sent to look after us. She wouldn't have coped without him, his love and support. He has been her rock and stood by her ever since.

It was late afternoon when we arrived in York. I have never seen such devastation as when I walked through the front door of our family home. I could hear uncontrollable sobbing. Pushing past a blur of faces, I saw Mum sat in our living room surrounded by tissues in her old tracksuit. Her eyes were completely bloodshot, and her nose was red raw. In that moment, I knew her heart was broken and that she would never fully recover. It destroyed me even more, if that was at all possible. We sat and hugged for the longest time, she couldn't speak and we both wept on each other's shoulders. There was nothing either of us could do. We rocked backwards and forwards. Mum kept asking me, "Why? Why Caroline?" I had no answers. All I could do was rub her back and try to console her.

After a time, when we had caught our breath, I asked, "Where's Grandma? Have you been to see her?"

Grandma had spent a lot of time with Caroline, when she was growing up, and had taught her how to be respectful and kind. I knew she was very proud of what Caroline was doing and the confident young lady she had become. They talked a lot together about her backpacking adventure and going to university when she returned.

Mum said through her tears that she had rushed around first thing this morning before Grandma could see the story on the news. She lived by herself and was always up with the birds. Understandably, Mum wanted to tell her. Grandma was absolutely devastated; her beloved granddaughter had gone. She didn't want to be around people, she needed quiet time, it was all too much for her. She had said, "Why not me at the end of life? Why Caroline? She had so much to offer."

Mum stayed with her for a while but had to come back home. Her close friends were already on the doorstep offering their sympathies and willing to help in any way they could. The police were also there for support and to make sure we were protected.

When she was calmer, I left Mum for a short time to call Dad from the house phone. He was in Scarborough, his partner Janet had travelled over from Birmingham to be with him. Speaking to him was very emotional, but there was nothing we could say that would make any of it any better. He was in no fit state to leave the house. The worst thing that could ever happen, had happened. Dad and Caroline had a special bond and were very much the same kind of people.

I needed some time to collect my thoughts. My eyes were red and sore. Everything felt so surreal. I walked out into our garden. It brought back everything our family home used to be; a place where we had taken our first steps, grown up together, learnt to ride bikes, told our first jokes and laughed as a family. There were five years between Caroline and I, so I was always overprotective. All the times we played as kids in the garden flashed haphazardly through my mind. I didn't want to go back into the chaos and misery of our reality, but I had no choice. Mum and Dad needed me to be strong.

Walking back inside, I said hello to family friends who had filled our kitchen and living room. They all had tears in their eyes when they hugged me. Everyone was in a state of complete shock. Most had been friends since Caroline and I were young, we had all grown up together. I knew in the back of their minds they were thinking that this tragedy could have happened to any one of their own children. I was introduced to a team of police including Sergeant Richard Crinnion, who was our Family Liaison Officer. He seemed a kind and sensitive man. I liked him straight away. He was calm and very respectful, offering support when we needed it. I asked after Caroline's friend Sarah who she was travelling with, and Ian who was Caroline's boyfriend and still in the UK. He told me Sarah was with police in Bundaberg. They were looking after her and she would be flying home as soon as possible.

I had always liked Sarah; her and Caroline would bounce off each other and used to laugh a lot. I couldn't imagine what she was going through. To be on the other side of the world, one minute having the time of her life with Caroline and the next to be alone surrounded by police. She had no one she could turn to for support and I was sure the police would have had to question her. She must have been going through hell.

The police had been in contact with Ian and his family. He had been going out with Caroline for a while and they had decided to stay together while she was in Australia. I'd met him a couple of times and he seemed like a good guy. It must have also been absolutely horrendous for him.

I thought of Caroline's school and college friends. Do they know yet? What must they all be thinking? The story was out there now and if they hadn't watched the news, they would find out from someone else. The more I thought about people who had known Caroline, the more I was beginning to see how real this was becoming. Her death had not just destroyed our lives but was going to have a lasting effect on a lot of other people.

Outside our home the media had congregated hoping for an interview. The story of an English backpacker, travelling in Australia, who had been thrown from a bridge in Bundaberg spread across the country making the national news here and in Australia.

I can honestly say that I never thought anything like this would ever happen to our family. There are horror stories every day in the news, horrific events all over the world but we are emotionally detached, we have to be, or we'd go insane. I used to share fleeting thoughts of sympathy for the people involved, not really understanding the ripples of devastation that happened around every tragedy. It was all too real now, and I knew exactly what death and murder can cause to loved ones, family and friends.

The post had been delivered that morning and someone had put it aside for us. A carefully wrapped parcel sat on our kitchen worktop, postmark Australia. I knew immediately from the handwriting it was from Caroline. We couldn't open it, none of us were brave enough. We just couldn't take any more. She must have sent it last week.

It was all too much, and I had to escape upstairs. Caroline's bedroom door was open, her room was next to mine. My heart went through the floor, tears welled up in my eyes again and my throat closed. Wave after wave of devastation bombarding me with extreme pain and emotion. I couldn't go in.

After looking out of the window on the landing for a while I plucked up the courage. Steadying myself, I took a deep breath and walked in. She had, of course, left it tidy before her travels. It was completely unreal, the last time I stood here she was alive. Everything in the room had been touched by her. She had carefully placed all her ornaments and trinkets on the shelves, her books had bookmarks and folded corners where she was reading and researching for university. The room still had her smell and energy, I felt as if she could just walk in at any moment. I didn't want to touch anything, so afraid I would be destroying what was left of her delicate essence. It was all we had left. Her favourite teddy, a little battered lamb I had bought her many years before, was still sitting on the window ledge. I picked it up and held it to my chest, my legs gave way and I slumped on the floor and wept.

Chapter 3
The aftermath

We were all completely different people from the very moment that we found out about Caroline's death. I didn't recognise myself, my parents or our family. My friends looked at me in a way I had never seen before. They looked at me like I was a complete stranger. The people I loved the most looked like different people. I was in a new world, nothing would ever be the same again.

Some parts of the week that followed are still very much a blur. For self-preservation I think my mind has compartmentalised everything, tightly boxing away the cataclysmic truth to save my sanity. Over time I have reopened some of those boxes but certainly not all of them and I'm not sure I ever will.

Waking up the first morning in my own bed, I didn't know where I was. Reality hit me immediately as it did every morning for many months after. Caroline was dead. All I wanted to do was pull the covers over my head and pray it was all a terrible nightmare.

Watching the morning news, Caroline's story was the main headline. They showed a picture of her, which I remember having been taken before she went out for her school leaving party. Her hair had to be just right. I vaguely remembered someone asking about photos in the chaos of yesterday.

Mum couldn't watch TV, she just sat in her pyjamas, crying and cuddling one of Caroline's teddy bears. I didn't know how to help her; I was at a loss for words and felt absolutely drained. Nothing I could ever say or do would change the fact that Caroline was gone. It felt like we were floating around on an endless ocean of grief with no idea when the next wave would hit. It didn't matter in which direction we swam, there was no safe haven in sight.

I am a practical person and like to have something to do. There was only one thing that mattered and that was to bring Caroline home. We started talking to Richard Crinnion and the police. They were still carrying out the inquiry in Australia and there was a lot to sort out. David stepped in again. Over the next few days, he talked with Megan Hunt who was our contact at the Foreign Office in Australia. He helped to arrange all the necessary paperwork including obtaining her dental records and finally managed to fix a date when she would be coming home. Sending her dental records, the thought of it just turned my stomach.

Cards of sympathy and bunches of flowers were arriving all the time in the days that followed, not only from family and friends but from people who had heard the story and just wanted to let us know they were thinking of us. We also started to see photographs from Bundaberg. I had no idea where it even was in Australia and had to look it up on a map. Under the bridge where Caroline's body was found members of the public had started to leave flowers and other keepsakes in her memory. It was incredibly disturbing seeing the spot where she died. I didn't want to imagine anything further and had to stop my mind from wandering. Seeing these acts of love gave us some comfort, just to know people were thinking about us and Caroline.

Our home phone rang constantly, friends were calling to offer their condolences and the media wanting interviews. There were so many people milling around the house, I didn't really take too much notice who was who. One of our friends spotted someone that nobody knew, asking who she was. It turned out she was a journalist from The Sun newspaper. We were so angry. It was incredibly disrespectful and such an invasion of our privacy. Especially at the hardest time our family had ever faced. She was soon ushered out of the door with a few choice words and we never gave an interview or had anything to do with The Sun from that day onwards. The majority of reporters and journalists we met were all very respectful of our privacy and over the years always supported us.

The following morning, I had the same realisation as soon as I woke. Caroline was gone, and nothing would ever change that. I had no idea how I was going to feel from hour to hour. Even when I thought I couldn't cry any more, another wave of emotion would hit and I would spontaneously burst into tears.

Sitting on the sofa with Mum, our bodies completely drained of tears and emotion, we were able to think a little clearer. I hadn't seen her for five months. We had only spoken once a week on the phone, whilst I was in Meribel. Over the last few years, I had been working away for the winter seasons, followed by a couple of months painting around the south of France before coming home for the rest of the summer. Mum and Dad were married for 30 years and built their business together. The story goes, they were looking for a flat in York, my Grandad found one on Micklegate. It needed a lot of work, but they still moved in. It was above a pet shop. A few years later when the owners retired, they offered the space to open a gallery. People said it would last six months. Dad would go out painting, Mum would help to run the gallery, work with agents and other businesses to sell the artwork. Thirty years later and they still had the gallery in York and a second in Scarborough. Since their separation five years ago they had only spoken to discuss business and talk about Caroline and myself. Mum had been running the gallery in York full-time while Dad spent his time between Italy and Scarborough. Mum and Caroline lived at home and had become really close. Grandma was always around and the three of them would hang out, drinking tea and chatting.

Mum wanted to tell me about the last time she had spoken to Caroline and what happened in the few days before her death.

"Caroline called on Sunday from Bundaberg, chatting at double speed about everything she had been doing. Her and Sarah had been staying in Byron Bay. She said it was one of the most beautiful places she had ever visited. It had perfect beaches and an amazing lighthouse that they had walked up to. They had been on a dolphin cruise and seen a pod of dolphins swimming next to their boat. They spent a lot of time on the beach and were both learning to surf; she said she was getting pretty good. I can still remember her voice; you knew when she was chuffed with herself."

I smiled and could see she was starting to get emotional.

Mum carried on, "She was actually starting to get a suntan which was amazing; she was fair skinned and always blamed Dad. She said that you would absolutely love Byron Bay. It was your kind of place, full of chilled out surf dudes. She loved you very much you know."

"I know Mum," I was welling up and could feel her emotion.

"She said she loved Brisbane and visiting the Koala Sanctuary was one of the best bits. You know how she loves animals, she said they felt funny to hold but made her feel relaxed and calm. Then she said they were in

Bundaberg."

"Caroline called Grandma on Monday to wish her happy ninety-first birthday, that meant the world to her. She said Caroline was chatting as usual. Talking about Byron Bay, Brisbane and telling her they might have to do some fruit picking work in the next couple of weeks. She told her she missed her and loved her. She said she couldn't wait to visit the Great Barrier Reef and do some scuba diving."

I knew Mum felt better just to talk about Caroline, it was difficult to speak about her in the past tense. Mum carried on talking, she told me about Tuesday night.

"I heard banging on our front door but for some reason I was already awake. It was 3 a.m. When I got downstairs the police were stood there. I immediately thought something had happened to Grandma, I was almost prepared for it, I was just going to turn to go and get my dressing gown. They then said it's about Caroline. That was it, I burst into tears. I still can't believe it"

Hearing Mum telling me about the last time she had spoken with Caroline sent me into overload. My head felt like it was going into meltdown, I had to run upstairs and was physically sick. It took me a while to be able to catch my breath and calm down. Going back downstairs Mum knew it had been too much for me. We hugged and cried, trying our best to comfort each other.

Thinking of Dad and I felt I had to speak to him. He needed to know he had our love and support. I called him, he was in pieces but said he was getting looked after by Janet and the police. He couldn't face going anywhere or really seeing anyone. He had been getting calls from reporters for interviews but declined most of them. All I could say was, "I am thinking of you, love you and I will come over to Scarborough to see you soon."

The next day, Richard Crinnion and the police liaison team arrived early. They had an update from Australia. Slowly we were piecing together what had happened. It was difficult to hear. After talking to her boyfriend Ian from a payphone in Bundaberg town centre, Caroline had called Sarah to say she would be back soon. It was around 9:30 p.m. when she started the fifteen-minute walk back to the campsite. It was dark and the route took her over the Burnett Bridge which was very badly lit. Nearing the far end of the bridge, someone or a group of people had stopped her, wanting to steal her bag, money and mobile phone. I knew Caroline and she wouldn't have wanted to let them go. There was a struggle and she would have fought back. Only a little over five-foot-tall she was overpowered and thrown over the railings to her death. It wasn't her fault. It's a natural reaction to want to protect your belongings and she wouldn't have even considered that the fight would have resulted in her death. She had just found herself in the wrong place at the wrong time, against people who had no regard for life.

We received news that Sarah had arrived back in the UK from Australia and was now with her family. I could only imagine what she had been through. I was pleased she was home. I had read in the news that the police had been taking care of her but seeing the photos in the papers she looked broken. It was hard to think she was home and Caroline wasn't, as they had both left together a few months earlier.

One of my best friends, Matty, who I have known since school, called round to our house. We had always been able to talk and were both on the same wavelength. The media were no longer camped outside our home and we managed to escape for a few hours. Walking through Huntington, we zipped down the snicket into New Earswick and along the river. We knew the place like the back of our hands. Finding a secluded spot, we sat and had a smoke, chatting about normal life. I hadn't seen him since before I left for France and he was aware I needed an escape from reality. We talked about cooking and food as Matty was a chef too. Caught up on what our friends were doing and where everyone was working. Caroline came into the conversation and we joked about a couple of things she did when we were young. It was one of the first times since the telephone call that I had smiled.

Walking further along the river and the conversation turned to what was happening now. I knew he was there for me, and it made me feel better knowing he could understand a little. We hugged, I felt recharged and went back home to look after Mum. All of us were just trying to get through each day. This was how life was for the foreseeable future; I couldn't see any light at the end of the tunnel.

I had another bad night's sleep. I was feeling shattered. Sarah came around to see us. She had recovered a little from the travel but was visibly distraught. None of us were ready to talk much about the good times they

31

shared. It was far too painful. I don't remember how the conversation began, but one thing Sarah talked about was seeing a rainbow the day after Caroline's death. It was bright and full, and she felt some peace for a brief moment. She said it was like Caroline was looking down over her telling her it would be OK. The way she spoke was very powerful and we grasped onto that feeling, we liked the idea of Caroline showing herself in all the colours of the rainbow. It seemed to fit her personality and the beautiful girl we all knew and loved.

Caroline's boyfriend, Ian, called with his family. He looked devastated. I could tell he had no idea what to say to us. We knew Caroline had been on the phone to him before walking back across the bridge. I thought he might think we blamed him, but of course we didn't. We weren't really friends, but if Caroline liked him enough to be with him then I was sure he was a good guy. We took a walk around our garden and he opened up a little. I tried to reassure him although I wasn't sure if it made a difference. We never discussed what he and Caroline talked about on their final conversation. It was not my place to ask and to this day I still don't know.

Caroline's story was still making the national news, the police were making inquiries but had no new leads. It seemed to have also sent shockwaves through various travel communities. People were talking about Australia as an unsafe place to visit and gap year students needed to be better prepared.

I had been back nearly a week but had no real concept of time. On April 16th, we had news from Megan Hunt at the Foreign Office saying that a memorial was going to be held in Bundaberg in memory of Caroline. I thought this was a wonderful gesture of love and support. Megan told us that the whole community was in shock. Nothing like this had ever happened before in their town. Bundaberg was a quiet and peaceful place, known to backpackers who wanted to do some fruit picking or farm work for extra cash whilst on their travels. It told us a lot about how much the local people cared. We gave a few words about Caroline saying about the type of person she was and that she was having the time of her life in Australia. It was to be read out during the service. We also offered our greatest thanks and respect for everybody's support.

We had hundreds of sympathy cards and dozens of bunches of flowers around the house. They were all for Caroline, recognising the wonderful and positive person she was. I thought people could really identify with her. A clever, talented girl fresh out of college, deciding to take a gap year with a friend before starting university. It was a common story. She was my wonderful sister, but also like many other sisters, daughters and granddaughters around the country. What happened to Caroline could have happened to anyone.

Later that day, Mum and I found a quiet moment and finally had the courage to open the package which had arrived from Australia. It had been meticulously wrapped and well-sealed. I carefully cut through the packaging. Inside was a pair of beige jeans which Caroline had told Mum on the phone were for university. There was a photo of her (she was smiling and looked so happy) along with a couple of brochures from places her and Sarah had visited. Also, a handwritten letter addressed to Mum.

'Hi Mum,

This time I am sending back my new jeans which I am very pleased with! I hope you like them. Also enclosed is a 'Dreamworld' brochure that was the theme park we visited in Surfers Paradise so you can see all the big rides we went on and the animals we stroked. It's our last day in Surfers today, we're leaving for Brisbane tomorrow morning so I'm looking forward to seeing a new place but I'm not looking forward to having to work, we really thought we wouldn't have to work because we cut down our time but you were right, we have to. I didn't realise how quickly and easily money goes! I hope Gran's OK and you're still having fun.

You've probably been on your first date with 'David' now, hope it all went very well, I'll be really pleased if it all works out for you because you deserve someone really nice who'll treat you well. I'll look forward to hearing all about it anyway! How's the diet going? I hope you're trying your best to lose some weight because you don't want to keep getting bigger because you won't like it when you won't fit into anything and it's a health risk! I love you however you are though obviously, but I don't want you to become really unhealthy as its bad for you.

I'm still having loads of fun over here but I'm beginning to miss home a bit more now! Yes, I miss you before you wonder! We've still got loads to look forward to, not only things like scuba diving in the Great Barrier Reef but another 3 countries too! I'm so grateful to you for helping me do it all.

And of course, Gran, without her money I would have found it a lot harder!

How's the house coming along? Nice and tidy I'm sure, ready for when I get back! It doesn't really matter though, after living in hostels for the last few months, out of a rucksack, home is going to seem like a palace! So, don't worry, I know how busy you are so I'm not really too fussed any more, I'll just be excited about having my own room and wardrobe again — what luxury!

I really enjoy our phone calls now, been out here has really chilled me out and I've learnt a lot about what kind of person I want to be so hopefully when I get back, we won't argue!

Anyway, I'll speak to you soon.

Miss you loads, lots of love Caroline xx'

After reading the letter we were completed drained, lightheaded, and tears poured down our cheeks. We wanted to hide away from the rest of the world. She must have only written it a couple of weeks ago. How was it that she was no longer here? It still just didn't seem real. It sounded like she was having the most amazing time and enjoying every moment. The only peace I could find was the fact that she was doing what she wanted to do: travelling the world and following her dreams.

Since the telephone call in Meribel I hadn't been sleeping well, usually collapsing at the end of each day through mental exhaustion. Some nights I would have the most vivid dreams. Well, nightmares really. They started in different ways but always ended the same; it was night-time, on a bridge, getting pushed towards the railings. I felt like I was seeing through Caroline's eyes. The moment that always terrified me was getting pushed with force by a hooded figure and tumbling backwards over the railing. Reaching out to grab the bars, missing them and my arms frantically waving but there was nothing else to grab. The fall was always in slow motion and I had the clarity of thought. This is it, I won't survive, I'm dead.

This nightmare has haunted my sleep ever since. As I tumbled, I felt myself grab the bed and would suddenly wake up sweating. Moments after I got a sense of relief that it was only a nightmare. Then the realisation hits, it's not just a nightmare, this actually happened to Caroline. She experienced that horrendous moment, reaching out in vain with nothing to grab and falling to her death.

I read in one newspaper that a woman who lived near the bridge had heard an ungodly scream, like nothing she had ever heard before and immediately called the police. What haunts me the most is the moment where Caroline knew she was about to die, screaming for her life and the split second where she knew this was it, her life was over.

The days were still 24 hours and time never stops; we had no choice but to start making some decisions about Caroline's funeral. As difficult as it was, it was more important than our grief. We had to do our best for her. Dad arrived at the house. It was the first time Mum and I had seen him. He looked like a completely different person, a shadow of his former self. He had always been the central pillar of the family, our strength. We embraced and he sobbed uncontrollably on my shoulder and I on his. We didn't have much to say, it was completely pointless to ask how each other felt and if everything was OK. We both knew nothing was OK and we weren't all right, our lives would never be the same again.

The funeral director and vicar came to see us. I knew they dealt with bereavement every day and both had a unique ability to put us at ease. They were very patient, even when our emotions got the better of us. I remember sitting in the living room with Mum and Dad talking about what we could do for Caroline. The service was to be held at our local church in Huntington. We thought there might be quite a lot of people attending but didn't know how many. We talked about what she liked, which brought more tears. We made decisions about who was going to speak, songs she would have liked to be played and the hymns we would sing. A friend had offered to arrange the flowers. Rainbows had become very significant after speaking to Sarah and we thought it would fit perfectly as a theme. Mum and Dad had the horrendous job of choosing Caroline's coffin, which must have been absolutely heart-wrenching. All I could think was that they should have been talking about what she needed for university, instead they had to choose the type of box she would be buried in.

When everything was finalised, we had a coffee and took some time to talk just the three of us. We found ourselves united by Caroline's death and shared each other's pain for a brief moment. It was very special but incredibly harrowing. The three of us together without Caroline was unbearable and shortly after we had to leave each other's company.

The house was quiet, it had been another emotional day. Dad left, heading back to Scarborough, and Mum had gone for a lie down. I decided to go for a walk. There was an anger burning deep inside of me. I had managed to suppress it with the whirlwind of everything that had been happening, but I could feel it starting to boil to the surface. Everything was directed towards a faceless figure, there was nobody to channel my hatred towards. Why hadn't the police found the person or people responsible yet? How could anyone do this? Hold my sister's life in their hands and push her to her death for a few dollars and an old mobile phone. It just didn't make any sense.

My pain cut so deeply it was agonising, I could feel it turning into hate. I remember thinking: breathe, don't be consumed by this, it's not who I am. Caroline was a happy person, inspired by life and interested in everyone and everything around her. She wouldn't want me to be like this. I pushed the feelings aside. It wasn't a good use of my energy and I was completely exhausted anyway.

Over time, the devastating heartache and chaos of that first week has faded, but the fact will never change; it will always be the most horrendous week of our lives. I remember moments where we had an overwhelmingly strong feeling of wanting to do something positive in Caroline's name. We all knew a happy, vibrant, intelligent girl, who could make us laugh and tell a good story. We felt her life force was too powerful just to let go. Through all the pain we could see she was doing what she had always dreamt of, exploring the world and living her life to the fullest.

Mum and I talked. We had no idea what we were going to do or how we were going to do it, but Caroline was going to live on. She would want us to help people.

Death can strangely unite people and they become driven by loss. Well-meaning ordinary people who find themselves in extraordinary circumstances, just like us. We wanted to prevent what happened to Caroline from happening to other young backpackers, and to stop other families going through what we were experiencing. We wanted to make a change and create something positive out of our tragedy. Somewhere within those initial conversations, a spark of an idea came to light. We made the decision to start a charity and the seeds were sown for what would become 'Caroline's Rainbow Foundation'.

Chapter 4
Laying Caroline to rest

April 18th, and Caroline was finally coming home.

Richard Crinnion drove Ian and I over to Manchester Airport to collect her body. We were all in a very sombre mood and there was not much conversation. I felt a small sense of relief, she was nearly home. When we arrived, her body was already loaded. Just knowing she was in a box in the back of a van turned my stomach and made me feel sick.

We followed in convoy back to York. None of us ever imagined she would be returning from her Australian adventure in this way. I hadn't realised before, but the Coroner's entrance was just next to the main hospital. We watched as the box was unloaded. I burst into tears, unable to control my emotions any longer. Lighting a cigarette, I needed to compose myself. We had to leave her at the Coroner's, there was nothing more we could do. Richard dropped me off. I saw Mum and told her my little sister was home.

The following day, Dad arrived from Scarborough. We met at York Hospital and with tears in our eyes we hugged. Neither of us said a word, we knew Caroline was home. It was all we needed to know in that moment. Dad always had a special bond with Caroline. In many ways she had very much taken after him: very creative, independent and strong-willed. He had the horrendous job of officially identifying her body. We walked into the building with the police and were taken to a waiting area. Only Dad got to see her. I wanted to go in with him but was told it was better to wait until they had cleaned up her body. I had no idea what he went through as he saw her laying out on a metal slab, but I have seen enough episodes of *Silent Witness* to be able to imagine the procedure. When he came out, I could see immediately he was a changed man, things would never be the same again. A part of him was gone forever. He looked visibly weaker and more vulnerable. Someone had completely and utterly destroyed his world. I gave him a big hug and he wept uncontrollably; finally, he said through his tears,

"She still has blood on her face." I could feel a surge of emotion from my very core, I tried to remain strong and hugged him tighter. I knew he would never be able to forget what he had just seen. The police drove him back to Scarborough.

There were only a few days to go before Caroline's funeral. Everyone was so supportive and wanted to do the best for Caroline. I realised I didn't even own a black suit, we had to go out and buy one. Afterwards, I took a walk along the riverside and down to the church in Huntington, passing only a couple of dog walkers on my way. It was quiet and I was aware of the beautiful setting around the church. I tried to imagine what it would be like when we would be walking behind Caroline's coffin. My brain wouldn't let me think about it. I felt it had completely shut down major areas since getting the telephone call. I knew this was my mind's way of saving me from so much pain, but it was scary to think I had no control over it. I wandered around the many graves and found a seat. I must have sat for over an hour, lost in thought but not really thinking of anything. What struck me was the fact that people's bodies were actually buried under the gravestones. Obviously, I knew this before, but the reality of knowing that I would one day soon be visiting a plot with Caroline's body laying six feet underneath was difficult to take. Everything was amplified; whatever thoughts I had were made unbearable knowing they applied to Caroline in some way, shape or form.

People started arriving in York in preparation to attend the funeral. Our Aunty Jean, who was mum's half-sister, and one of her sons, Grant, had arrived from Canada. They were welcomed and stayed at David's house, which I thought was very kind of him. They couldn't believe what had happened and there was a great deal of emotion between us all. When we relaxed, we talked of happier times. Our last family holiday together had been to Canada around eleven years earlier. Aunty Jean lived in Niagara Falls and when we visited, she welcomed us with open arms. I will always remember the first time we walked up to Niagara Falls and saw the water powering over the edge of the rocks. Caroline and I stood on the railings together in absolute amazement. Afterwards, we went shopping to one of the big shopping malls. Caroline was in her element. She loved trying on clothes and they had every shop she could have possibly dreamt of. I remember her, Mum and Aunty Jean's daughter Tracy going off for hours and coming back arms full of shopping bags. We had great memories although everything was very different now.

Aunty Mildred, who had looked after Dad when he was young, had driven up from Crewe. She had a wicked sense of humour but this time I saw none of that. I had never seen her so serious and upset. We had visited her many times. Caroline shared her love of animals and always enjoyed playing with her little dachshund. Caroline had wanted a dog for years and Dad had always refused. I agreed with him. It would just make our house smell. Eventually, like always with Caroline, he had given in and we got a black labrador from the rescue centre which she absolutely adored. The dog was called Jude and she used to take her on long evening walks across the fields. It made her so happy.

On April 22nd, we all went to see Caroline for the last time at the chapel of rest. I felt like I had no choice, out of respect and for my own peace of mind. I needed to see her one last time. I was extremely nervous. I had never seen a dead body before and didn't expect my first to be my sister.

I had a cigarette outside. It was a bright day but very windy. With a deep breath I tried to steady myself. Standing in the chapel doorway I could see her coffin surrounded by flowers, my heart was pounding. It hit me that Caroline's heart would never beat again. I went in alone and shuffled closer to peer over the edge of the coffin. My heart sank to depths I never knew existed. If it was unbelievable and hard to comprehend before, it was certainly cemented in reality now. There she was: no life, nothing that resembled the fun-loving, passionate girl who was full of energy. Just a body, lying cold, expressionless and peaceful in a box. She was laid to rest in her new jeans, a pink jumper to keep her warm, and black socks with pink toes because everything had to match. It didn't look like her. Her soul was gone and just a shell remained. I touched her hand; her skin was icy cold. I was not religious but knelt down and prayed, asking for forgiveness for all the childish things I had done. I told her I loved her very much and wished her well on her journey wherever she may be going.

Dad had three small crosses he had bought in Assisi, Italy. He put a wooden one in the coffin with her, one he kept, and the other, a gold cross, he gave to me. I wore it on a chain around my neck. It was a lovely gesture and in a small way would keep us all connected.

Outside I was shaking. The world seemed completely flat and monotone. I lit another cigarette and looked to the heavens shouting to God in my mind, 'Why has this happened? Why, why has she been taken away from us?' Tears poured down my face again and I felt utterly worthless. What was the point? There was nothing we could do. Nothing really mattered any more, I had just said goodbye to my little sister.

Caroline's funeral was held on the April 23rd 2002. Rainbows were now of huge significance and the florist had made a beautiful rainbow-shaped wreath that sat prominently on top of her coffin.

The cars pulled up outside. All of us had been dreading this moment but the time had come. It was only a short drive to the church. Mum wouldn't get out of the car. It would become all too real and meant her daughter had actually gone. I walked around to her side, gave her a hug, and with a few words about having to be strong for Caroline, helped her out.

Waiting for the coffin to be lifted, we composed ourselves as much as we could. As Caroline was carried in front of us, we slowly walked towards the church arm-in-arm. Tears were still pouring down Mum's cheeks. I tried to hold it together. A horde of media people were gathered outside the gates waiting for their photos. I looked straight through them and saw hundreds of people, some gathered at the entrance of the church and others stood in groups all around the grounds. I couldn't believe how many people were there. There were faces I recognised and faces I didn't. Many of them were around Caroline's age and were friends from school and college. I had never felt such an outpouring of love. I had no idea that my little sister had touched so many people's lives. We had shared many special moments together, but she was always my little sister. How she was regarded by her friends was a mystery but something very special. She was more loved by others than I think any of us had appreciated.

Over four hundred and fifty people were there to pay their respects for Caroline. The small church was packed, many people spilling out into the grounds. Speakers had been set up outside so everyone could hear the service. It was completely humbling to see. Grandma, Aunty Mildred, Aunty Jean, Grant, Janet and David, who had been pushing Grandma in her wheelchair, joined us on the front row for the service. I sat between Mum and Dad. The service was taken by our vicar, Chris Cullwick, who had known Caroline for nearly all of her nineteen years. He was visibly upset; every word was said with feeling and pure love. We played a selection of her favourite songs including *My Heart Will Go On*, by Celine Dion, which Caroline used to play on the organ, *Let It Be* and *Hey Jude*, by The Beatles, after our dog she loved so much. We sang *All Things Bright and Beautiful* and *Abide with Me*. Caroline's tutor from college, Jo Barrett, gave a wonderful eulogy. I could feel the energy and emotion in the church. Everyone was in floods of tears.

After the service we stood outside and shook everyone's hands. Her friends shared moments they had with Caroline and offered their sympathies and prayers. This meant a lot to us and even now brings comfort to think of how much she was loved. Our old schoolteachers paid their respects. In the complete confusion and chaos of my mind I only remembered some of them. It wasn't until afterwards that I could place everyone. I had thought more about the past in the last couple of weeks than I had for many years.

We followed Caroline's coffin the short drive to Huntington cemetery. It was only a ten-minute walk from where we grew up. As we walked over to the hole in the ground, where Caroline would lay for all eternity, I thought it was a beautiful place for her to be. We held each other up as our legs were giving way beneath us. The vicar said a few more words and we all prayed as she was lowered into the ground. We gathered closer to have a final moment together as a family. Each of us dropped a yellow rose, signifying love, on top of her coffin. It was another of the hardest moments to see both my parents and Grandma in tears, my sister in a box in the ground and absolutely nothing I could do to make anything any better. I had written a card and later left it on the freshly laid earth in amongst the flowers. On the card I wrote, 'What you didn't achieve in life may you achieve in death'. There must be an afterlife. I had to believe.

The wake was held at the Bowls Club in Huntington. I couldn't eat anything. Time went by quickly and the details are still unclear in my mind. Everyone handled it differently. I spoke with a lot of people, who offered their sympathies. Some people simply put a hand on my shoulder or gave me a hug, they didn't need to say a word. Others avoided eye contact and didn't say anything, which was completely understandable. What could anyone say at a time like this? It was obvious it wasn't only us who were struggling to come to terms with Caroline's death. This gave me a new perspective and a feeling that we were not alone.

After the wake, a few of us went around to a friend's house and had a beer in respect of Caroline. She would have wanted us to celebrate her life. I told a few stories about when she was young and tried to stay positive, however there was no escape from the thought that her life had been unfairly cut short. We all promised from that moment we would try to live the best lives we could.

When I arrived back home, I was devastated and completely shattered. I had been running on adrenaline for the whole day and just collapsed. Thinking back over the day I couldn't dwell too long on any part of it. Only a couple of weeks ago, someone had chosen to take my sister's life, not only destroying our family but also leaving lasting emotional scars on her friends and everyone who knew her. It wasn't only us who would never be the same.

Caroline and I had been brought up to be independent and learnt to deal with our own problems. Her death had united our family again for a brief moment, but the three of us were hurt so deeply and reminded each other of our previous life together. It was just too difficult. We all needed our own space and time.

After the wake Dad went back to Scarborough. He wanted his own grief, some peace and time to remember Caroline. He would spend the next couple of weeks visiting places that they had visited together. Mum could no longer stay in our house as it was too painful, so she decided to move in to one of David's spare rooms. His home was just outside of York. I thought it would be good for her to be away from the house, there were just too many memories.

I felt I couldn't leave our home; it was all I had left of our family. I needed to be alone. We all had our personal grief to deal with and even then, I don't think any of us could actually believe she was gone. I knew tragedies happened all the time, but never to anyone I had known directly. There was no one I could really talk to about how I was feeling, I felt like no one would understand.

Both Mum and Dad were in their own worlds of pain and grief.

Dealing with the loss of their daughter is one of the greatest burdens. How could I add to that? It was out of love and respect for them that I kept my feelings to myself and tried my best to remain strong when I spoke to them. I felt it was important for them to have something solid that they could recognise from their lives before the loss of Caroline.

Over the following weeks, our friends stayed in contact. Everyone had already helped us far more than they needed too. Understandably, they wanted to return to a bit of normality, their own lives and families. They were still there for us but understood we needed time to grieve just as they did. We will always be forever grateful for their love and support.

I found myself completely lost and trying to find a route out of this hell. I didn't feel ready to really do anything or see anyone. I felt like people were whispering behind my back, there were discussions and conversations about Caroline. 'Don't mention it, his sister was murdered.' When something like this happens, they say you find out who your friends really are. People didn't know what to say, they didn't know how to act around me. Some tried to get on with life, in their head taking my mind off everything would be the best course of action. For others, they thought it best to talk. 'I am here for you if you need me,' they'd say. I knew they were well- meaning; whichever way people chose to approach Caroline's death I appreciated it. My friendship circle got significantly smaller, I felt I could no longer trust anyone, and I tried to turn off my feelings. It was for self-preservation. My biggest fear became anyone I cared about could also be taken away.

Now there was only me left in our family home. I started to spend time in Caroline's room, not touching anything as she would have been very annoyed, just sitting quietly and remembering the times we shared together. She was still in every part of the house.

Downstairs in the dining room was our organ. We both played and had lessons every weekend. I thought about all the times we would practise together and how over the months she became much better than me. She was naturally gifted and annoying like that. It made me smile. Looking out of her window, I remembered us pushing each other around in a red pedal car we had as kids. Although she was only half my size she was just as strong as me. We still had that little car locked away in our garage.

In the winter, when we were lucky enough to get snow, we would build snowmen. I would push the balls around and stack them as tall as I could. She would find sticks for the arms, stones for the eyes and mouth and ask Mum for a carrot, hat and scarf to finish our masterpiece. We had lots of happy times and I was starting to remember them fondly through lots of pain and tears.

One evening, I had gone to bed. It was late, I wasn't sleeping well and would have the same nightmare night-after-night. As I lay there, I heard sounds coming from downstairs and my ears pricked up. Had I locked the door? Listening closer, I could hear our organ playing… couldn't be, could it? I could hear the definite notes just like when we used to practise. I was petrified, too afraid to move. I curled up in a ball under the covers and just waited. After a few minutes the sounds stopped. I was sure of what I heard but was still too scared to go downstairs. Was it Caroline playing? Was there an afterlife and such a thing as ghosts? It never happened again, but to this day I am absolutely positive that's what I heard.

Early the following month, I was feeling a little stronger, a little more myself and went over to see Dad and Janet in Scarborough. It was nice to get away from York. As much as I liked my own space I sometimes needed to be around people. Dad had been doing a lot of painting and writing and told me about how it felt revisiting places he and Caroline had been to. It was nice for us to spend some time together. I had been living away a lot over the last few years, so we had not seen much of each other. I didn't know Janet that well, but she seemed like a nice lady and was very supportive of Dad.

Being back in Scarborough brought back many happy memories. When Caroline and I were younger he had bought the gallery on North Marine Road, which had a flat above it. It was where he was living now. It had always been our little seaside escape. I took long walks along the beach, remembering places where Caroline and I had played as children, building sandcastles and splashing around in the sea. I loved the space, fresh sea air and looking out across the water to the endless horizon. I always found it peaceful. It was just the time I needed to clear my head.

It had been over a month since Caroline had died. Sometimes it was like the telephone call was only yesterday and other times it felt like a lifetime ago. We talked about Caroline and one of our ways of coping was to laugh. We started reminiscing about our childhood and the silly things she had done. It felt like a long time since either of us had even smiled together. I told him the story of the organ playing, but he wasn't as shocked as I thought and could quite believe it. He told me about his work at The Arthur Findlay College, which I had visited years before, it was the most magnificent building and the grounds were beautiful. I remember feeling very relaxed and at peace as we painted together. Until that point, I knew little about the work they actually did. I knew Dad was a tutor and hosted a few weeks a year. The college is a place for psychic sciences and research. In part it was belief in an afterlife, the college was a place where people could go to learn more about energy, expand their sensitivity and understand their feelings. They also taught mediumship which was the practice of making contact with loved ones who had passed away. We were not in the right place to discuss it further, but it certainly piqued my interest.

Over dinner one evening, we talked about setting up a charity in Caroline's name and discussed the idea, Caroline's Rainbow Foundation could help other young people when they were travelling. I was very passionate about it, thinking we could do something positive after what had happened. Dad wasn't interested in getting involved. I couldn't really understand why, as we were doing it for Caroline. It was for her memory and to help other people. It was his choice and I respected that. He had to deal with everything in his own way, just as we needed to do what we felt was right. It hurt me deeply that he wasn't interested in what we were planning but I knew I couldn't change his mind. We were both in a very fragile state, so I didn't discuss it any further.

We had not heard much from the police about what was happening with the investigation in Bundaberg. We were told things were moving forward and the officers were putting in a lot of their own time. We really appreciated their work and knew they were doing everything possible. The BBC had invited us to go to Australia and visit Bundaberg. It would be incredibly difficult and emotional. I was unsure whether I wanted to make the same journey that was Caroline's last. However, it would be important for our family to show support to everyone who was working so hard on the case. It could also be a big step in dealing with our grief and part of our healing process. The thought of going was scary and filled me with dread; I would be facing many demons and because of that I knew I had to go.

A few days by the coast had made me feel better, I felt more comfortable. Mum was still in pieces but living away from the house I thought was good for her. I went over to David's house to see her. One of the first questions she asked was, "What are we going to put on her gravestone?"

I needed something to focus on and took hold of the challenge. Whatever I came up with would be carved on Caroline's headstone forever. I then realised the significance of my actions; some things were permanent. I felt a huge sense of responsibility. How was I going to do Caroline justice in only one sentence? I scribbled, changed and tweaked, looking at a host of usual phrases on the headstones of loved ones. After carefully considering who she was and the impact her death had had, not only on family and friends but people from around the world, I finally came up with something we all agreed felt right.

'Caroline Ann Stuttle 1982 – 2002

She only touched the world but the world was touched by her.'

Chapter 5
Caroline Ann Stuttle

Caroline was the other half of my childhood; she brought balance to me and made the fourth corner of our family home. I watched her grow into a bright, intelligent young woman loved by both family and friends.

Born on September 2nd 1982, I was five years old and welcomed my little sister into this world with a little bit of jealousy if I'm honest. I now had to share Mum and Dad, their attention was on the new baby and no longer only for me. Those feelings soon passed as it was impossible not to love her. She wanted to be just like me, always wanting to play with my things and do what I was doing. She was kind, confident and intuitive just like our parents taught us to be.

We had an active childhood, always playing in our garden. When she got older, she learnt to swim, we used to go to the local pool regularly and swam for our local club. She also had a terrific love of animals. We had a lot of pets growing up. The first that were completely our responsibility were a couple of rabbits, Bandit and Snowy; they were allowed in our living room and we would sit and play with them for hours. Weekends we had to clean out their cages, Mum said it was part of the responsibility. Caroline wanted a fish tank in her room and kept nagging Dad, and again he finally said, 'Yes'. I could never understand why as we had a pond in the garden full of fish. I joked saying it was like putting one in prison looking out to freedom. She also loved horse riding, which was just for her; I have always been afraid of horses, big powerful animals with small brains. They were not for me. I thought her very brave to get up on those large, majestic beasts, she had the confidence to take control.

In later years, her dog Jude kept her company. When Dad left and I was working away, Mum was working in the gallery, it was lovely for Caroline to be able to come home to a loving dog. I knew Jude gave her a lot of pleasure, which was also a comfort now.

Everyone who met Caroline loved her wonderful spirit and caring nature, over the years and probably partly due to my influence, she also developed a wicked sense of humour. It would be the little things that always made us laugh. Dad liked model aircraft and we used to build radio-controlled models together. Strensall Common was a short drive from our home and when the army were not doing manoeuvres it was the perfect space for us to go and fly. On one occasion some family friends had come to visit, they had children who were slightly younger than us, and we all trekked out to fly the aircraft. The common was uneven and you had to watch your step, our friend was walking along in front of us and suddenly disappeared up to his waist. Caroline and I looked at each other and absolutely howled with laughter. He had fallen into the ditch and was soaked up to his waist in muddy water. We suddenly both realised that we shouldn't be laughing, but every time we looked at each other it set us off again. Weeks later we still chuckled about it.

Some of the best memories I have of our childhood together were family holidays. One year we went to visit family in Canada, Caroline and I were uncontrollably excited.

Mum and Dad always encouraged us to write when we were younger, to keep a journal of what we were doing, especially on holidays. I wrote,

'Mum woke us before the sun was up, straight away we were super excited. It was the morning of our holiday. For Caroline and me holidays were up there with birthdays and Christmas as the most exciting, brilliant things ever!

Canada was a very, very long way away, we had been on holiday to places in Europe before which had been flying in the plane for a couple of hours, but this time the flight was over six hours! It has been ages; we had been talking about it for what felt like forever. Our bags and cases had been packed, repacked and packed again. I am 14 years old and Caroline is 9 years old, our responsibility was to stay close to Mum and Dad and looking after our backpacks. We both had a book to read and Caroline had a couple of toys, Mum and Dad let me take my skateboard which was the most important thing in the world to me.

The airport was a big deal, we both loved planes and Dad took us over to look out of the big windows at the runway. Mum had all the passports and looked after the paperwork, Dad had the money and his paints. Mum always liked to be early, we had lots of time to have breakfast and look around the shops.

It was finally time to get on the plane and we were very, very excited! I loved the window seat, Caroline did too, and it always caused a fight between us. I won because I was a boy and boys like planes, and I was older. Taking off was the best part, pushed back in our seats and going up in the sky. Our ears popped which didn't feel nice, but we got sweets from the cabin crew which made it all better.

I looked at the map with Dad, we were crossing the Atlantic to land in Toronto. Our cousins lived in Niagara Falls and we would be staying with them.

It was all very exciting as we landed, the sun was shining and we got picked up by my Aunty Jean. She had a nice big brown car with a private number plate and got all of our bags in the back, I kept my backpack and skateboard with me. We drove to Niagara Falls and her house, I liked the drive, everything looked so different to home, I liked it.

The four of us, with my Aunty Jean walked down to see Niagara Falls. I was amazed by the amount of water, over a meter deep going over the falls. It was incredible. We walked along and stood on the railings looking over where the water went over. I found it beautiful, the water was so clear, and I could see though to the rock edge underneath. I wanted to reach out and touch the water.

We got on a boat called The Maid of the Mist which sailed right up close to the Horseshoe Falls, we all had yellow ponchos on which were huge on me and Cas and we got absolutely soaked but we didn't care. It was amazing!

My cousins are Grant, Kevin and Tracy. They were all grown up but liked playing with us, they were fun. The holiday was the best time, it seemed like we were away for ages! Caroline would follow me around which was OK, but sometimes we did things that were just for boys, so she couldn't join in. Sometimes I liked it when she was with us, especially when we went to the big shopping mall. I held her hand as it was so big and I didn't want her to be scared or get lost.

It was Caroline's turn to sit by the window on the way home and I didn't mind, I could still see out and the fun bit was getting pushed back on our seats, planes went really fast! Caroline and I both agreed, it was the best holiday ever!'

Thinking back to this happy time, it was one of the last family holidays we were all together. I recently visited Canada and went back to Niagara Falls and caught up with our cousins. All the memories came flooding back. Walking along towards the Horseshoe Falls this time arm-in-arm with my wife Sarah. Last time was with Mum, Dad, Aunty Jean and holding Caroline's hand. Caroline and Aunty Jean were both no longer with us. My memories were completely raw. I hadn't thought about these moments for many years, I unlocked feelings and images in my mind that were not distorted, unlike a lot of other memories. I didn't realise how much I had forgotten. It brought a tear to my eye. I had a fragile glimpse again of our family as a whole. I felt the same wrenching pull on my heart and stomach that I have felt many times over the years, the realisation that now we all lived a completely different life. We stood looking over the Horseshoe Falls in the same spot I had looked over those many years before, I didn't have to stand on the railings this time but still had that teenage excitement of the water powering over the lip. It was completely mesmerising, I still wanted to reach over and feel the rushing water through my fingers, although now I knew it wouldn't be a good idea. I love Canada, now for many more reasons, the feeling of space and lovely people, everyone greeted us with a smile. Sarah and I talked at length about moving out to Canada; great country, plenty of space and a lovely way of life.

Creativity was in our genes. Caroline enjoyed expressing herself through drawing and painting, her GCSE Art was exceptional and blew me away; she was a natural artist. Her creativity also extended to music; from my room I could hear all different genres playing from her stereo. I thought, how can she like everything? Strange girl! Saturdays we took lessons learning to play the organ, she soon became more advanced than me, which was annoying. I had absolutely no sense of rhythm. One of her favourite pieces of music to play was *My Heart Will Go On*, by Celine Dion, wherever we were in the house you could hear her playing.

She crammed so many things into her life with such energy and enthusiasm. Caroline was definitely a people person, incredibly friendly and loved the company of others. Family and her friends were hugely important. When she was fifteen, she worked for a pizza place in York saving money for her future adventures. She would save her lunch and at the end of shift go out and give it to a homeless person she got to know.

She seemed to find herself at college and find out more about the person she was, she had a real passion for psychology. When we chatted, I got the feeling she could see straight through me, she knew exactly what made me tick and we had some very deep conversations.

When Caroline was at college I had moved out of home and was living in a shared house with four other chefs, we were all the best of friends. It was a great house, always lots of takeaway boxes in the kitchen, like most chefs we never cooked at home. We enjoyed a lot of space and freedom. Caroline wanted to have a party and I said she could have it at our house, she was super excited. I left her to arrange everything, which she did no problem. On the night of the party, I stayed for a while and watched her busying herself making sure everyone had a drink and was having a good time. It was obvious she genuinely cared for people. She wanted everything to be perfect.

Caroline had her heart set on a career in forensic psychology, I know she would have succeeded. She possessed all the right qualities, sensitivity, compassion and understanding to those who needed help. We both shared an adventurous spirit, and this became even more obvious when she chose to take a gap year. We talked passionately about travel, she was fearless. Nothing was going to be a problem for her. She was an optimist, if she got an idea in her mind, she would stop at nothing until she achieved it.

Chapter 6
Visit to the Alps

After my first winter season in the French Alps I was hooked, for me snowboarding was a natural extension of skateboarding. I got the same release of endorphins and sense of freedom. When I first stepped on a snowboard it took a week until I could ride pretty much anywhere. I felt connected with the mountain and found I was partially living in what Taoism called the 'Tao' or natural harmony with my environment. At certain moments I found myself in what could be described as a 'flow state' as detailed in Steven Kotler's book *The Rise of Superman*, although at the time I didn't have a reference for what I was experiencing. I was soon hooked on one of the most addictive states of being on Earth. Allowing the freedom to enter these states opens you up to taking in more information, processing it more deeply, learning more quickly and pushing the boundaries of what's possible.

In this state, your body is flooded with naturally produced chemicals: first comes dopamine, which offers a feeling of happiness and feeling good. Next up is norepinephrine, which speeds up the body, muscles and increases heart rate. Endorphins regulate the body and mediate stress and pain levels. Anandamide is then released, which gives the same sense of bliss as smoking a joint (which I knew well). It improves lateral thinking and can offer different solutions to problems that we might not have previously considered. It also inhibits fear, breaking down mental barriers and allowing us to push to new heights. Serotonin is the final release and offers us a sense of peace and relaxation, the bliss feeling we got after a good day's riding on the mountain. It took my awareness to another level, a place where I could live in the moment and feel so much more. Every breath meant more and grounded me, I felt extended and completely connected. When the opportunity came to do another season, I didn't hesitate.

It was March in 2001 when Caroline came out to visit me for a long weekend, the weather was getting better and we had sunny days. I was impressed that she'd arranged everything by herself, I picked her up from Chambéry Airport. Caroline was eighteen years old. In my eyes, she had grown from just being my little sister into a confident young woman. She could travel independently and start to enjoy the big wide world. It was the first time we had spent time together out of the country, apart from on family holidays. I was excited and wanted to show her a new amazing world I had discovered.

The mountains are mesmerising even if you don't ski or snowboard, I was proud to show her around Meribel and introduce her to my friends. I worked every morning and evening but had time free each afternoon. We went up to the top of the mountain for lunch and looked out at the breathtaking views. Caroline and I had become close friends, far more than just brother and sister. I thought of her as someone I could talk to, someone I wanted to spend time with, and I massively valued her opinion.

We had both been through a lot over the last few years with our parent's separation, it had definitely brought us closer together. I had been working away and was able to put everything aside for the occasional moment, but Caroline was still at home and had been going through her exams. It was devastating watching our family unit break up; neither of us saw it coming. How could this happen? Everything, we both thought was solid and true, felt like a complete lie. We talked about how she focused on her schoolwork and tried not to think about it. There were parts of us which thought it was our fault, although we knew that was ridiculous. Was there anything we could know to be the truth? We felt they had lied to us, but we still had each other. We could always rely on each other. We vowed there and then never to hurt or lie to each other again. We didn't know many other people whose families had separated; it was a strange concept to us.

We still loved Mum and Dad dearly, but also felt resentment towards them for splitting up. We couldn't understand why they had chosen to end what we both thought, was a loving family. At the time, I think Caroline understood far better than me but that doesn't change anything when you are caught in the middle of it all. My wish was that Caroline didn't have to go through it.

Despite everything that was happening, she had done really well in her exams, far better than I had done. She easily achieved the grades needed for college. I was recently reading through her school-leaving book, conscientious and organised of course, she had glued in pictures of her friends and they had written a few words about their school years. It made me smile and I knew she wouldn't be happy knowing I was reading it. On the final few pages, she wrote.

'After 5 years at Huntington School my compulsory schooling has ended. No more maths lessons with Cas and no more being told off for talking too much! No more French with Sophie. It's the end of our oh so exciting sociology lessons.

Thankfully physics, chemistry and biology have finished! Which means no more bulls' eyeballs, pointless equations or the periodic table.

Never again will I have to stay behind in textiles even though we had so much fun.

It's the end of an era which can never be relived or changed.

So, what do I take from that school?

A bunch of memories good and bad, knowledge that will fade but never disappear and my GCSE qualifications. I'll always remember the great friends I've made and the laughs we've had, I've had some of the best times I will never forget.

Although at times I've not wanted to go and sat bored in lessons I will always be grateful for the things I was taught and the people I've met.

I'll never be sorry, if I hadn't gone, I wouldn't have made the great friends I have!

My GCSE grades	
English Language	A
English Literature	A
Double Science	B B
Maths	B
French	A
Art	A*
Sociology	A
History	A
Textiles	B

Caroline loved her time at college. She talked with excitement about everything she had learnt, the amazing people she had met and their shared passion for the subjects they were taking. She chatted about the opportunities for her future and career. She knew exactly what she wanted to do and where she was going, which was the complete opposite to me. Each of us were blessed with different talents. I was very logical, had strong reasoning skills and was very practical. My reading and writing were appalling. She was academic, had a far sharper mind, understood people and could see past words to people's underlying intent. She had an incredible love for psychology and was incredibly good at it. She made me realise, if Mum and Dad weren't happy together any more then they shouldn't be together. Over time people grow apart and find themselves on different journeys. It was a taste of what could happen, a wake-up call that life was not always rosy even if you have the best intensions. I always learned a great deal spending time with my sister, she was far wiser than her years.

She would be finishing college soon and was planning to study criminal psychology at Manchester University. I knew she would do extremely well.

I had a picture in my mind of Caroline living in a New York apartment, floor-to-ceiling windows, large light-coloured sofas with huge cushions, glass coffee table stacked with books and an elegant reading lamp. A piano on one side of the room and her leant against it looking out over an electrified city skyline with a glass of wine in hand. Very tasteful.

We talked about travel, she felt a real affinity for Australia and wanted to go backpacking. She had been working really hard and wanted to take a year out before university, she had been talking with one of her best friends and they were both getting excited about the idea. I always thought of travel as positive, the mountains for me had opened up a new and amazing world. We talked about the distance between us and Australia, it was a very long way. You can't just pop back if you wanted to. The country itself was amazing, the Great Barrier Reef, Fraser Island, Whitsundays, Broome and, of course, Sydney. We had always watched the New Year's celebrations in Sydney on the TV. To be there at the Opera House watching the fireworks over the Harbour Bridge would be magical. Once in a lifetime. The weather was always amazing, the beach life. I mean what's not to love. I said I might go with her. I could go travelling with Matty and meet her in places we both wanted to see. I was easily excitable, she talked so passionately about wanting to dive, learning to surf and checking out all the wildlife, I wanted to be part of her adventure. I told her, "Go for it. Taking time out to travel can only be a good thing, you deserve it."

We were both still kids at heart. It had snowed overnight; on her last day we built a snowman like we used to as kids, but this time there was plenty of snow. I had a carrot, hat and scarf to finish the job. There were a few snowballs thrown and we were both soaked through by the time we had finished.

I didn't know it then, but her visit to the Alps would become one of those special memories I hold close to my heart. I gave Caroline my blessing to travel, in fact I encouraged her to go and explore the world. Of course, I had no idea what was going to happen. For many years, I felt guilty for encouraging her to go, I felt responsible for not properly explaining the risks and making her be more careful. These feelings weighed on my heart and shoulders like I was dragging a rock up a perpetual mountain.

It was only after the cloud of grief began to subside that I remembered her face lighting up when we talked about travel, hearing her excited voice on the phone when she called to tell me all the amazing things she was doing. I realised not encouraging her to travel would have been like keeping a Siberian tiger in captivity or clipping the wings of a beautiful golden eagle. I would have been denying who she was, who we had both grown up together to become. She did everything right, she was as safe as she could be. At nineteen, she was young, healthy, quick-witted and fast to react. There was only so much she could do to keep safe. You can't keep people wrapped in cotton wool and put them in a box like an ornament. Even Bernini's sculpture, the Ecstasy of Saint Teresa, arguably one of the greatest sculptures ever created, is on display for everyone to see in the Cornaro Chapel in Rome. There is risk of damage and vandalism, but the risk is acceptable for the infinite rewards. People need freedom to be able to breathe, to live and to enjoy.

One of the things I understand far more about today is intuition, listening carefully to your little voice inside. It's an inherent survival mechanism that has taken all of human evolution to perfect, hearing that voice in today's chaos only comes with time and experience.

Thinking back to our time in the Alps, we were both naive to this side of ourselves. We didn't hear the whispering voice whose job it is to keep us safe and point us in the right direction. I do wonder what Caroline's voice was saying to her and whether she even heard it. Whether something was telling her not to step foot on that bridge or told her to walk in the other direction. What continues to destroy me more than anything else is that she had the potential to achieve whatever she wanted in life. I truly thought we would have had a lifetime together.

Chapter 7
Our final conversation

October 2001, our home was full of excitement. I had decided to do another winter season, it was comfortable and my love for snowboarding had won me over. I was preparing to depart for Meribel. Caroline was packing and getting ready to leave for Australia.

We went for coffee, both of us were super excited. We talked at length, I thought Caroline was extremely brave to be travelling to the other side of the world, it was going to be her greatest adventure yet. Obviously being the older brother, I knew everything about travel and proceeded to advise Caroline, this is what to do and what not to do. Looking back, it was absolute rubbish, I knew the basics but that was it. I didn't really know the first thing about how the world worked or the main dangers and pitfalls backpackers faced.

Caroline had done a lot of research and planned everything right down to the final detail. The day I left for France I never for one moment thought I would never see her again. We gave each other a big hug, said we loved each other and wished we would both have the most amazing adventures.

This would be my third winter season. I knew many people who were going back, so felt pretty confident. I had taken my car last season and liked the freedom it gave. At the end of November, I boarded the ferry from Hull to Rotterdam and took a few days to drive to the Alps stopping for a night in Metz and another in Dijon. I had time to paint. After last season, I had driven down to the South of France for a few weeks painting around Cannes. I wanted to be there in May for the film festival again. I loved the movies and with so many people visiting the picturesque coastal town, I figured there was a good chance of selling my art.

Caroline and I were mainly keeping in touch by text, I had a French mobile and she had an Australian number, so it worked out cheaper. She also had a phone card and called my chalet shortly after arriving in Australia, she sounded so excited. Her and Sarah had arrived safely in Sydney, so far it was everything she dreamt it would be. The sun was shining, they were staying in a youth hostel close to the CBD or Central Business District and had already visited Bondi Beach. I was so excited for her and proud that she had actually gone and done it. She sounded so happy, full of excitement and energy.

We kept in touch over the next couple of months with phone calls and text, she liked to update me with her progress, two excited young ladies working their way up the East Coast. I was chatting more regularly with Mum, we would update each other on what we had heard, where Caroline was and what she had written on her postcards.

At the end of March, Caroline called the chalet again. It was lovely to hear from her; of course, her and Sarah had been busy doing everything they could. She talked a million miles an hour about everything they were still going to do. I got a sense that she was the happiest she had ever been, it sounded like she was having the time of her life.

We talked about the vibe in Australia, how the people were really chilled and relaxed. She joked that I would fit right in. Hanging out on the beach in most places they visited, there were surf dudes and skateboarders everywhere that looked just like me. She said I would absolutely love it. She was meeting a lot of other backpackers too, her and Sarah were both chatty and happy to talk to most people. I could easily imagine what they were both getting up to.

She was surprised by the amount of English people staying in the hostels, a lot of them were heading along a similar route. I joked about her getting a suntan, she had very pale skin and on our family holidays I used to go brown, whilst she would stay white. Apparently, she actually had a suntan now and hair straighteners weren't needed!

We always had interesting conversations, we talked about the culture and the Australian way of life. The people were so friendly, and it was all about an outdoors lifestyle. Everyone loved going to the beach, socialising in local parks and having a few drinks in the bars. The weather was amazing, they both hadn't worn anything other than shorts and t-shirts since they arrived. She laughed, saying the general dress sense wasn't great compared to people back home. Getting dressed up meant putting on a clean t-shirt, everyone wore flip-flops all the time whether they were going to the beach or for a night out.

I filled her in with how the season was going, she understood more after her visit last year. The snow was good, a few people that she had met last year were back and they asked after her. I started to get excited telling her my snowboarding was getting better, a few new tricks and the snow parks were good this season, but I could tell she didn't care. She was more interested in whether I had met any girls or had a new girlfriend yet. I said a few of course but I was here to snowboard. I asked after her boyfriend Ian, she was missing him a lot, but she knew it wouldn't be forever.

At the end of March, Caroline called the chalet again. It was lovely to hear from her; of course, her and Sarah had been busy doing everything they could. She talked a million miles an hour about everything they were still going to do. I got a sense that she was the happiest she had ever been, it sounded like she was having the time of her life.

We talked about the vibe in Australia, how the people were really chilled and relaxed. She joked that I would fit right in. Hanging out on the beach in most places they visited, there were surf dudes and skateboarders everywhere that looked just like me. She said I would absolutely love it. She was meeting a lot of other backpackers too, her and Sarah were both chatty and happy to talk to most people. I could easily imagine what they were both getting up to.

She was surprised by the amount of English people staying in the hostels, a lot of them were heading along a similar route. I joked about her getting a suntan, she had very pale skin and on our family holidays I used to go brown, whilst she would stay white. Apparently, she actually had a suntan now and hair straighteners weren't needed!

We always had interesting conversations, we talked about the culture and the Australian way of life. The people were so friendly, and it was all about an outdoors lifestyle. Everyone loved going to the beach, socialising in local parks and having a few drinks in the bars. The weather was amazing, they both hadn't worn anything other than shorts and t-shirts since they arrived. She laughed, saying the general dress sense wasn't great compared to people back home. Getting dressed up meant putting on a clean t-shirt, everyone wore flip-flops all the time whether they were going to the beach or for a night out.

I filled her in with how the season was going, she understood more after her visit last year. The snow was good, a few people that she had met last year were back and they asked after her. I started to get excited telling her my snowboarding was getting better, a few new tricks and the snow parks were good this season, but I could tell she didn't care. She was more interested in whether I had met any girls or had a new girlfriend yet. I said a few of course but I was here to snowboard. I asked after her boyfriend Ian, she was missing him a lot, but she knew it wouldn't be forever.

We talked more about Australia, she said it was the perfect place for me. She joked again, there were people who looked like me on every beach and I would be friends with all of them. I remember saying, "I would love to come out to see you after the season, it would be…"

The line suddenly dropped; our conversation was cut short. I was disappointed. I presumed she had run out of credit on her phone card.

I had an uncomfortable feeling, something felt wrong and just didn't sit right. I brushed it off. I really missed her this time, more than usual. I texted to say, keep on enjoying yourself, sounds like you are having the best time. I didn't know at that point I would never speak to her again. I never got to tell her one last time that I loved her or to say goodbye.

As I wasn't used to seeing her every day, in the days and months after her death my mind would play tricks on me. I would see her out of the corner of my eye, a fleeting glance walking down a busy street. I would start to race after the person with a small glimmer of hope, only to be reminded a few seconds later by my logical mind, it's not possible. She's gone, and a hard slam back to a reality. By nature, I am an optimist, and battled with my mind to accept the truth. It didn't matter how much I hoped, or wanted to believe, it would never change the fact that she was gone.

Every now and then I would find myself so caught up in what I was doing I would forget what had happened, we were a happy normal family again. Bang. I would remember and plummet straight back down to earth.

I grasped for meaning in everything, thinking back to our final conversation, why was it cut short, why did I get that uncomfortable feeling? Was my subconscious trying to tell me something? If it was why didn't I listen? If I had listened what could I have even done about it? These questions ran through my mind, but there were still a lot of bigger, unanswered questions. I caught a glimpse of a time in the future when maybe we would have some answers. Other questions would never be answered. I struggled with 'why' not in a sense of why was she murdered, but why did this happen to our family.

There was another 'why' that haunted me. Why wasn't I there when she needed me? I felt it was my job to protect her, that's what big brothers are supposed to do. What if I had been there? Could I have changed something? There were no answers, there was no right way to think and it has brought me to tears on many occasions. The optimist in me still hoped that one day, maybe I would see the bigger picture and would understand the reasons 'why'.

I know life's not fair and there is no reason why it should be, my heart wanted to believe in a higher purpose. A lot of people who have lost loved ones, I'm sure go through the same emotions, they want to know their loved one's life counted. I felt an overwhelming sense of guilt. Why did I still get to enjoy my life and she didn't? This tore me apart; my self-worth went through the floor. She was smarter, did better in her exams and knew what she wanted to do with her life, more caring, held in high regard by family, her peers and contemporaries. She fitted in. I was a skateboarder, a snowboarder, a chef working unsociable hours, I smoked weed and drank beer. Deemed a misfit, or at the very least unconventional by society. The guilt of still being alive began to weigh heavily, at times I found it hard to control.

The one thought that always brought me back was the incomprehensible realisation that it was actually a billion to one odds, I was even born in the first place. I understood how magical and precious life is. There was no way in the world that I could throw that away, no way I could give up on the blessing of life that has been denied to so many others.

Chapter 8
Starting a charity

In the days and weeks after Caroline's death we felt we had to do something positive. The more we began to associate Caroline with rainbows, the more energy we had. A rainbow of hope driven by love, we officially announced we would be setting up a charity in Caroline's name called Caroline's Rainbow Foundation.

Our thoughts were simple. We wanted to prevent what had happened to Caroline happening to another young backpacker. We wanted to prevent other families from going through the hell we were experiencing. We had to do something, and it just felt right. She was such a positive person, so full of energy and life. I could imagine her giving us a big kick up the backside and saying, "Come on, get on with it." We wanted to use Caroline's outlook on life as the basis for the charity. She inspired others, her passion for life, interest in exploring different cultures and learning about people. Her conscientiousness towards travel fit perfectly.

Mum had a lot of friends and contacts she knew through thirty years of working and living in York. When people heard about what we were planning, they immediately wanted to help.

One of Caroline's close friends, Ben Fogerty, was also travelling in Australia when he heard the news. Out of respect he flew back for the funeral. We had a chance to talk; when we discussed the charity, he thought it was a brilliant idea. He talked passionately about travelling, after the funeral he was planning to resume his travels and fly back to Australia. "It's what Caroline would have wanted," he said with conviction.

I completely agreed. It was his generation that should be out there experiencing the world, they shouldn't be afraid of what's around the next corner. It was now our mission to make sure backpackers had the knowledge and confidence to travel, we wanted to prepare them for whatever life had in store.

When he finally returned from his travels, he gave a moving interview.

'After Caroline's death, Ben Fogerty returned home to say goodbye, and then continued his travels in Australia and Asia. As he explains, to stay at home would be to go against his friend's love of travelling.

Have you ever looked into the sky and wished you were a bird, free from the shackles of the Earth and blessed with a whole new perspective on the world?

As a child it was something I often wished for and as time went on, I found a suitable alternative for this impossible dream. I wished to travel, free myself from the shackles of home and receive a new perspective on the world and the people in it. Just the thought of having such an opportunity filled my heart with joy and, as my wings spread so did my smile.

Yet birds in flight are often brought to earth, by God, by another's selfishness, nobody knows. My friend Caroline was one such bird who, in tragic circumstances, was awoken from her dream. From that day forward we all, both at home and abroad, carry her dreams with us.

After having travelled home to say farewell to Caroline, I returned to continue my journey in Australia and into Asia. At home, family and friends came together and formed Caroline's Rainbow Foundation in her name.

I have often asked myself whether I would have continued my flight had it been another who had passed away. Caroline was passionate about her travels, credit to her, joy is the song which Caroline and Sarah wrote whilst in Australia. They would often bore my travelling companion Jimmy and I with renditions of it.

Yet it was only after April the tenth that I understood the full significance of this song and so turned it into a poem in her memory.

With this new-found wisdom I decided that it would be ludicrous to even contemplate staying at home. After all, I didn't wish to upset my friend and I came to realise that remaining on my perch would only achieve that which I wished to avoid. As it was the duty of those at home to consolidate her dreams in a foundation, it was mine, and the others who continued travelling, to carry her dreams as far as we could. It was without doubt the most difficult and cathartic task I have ever carried out. Oftentimes I wished to lower my head, perch and not move. Yet her strength, her soul enabled me to continue. All I would need to do is think of her and her ambition and off I would fly.

By this strength we are all able to continue, her memory has taught us many lessons: we must follow our dreams, life is precious, we must take care. Caroline's character is now manifested in her own Rainbow Foundation whose aims are so closely intertwined with safety and enabling people to follow their dreams.

Some dream that at the end of any rainbow there is a pot of gold. Needless to say, these same people will be searching for eternity to find fulfilment in their minds' prophecy.'

A new chapter in our lives was just beginning, something none of us could ever have predicted. We again had a reason to get out of bed each morning. Our new headline read 'Charity born out of tragedy'. We had something positive to talk about after all the negativity and heartache. We felt it more aligned with Caroline's spirit and the person she was. I had absolutely no doubt in my mind we were doing the right thing.

Mum and I had no experience of running a charity and very little knowledge of the travel industry. We sat around a table with a group of close friends and colleagues. We asked, what are we going to do and how are we going to do it?

Our mission was twofold:

- To keep young travellers safe when travelling.
- To support families who have lost loved ones in travel-related incidents.

Mum and David used their contacts to pull together an incredible group of people who were all interested in helping, they offered their time freely and wanted to build something special for Caroline. (There are too many people to mention who helped the charity, but please know that we offer our eternal gratitude for all your love and support.) Everyone wanted to prevent what happened from happening again and to potentially save the lives of other young backpackers. We laid out our objectives and applied to become a registered charity. People started to donate, and we started to build up funds to put towards helping backpackers.

After long discussions, one of our initial ideas was to set up a telephone line for people to call if they got into trouble. We could offer phone support and importantly leave funds which could be accessed by the nearest embassy to help backpackers if they had their bags stolen, lost their money or worse. They would be able to access money and we would pay for a night's accommodation to help keep them safe.

Mum and David travelled down to London by train for a meeting at the Foreign and Commonwealth Office, to see how the idea could work and discuss other ways we could help the backpacker and travel communities. As they left York, I knew Mum was very nervous. From Kings Cross train station, they got a taxi, the next one on the rank amazingly had rainbow colours on the side.

This went further to cement the thought that Caroline was still around. This could have just been coincidence but whenever we saw a rainbow, we thought Caroline was supporting us in whatever we were doing. The meeting went well and there was a lot of opportunity for us to help and work together in the future.

We made contact with Diana Lamplugh; she was an inspiring lady who had set up the Suzy Lamplugh Trust after her daughter Suzy had gone missing in the UK. Suzy was an estate agent, who had gone for a viewing to show someone around a property and just disappeared. Diana had set up a charity focusing on personal safety when travelling to and from work. We went down to her offices to meet Diana and her husband. Her story was heart-breaking, Suzy's body was never found. Diana never found closure. Her grief must have been horrific, different to ours although we could empathise with each other's story. She would still have had hope, maybe one day her daughter would come home. Diana inspired us really connected with Mum and what we were doing. Our charities would be able to work side by side helping people stay safe.

I looked through their information; one thing surprised me, but when I thought about it made perfect sense like most things related to safety. The most dangerous time for people travelling to and from work was the fifty metres before they reached their front door. People are distracted, keys in hand, daydreaming about what they are going to have for dinner or watch on TV. They are not concentrating on what they are doing, they are not present in the moment or aware of their surroundings. This really resonated with me, we had to make sure people's awareness was raised in the moments they were at most risk.

Offers of support from people extended to building a website, registering a domain name and pulling together travel safety information to put online. I was very interested in this side of things, at the time websites were still relatively new for businesses and charities.

After registering www.carolinesrainbowfoundation.org we started writing content. Our focus was travel safety awareness. We had to raise awareness of the potential dangers. I needed to better understand what this meant. I had done some travelling and prepared a little, but honestly, found myself relying on my wits in many situations.

Travel safety awareness to me was about understanding the risks, preparing as much as possible to make travel stress free and more enjoyable. Through knowledge, travellers would be forearmed for what could happen, ultimately, they would have more confidence and a safer experience.

Our focus online was to help backpackers by better preparing them for their travels. Offering tips and advice about recognising potential dangers, and the steps they could take to reduce risk. We produced our first list of top tips, which still features on our website today.

Research before you go — Knowledge of the country or city you are travelling is essential. Make sure you are aware of what to expect before you arrive.

Visit your doctor — Get an appointment before you travel. Check if you need any inoculations or vaccinations for your chosen destination.

Travel Insurance — Make copies of your documents in case you need to prove who you are. Always check the details carefully, read the small print and make sure you are fully covered for any activities.

Gap year companies — Check to see if the company is offering what you want. Read testimonials from other travellers who have already done it.

Local language — If travelling to a non-English speaking country, try to learn a few phrases. You will find you get a lot more respect and interaction from the locals.

Try your gear — Use your bag and walk in your shoes before you go. Get used to using your gear, so when you leave for your travelling adventure it feels familiar and comfortable.

Watch your belongings — Split your money and keep it close. Keep an eye on your bags at all times, this could save you a lot of trouble and expense.

Accommodation — Book your first night's accommodation and know how to get there. This will make things easier and you will be less of a target for opportunists.

Keeping people informed — Always let your friends know where you are going. They are less likely to worry if they are informed and can quickly raise the alarm in case of emergencies.

Be aware — The more aware you are, the earlier you can recognise warning signs, the easier it will be to avoid potential problems. Always keep your wits about you.

Taking offence — Travelling you will meet a lot of like-minded people, but not everyone will want to be your friend. Be confident, don't take what people might say personally.

Follow your instincts — You will know if something feels right. Always listen to yourself and don't be dragged along with the crowd.

We felt all the tips were relevant, one tip rang uncomfortably true. Insurance — read the small print and make sure you are fully covered. Caroline had gone through a company who provided an insurance policy, we naturally assumed that the insurance would cover all of her needs. If she wanted any extras they were listed, scuba diving, skydiving etc… no problem. What we never thought to check was that her life was covered. It turned out it wasn't. A travel insurance policy that covers you to go scuba diving but doesn't cover your life. We were absolutely gobsmacked. Please, read the small print. Check you are covered for everything you are planning to do.

After speaking with Caroline's college tutors, including Jo Barrett and Jill Sissons at York College, they were very pleased to support us in any way they could. They had the idea to set up an annual psychology prize. Caroline was an excellent student and was really passionate about the subject. The prize would go to the top student in the year group. We thought it was a lovely positive tribute, people would know Caroline's story and she would inspire them to be the best they could be. We were very proud; it was the only prize of its kind the college offered students.

The winner of the first Caroline's Rainbow Foundation Psychology Prize was Elly Pegg. Elly had planned a gap year before going to Sheffield University. She intended to work for the Children's Trust in Surrey for six months, and then spend a further six months working in Canada on a special needs project for the YMCA. It was great to see someone who was similar to Caroline with the confidence to step out into the world and do what they wanted to do.

At the College we offered students in the Design Department the task of designing the logo for the charity. They were extremely excited and came up with some fantastic designs, we had a shortlist to choose from. After a lot of thought, we finally decided on an arc of stars that had the colours of the rainbow running through them. It was perfect.

We produced rainbow star pin badges, travel notebooks, pens and umbrellas. Caroline had created some paintings, her art teacher contacted us asking if we would like them. There was a set of three lilies, and we thought they looked really vibrant and fresh. With the art link in our family, we printed them to help raise funds. A set of the pictures also hangs proudly in the library at the College. Dad also donated a limited-edition print run of a scene of the west front of York Minster.

We had great momentum behind us, and wanted to reach as many people as possible, we needed to let people know it was still OK to do a gap year. Caroline was doing what she wanted, a phrase that was constantly mentioned was 'she was following her dreams'. This quickly got turned into 'follow your dreams' and became the charity's motto. We were promoting travel, with the caveat, prioritise your safety and minimise risk.

A lot of my free time was spent thinking about ways we could help people. I had always been interested in travel but realised it had only really been superficial. I liked visiting different places and seeing new things but that was as deep as it went. When we were younger family holidays were primarily to have a break, play on the beach and recharge our batteries. I started to look more in depth into travel and what it actually meant to have an opportunity to see the world. Travel was a privilege, to visit another country, dive into another culture and experience something completely different was incredibly special. As human beings we are tactile, our bodies are built for soaking up sensory experience. That's after all one of the main reasons we are here, to experience life. I began to understand why we should travel; it can not only educate but also contribute to defining our future.

We turned our attention to the travel industry to understand what worked and what safeguards were already in place for backpackers.

Travel was redefined in 1994 by the United Nations into three distinct categories:

- Domestic Tourism, involving residents of the given country travelling only within this country.
- Inbound Tourism, involving non-residents travelling in the given country.
- Outbound Tourism, involving residents travelling in another country.

We were primarily concerned with Outbound Tourism. We were keen to see how we could work with different companies to try to bring travel safety into the forefront of people's minds. Gathering together travel guides and books, I was surprised to find that there was only a paragraph or so in each book that related to travel safety. We had our work cut out. I started to contact travel companies to see if we could help expand the safety sections.

As we gained momentum, Mum became the figurehead of what we were doing. We found ourselves giving a lot of interviews, she talked passionately and emotionally about Caroline and the risks when travelling. We became friends with a few of the TV presenters and journalists.

It took some time, but it was now official. Charity status had been granted for Caroline's Rainbow Foundation. We were all so proud, but it also meant we had a lot of work ahead of us and a responsibility to the Charity Commission.

We were talking with the Bundaberg Police about what we could do to improve safety for backpackers in the town. They thought additional lighting on the bridge would make a big difference. No one had really thought about it before, but like all these things, it's not a problem until something happens. It was an obvious place for people to hide or somewhere opportunists could use to take advantage of someone else. The council quickly installed additional lighting along the route. We thought we had already made a difference in our challenge to keep backpackers safe. Symbolically we were illuminating the people who try to live in the shadows and take advantage of backpackers. As a result, the council reviewed all the lighting around Bundaberg to make sure everywhere was lit adequately after dark. Especially the backpacker hangouts and routes to youth hostels, hotels and other accommodation.

In all our work setting up Caroline's Rainbow Foundation and having something positive in our lives again, we never stopped to think that it would be a constant reminder of Caroline. Talking about her every day in some way was like she was still with us. None of us were ready to let her go.

Chapter 9
A flying visit across the world

July 2002 and we were waiting for new information on the case. Our family was invited to go to Australia and visit Bundaberg, primarily to put out an appeal and help with the police inquiry. I knew I had no choice but to go, anything we could do to help Caroline. It was decided, Dad and I would go with Richard Crinnion, Dad's partner, Janet, and a team from the BBC lead by Christa Ackroyd.

The trip sent my emotions into overdrive. In one way, I was excited to be travelling to one of the places I had always dreamt of exploring, on the other hand it couldn't be a worse situation. We knew it would be a complete rollercoaster, but our focus was firmly on helping the police find Caroline's murderer. I was still learning to cope with getting up each morning and my first thought always being 'Caroline is dead'. We had to be strong. I knew we would be on show in front of the media. I had seen these kinds of appeals before on TV and could only imagine how difficult it must be for the family. At some point very soon, it would be us sat in front of a bunch of microphones, with cameras flashing, answering questions about Caroline and asking the public for help. It was a very scary thought.

I had an understandable but probably unfair resentment for Australia; an ignorant person had single-handedly managed to destroy our family. This person needed to pay for their crime. I was sure it wasn't a true representation of the country and the Australian people, but I had to find out for myself.

Thinking back over the last few months a lot of it was a blur. I started to keep a diary, partly to try to make sense of my thoughts and feelings, but also to keep a record of what was happening. I knew this visit was going to be significant for us and hopefully in Caroline's case as well. We would be experiencing a lot of painful emotions and reliving some of the most horrendous moments.

It was going to be a long flight, travelling at 34,000 feet, around 500 miles an hour, destination Australia.

9/7/2002

She is my sister! Even though I can't see her it doesn't mean she is not around. I have been going to the grave daily, desperately trying to make peace with her, God and everyone else who matters. Up to now I have had no comfort or words of wisdom that have made life any easier.

Here I sit on the same flight she took months ago. Little did she know at that time that it would be her last, the thought makes me cringe and crumple inside. I imagine her so happy and excited chatting constantly for the whole flight, looking forward to her adventure of a lifetime. I feel like a member of the audience in a horror film. Two girls travelling, having the time of their lives not aware that anything could happen, but I know, the audience knows… this is not going to end well.

Twenty-four hours flying, plenty of time to think. All the stupid mistakes I have made, close calls, I am so lucky to still be here. If it was my time now how many things would be left undone, unsaid and unfinished. I haven't done enough in my life, I feel like I have pissed away the days, weeks and years. My time has flown by, thinking back now I can't seem to remember half the things I have done.

We are flying over Calcutta.

She was amazing, she seemed to know what she wanted and would go out and get it! Working hard, playing hard and doing it all by herself. No handouts. I admired her determination and willpower immensely. This still makes her death so hard to comprehend, she just wouldn't have let it happen, yet it did. She had so much potential, it's such a waste. I feel a huge sadness looking at a world without her.

Caroline's Rainbow Foundation — her new manifestation in this world. She will always be with me in my heart. We can only hope she will help more people in death than she ever could in life. But does it really matter? Nothing will ever bring her back. I am having trouble accepting the rest of my life without her, I don't want my children to grow up without ever knowing hers.

It's -44 degrees outside, feel like shit only three hours of sleep, about an hour out of Bangkok.

10/7/2002

Back on the plane for another ten hours heading to Sydney, we arrive at 6 a.m., then fly to Brisbane and on to Bundaberg.

Flying over Alice Springs, 4 a.m. local time, I have no idea what time it is in the UK. The distance we are travelling is immense. I looked over the wing and saw more stars than I had ever seen before. Looking down to Earth there were only the lights from the city and road networks which offered a perfect layout. No other light for as far as I can see. I thought a lot about the Foundation and what we were planning, there was so much to do and so much I had absolutely no idea about.

We finally arrive in Bundaberg after four planes and two days travelling.

As we pulled into the small airfield, I could feel the adrenaline starting to pump through my veins which made me feel sick. From the window I saw a gaggle of media at the airport exit. Were they all for us?

The cabin crew escorted us from the plane straight into the back of a car, we were driven out as flashes from the cameras blinded us. We stopped in the town centre at the council offices, where we were introduced to Mayor Kay McDuff and her team and had a bite to eat. The police had arranged interviews for the following day and a television appeal for anyone to come forward with information relating to the case. They had also kindly arranged for us to stay at a bed and breakfast just outside of the town, run by an English couple, Kate and David Brant. They had a lovely place with traditional English comforts, they immediately made us feel welcome. There was a pool in the backyard, I was straight in for a swim. My body felt cramped and needed to stretch after twenty-four hours travelling. We were all absolutely shattered and fell into bed.

11/7/2002

At 6 a.m., Dad walks into my room saying we are going down the beach to watch the sunrise and start a watercolour.

By 7 a.m. our thoughts were to head to the bridge but when we checked the area it was already full of journalists and photographers. We decided to go back to the B&B for breakfast. Fresh fruit and a full English, very welcome.

The police arrived at 9:30 a.m. and drove us over to the police station. We met the Chief Superintendent. He took us around the station and introduced us to the team in the M.I.R (Major Incident Room) for Caroline's case.

I had a lot of confidence in what I saw and what everyone was doing. There was a press conference happening shortly, my heart was pounding but I held myself together. Dad and I sat down behind a desk with one of the lead detectives. In front of us was what I had imagined, a room full of cameras and reporters. I talked briefly about Caroline's Rainbow Foundation, but more importantly put out an appeal for anyone with any information to come forward. It seemed like it was over in a flash.

After lunch, we had time to gather our thoughts and met the Mayor at the Botanical Gardens, we were shown a tropical birch tree that had been planted for Caroline just nine days after her death. It reminded me of the trees in Strensall Common where we used to fly our model planes. I smiled. It was a beautiful spot by a peaceful lake and an old English semi-detached house. It had been brought over brick by brick from the UK many years before by one of the landowners. Strange how much it looked and felt like home. The media were all over us, but I was learning to smile, not look at the camera and focus on what we were doing. Dad and I were very moved by the tree, it was a privilege to spend time with the councillors. We did a short piece to camera with Christa for the BBC while we were at the tree. I spoke about my feelings for Caroline, how I missed her every day and how I felt about being in Australia. I was pretty honest but didn't go into the despair and sadness that constantly plagued me.

Driven on to our next appointment. We were introduced to the MP for Bundaberg and the Deputy Prime Minister John Anderson. This was a great honour and gave me a sense of how much Caroline's death had affected people all across the country. Mr Anderson told me about how he lost his sister in a sporting accident so could somewhat identify with what I was going through. He was a lovely man and I had a few minutes chat with him alone, it meant a great deal.

We were pushed through to another press conference before heading back to the police station and down to the radio station for a live broadcast. I was starting to know what to say and the questions the journalists would ask, I tried to be brief and to the point but pretty sure I waffled on just like Caroline would have.

Dad and I were both flagging, we went back to the B&B and crashed out for a few hours. In the evening I went with Christa and the BBC guys to send the broadcast back to the UK, which was airing at lunchtime. The work was done for the day and we went for a beer and pizza.

It was an incredibly difficult day for all of us, we had been thrown into the spotlight and done our best. I was so pleased that Dad was with me, we supported each other. His presence gave me more confidence. I could stand up taller knowing that he was behind me, supporting me and giving me the energy to carry on. All we could hope was the interviews and appeal had made a difference and would help the police track down Caroline's killer.

12/7/2002

A good night's sleep but the jetlag was starting to catch up with me; luckily, we had a quiet day with no interviews. We had time to reflect on where we were and what was happening around us. We went down to the beach and got some nice photos; it was a beautiful coastline and such a picturesque place. Nothing like I would ever have imagined. Met up with Kay and her husband for dinner, they were lovely people and genuinely devastated by what had happened to Caroline in their town.

We were leaving Bundaberg tomorrow for Sydney. It had been an incredibly difficult time, but the people of Bundaberg couldn't have been nicer. I felt it was all done with love. They were used to backpackers regularly passing through and it was considered a safe place. The councillors and residents were still in shock and couldn't believe this tragedy could have happened in their peaceful town.

13/7/2002

A bad night's sleep, my usual nightmare again. I was up and showered by 6:30 a.m., we went down to the bridge. It was our first opportunity with no media. I had been thinking of this moment for a long time, it was very emotional. Dad and I wept together and left blue flowers which were local to the area. Under the bridge there was a white cross and bunches of flowers, local people obviously visited regularly leaving their thoughts and regards.

It was one of the hardest moments of my life, words cannot express the sadness, anger, loneliness and emptiness I felt in that moment. I was pounded by the longing, wanting her back so badly, but knowing it's the one thing that I could never have. I miss her more than life itself, the old saying, 'you don't know what you have until it's gone' has never resonated so strongly.

We walked part way along the bridge. I have a vivid imagination and think in pictures. We stood at the point of the bridge where she had the realisation she was in trouble. Thrown over the railings, reaching for something to grab but there was nothing. Her life was over! It had plagued my nightmares for months and repeated constantly in my mind. I felt an intense stabbing in my heart every single time. My heart and soul fell to depths deeper than I had felt before. Caroline and I were part of each other, I had just mentally experienced her final moments. Dad and I had a few minutes of silence together, lost in our own thoughts.

I lived my nightmare; visiting the Burnett Bridge had only made everything more intense, cementing a reality to her experience in my mind.

Afterwards, I thought back, the railings were high, Caroline would have only just been able to see over the top, it would have taken a lot of effort to push her over. It was a long bridge, crossing over the Burnett River as well as Anzac Park. What killed me was thinking, if it had happened closer to the Bundaberg town side she would have maybe landed in the water and could have survived.

We drove around to the campsite where she was staying, it was strange. Dad and I walked the route Caroline would have taken, it was unbelievably upsetting and only solidified our reality further with every heavy step. Both of us had seen and felt enough, it was time to leave.

We went back to the beach, tried to clear our minds. We thought of Caroline again and how she would have walked along this beach with Sarah and probably watched a sunrise or sunset here.

David, Kate and their daughter, Claire, were lovely people. They had looked after us really well giving us everything we needed, it had been our little oasis away from our crazy reality. We will always be in their debt. The police picked us up and drove us to the airport; as we arrived Kay and her husband were waiting. They had a card from the local school, the kids had made it and all written their names on for us. We got to meet some of the kids and their teachers, it was touching how much they cared. We were so humbled and had an overwhelming feeling of love. It had not in any way been the experience I had expected from Bundaberg and certainly changed all preconceptions I had. Thanking everyone, it was time to leave.

We flew back to Sydney, I was feeling a sense of pride, we had achieved what we set out to do. We felt so very grateful for all the love and support we received from every one of the councillors, the police and the town as a whole. I was overwhelmed by the amount of work and care the police and detectives had put in to help Caroline. We were hopeful that the TV appeal and other interviews would help to shed some light on the case and get us one step closer to catching Caroline's killer. We were staying at the Hilton, not far from Circular Quay, my room had an amazing view of the city. I went for a walk around the CBD, it was nice to have a bit of anonymity after the last couple of days in the spotlight. Arriving back to the hotel late I had a drink in the bar. I wasn't tired so put a movie on in my room, *The Time Machine*. It was about a guy who lost his girlfriend in a robbery, this spurred him to build a time machine to go back and save her. Which he never could, because if he saved her, he wouldn't have built a time machine in the first place. A strange and poignant story; we are unable to change the past, no matter how much we want to.

14/7/2002

Up at 6 a.m., strange dreams again but different. I was in a house I didn't recognise. Mum and Grandma were there. Mum stopped breathing and I was fighting to help her, there were people pulling her away. I knocked into Grandma, she fell backwards in slow motion and hit her head. I was still fighting but couldn't save either of them. I picked up both bodies and laid them outside on the grass, I went back in the house through to the kitchen. Caroline's body was on the sideboard, all three were dead. Just Dad and I left now, the others were gone.

Showered and tried to refresh myself. Went down for breakfast, the buffet had some of the most flavoursome fruit I had tasted, sun-kissed! Completely different from the produce we had in the UK. We all met up and headed out for the day, driving to Milsons Point; we found a lovely view of the Harbour Bridge and Sydney. Dad and I both painted, relaxed and soaked in the atmosphere.

I went to see Bondi Beach. It was a dream moment walking up and seeing the beach and surf. The water was full of surfers and the beach was full of beautiful couples and happy families. Caroline must have loved the energy here, the feeling of the place and vivid colour. I felt a sense of happiness for the first time, appreciating the good times she must have had before Bundaberg. Her travels must have been so exciting, she would have stood on the beach with Sarah, soaking up the view and thought she was in paradise.

As I wandered around, I felt strangely at home, even though nothing was further from the truth. Geographically, I couldn't be much further away. I had a skate, it was good to clear my mind and be fully present in the moment. I needed the escape.

Dinner at Doyle's restaurant, one of the city's finest. The food was amazing, steamed king prawns to start, grilled John Dory for main. The atmosphere was great and the view was incredible, a blend between the natural world and big city lights. I loved it.

15/7/2002

Our last day in Sydney, we were flying out at 8 p.m. I had the whole day to see as much as I could. I visited the Opera House, incredible. I would love to see a performance one day. Walking around the point I saw Dad painting across the harbour, he was back doing what he loved and looked relaxed. I sat in the Botanical Gardens and wrote, caught up with everything. I had my skateboard with me, a great way to see more of the city in less time. Picked up a few gifts for Mum and people back home, I seemed to be able to escape in the beauty of the city for an hour or so before everything came flooding back.

Sydney is a big place, but I still felt safe and more comfortable here than I ever have been travelling around Europe. I guess that's part of the appeal. I think it's to do with the culture, to me it feels more akin to life in the UK. The city is clean, architecture is modern. Not only that it's also the life we dream about, plenty of space, great weather and relaxed people.

16/7/2002

Going back home. I felt different, more confident and a huge relief the trip was done. In some ways a weight had been lifted. I feared setting foot on

Australian soil, but we were offered such a warm welcome and the country is so amazingly beautiful. All my preconceptions had quickly disappeared. The horrific tragedy that happened to Caroline had become compartmentalised in my head. I was pleased it had not tarnished my view of the country as a whole.

Caroline's Rainbow Foundation was now our focus, everyone I spoke with took it in a positive way and thought a charity to help backpackers and other travellers was a great idea. It felt like we had the backing of people in Bundaberg and the rest of the country. We need to do it for Caroline, had she been here she would have wanted us to help others.

This trip has undoubtedly changed me, probably more than I know at this time. I liked talking to people, they listened when I was speaking and seemed engaged with what I was saying. I couldn't get away with saying what I liked any more or be ignored when I said stupid things. I felt I had a bigger sense of responsibility now, I moved on to the next chapter of my life. Life is different, Caroline has gone and we must rise up and get on with it!

17/7/2002

Touching down, I saw the UK in a different light. We headed through Kings Cross Station to catch the train back to York; it was dirty, soot on the buildings and graffiti on the walls. The sky was grey, and it looked like rain. Finally, we made it home, another long journey. It was heart-breaking, but I also thought we had achieved something. We had done something for Caroline hopefully to help bring her killer to justice. We had also done something for ourselves, confronted some of our demons and lived to tell the tale.

The trip was over, Mum was so pleased to see me back. She wanted to know every detail. Living with David she was feeling slightly better, David was looking after her well. Dad went back to Scarborough and painting in his studio. I was back in our family home and took time alone to process everything. We waited every day for news from Australia, I must admit I was still struggling.

I needed some routine and of course still had to earn a living. I went back to work, part-time at first, as a chef, at The Grange Hotel in York. It was a beautiful characterful hotel offering guests a high-quality stay and a fine dining experience. They also hosted weddings and events which made the kitchen side of things very busy. I knew the place well, they were really good to me and always had me back when I was in York. Many of the chefs from that period have become lifelong friends and have been an amazing support throughout the years.

My head chef at the time, Michael Whiteley, was very understanding. I was still a complete mess; some days were better than others. To have some kind of routine in familiar surroundings was very welcome. Kitchen life was always intense, with such a huge workload we all had to focus. One of my first jobs of the day was to make bread, flavoured rolls for dinner service and events. I loved it; it became my therapy. Mixing dough, proving, knocking back, adding flavours and second proving hundreds of perfectly shaped rolls. The fresh bread smelt amazing. It gave me great satisfaction and helped me to process everything that was happening outside of kitchen life. I found it an immersive experience, nothing was trivial, everything had to be spot on to get the perfect result. I felt my mind could switch off from my other life. Chef was great, he let me have time off when needed for different charity events, interviews and meetings. The kitchen boys helped me find some peace, when I had my whites on, I was no longer the guy whose sister had been murdered. I was just another chef and part of the team. They were supportive when needed but also gave me a reality check, we all worked hard and played hard together.

10/10/2002

Six months since Caroline's death. My nightmares were starting to become less frequent, it has undoubtedly been the worst time we have ever faced. There were lots of phrases going around our family. 'These things are sent to try us.' 'You are never given anything you can't handle.' There must be an element of truth to it as we were pulling ourselves together and trying to gain strength. It was our choice to step up and get on with it. The other option was no option for me; lay down and let grief wash over us.

No matter how I tried to act, how I tried to change my mindset there was always an anger deep inside. I could feel it deeper than I had ever felt anything before, it wasn't in my heart although I knew that was broken, it was in my gut or even deeper if that's possible. When people annoyed me,

99

I could feel that anger begin to build. If anyone were to push me too far, I was afraid that the whole lot would boil out of me and I could bloody kill someone.

I visited Cambridge, where I used to live when I was Caroline's age, nineteen. I parked up and took a wander around the old city. I was young, trusting and amazed by the world. I couldn't have imagined having the confidence to go to Australia back then, my respect for Caroline grew even more.

Fond memories, I had a good job and worked hard. I didn't think people had different agendas to what they told me, looking back I was very naive. I am more suspicious now of what people say but more importantly why they're saying it.

Walking through the streets I felt safe. There didn't seem to be anything untoward and I remembered the happy times, but maybe the bad bits had just faded away.

When all our beloved possessions lost their sparkle and got thrown away, all we have left are memories. I now realise, they're what's precious. What are possessions without the memories surrounding them? It's the story behind them that gives them value.

I was starting to think, ignorance was bliss; when I lived here our family unit was still complete. We had a lovely childhood. I am sure there were still many problems, but I was just unaware. I was ignorant to the fact the bills had to be paid, I didn't know first-hand anything of loss or devastation, I was naive to these experiences and emotions. I didn't understand the long-term consequences of one's actions.

Leaving Cambridge, I travelled on to London, catching up with friends from winter seasons. We went to the annual snowboard show at Battersea Park. It was a taste of normality and took me back to life before the telephone call. For the first time, I remembered the good times we had on my last winter season. It was OK to feel happy again, it was good to smile and not feel guilty.

I got a call from Mum. The police had been in touch from Australia. They had found evidence linked to the case in a local farmer's field. I was hopeful the police were one step closer, although we were still in the dark as to the biggest questions, who and why? It brought it all back and I could feel my anger brewing inside. Given the chance I would happily inflict serious pain on the son of a bitch responsible! I had imagined what I would do in the most grotesque ways, I know it won't change anything but right now it would make me feel better.

Back in York we met up with Richard Crinnion. He wanted to talk face-to-face, some information was confidential and other parts would be released to the media. Caroline's handbag had been found in a field just outside Bundaberg and the police had found evidence linking a man to the case. They had also found graffiti on a picnic bench near the bridge that read 'I throw the girl off the bridge. I am sorry.' A man known to the police as a drifter and drug addict, he was already in prison for other offences. They had potentially identified the person responsible for Caroline's murder.

Following a series of police interviews with the man and associates they had enough to make an arrest. The police were extremely confident they now had their man.

News of the arrest had given us a sense that justice was going to be served; in the back of my mind, I knew there would be a trial and that I would have to be there.

I made a decision to go travelling to Australia, I wanted to follow in Caroline's footsteps and see places that she had talked about so passionately. I also wanted to visit the places that she had never got to see, a part of me wanted to finish her adventure. We had Caroline's Rainbow Foundation now and I wanted to understand what life was like as a backpacker to see how we could really help.

Mum and David were working hard every day for our charity, they were living together and getting on really well. He had asked her to marry him. It was a shock, but I was assured nothing was going to happen quickly. He just wanted her to know he loved her. If they made each other happy then it was the right thing to do. Life had to carry on. I could tell that he adored her and knew she would be looked after. I am sure Caroline would have approved.

Chapter 10
Caroline's Rainbow Foundation

Throughout this book when talking about Caroline's Rainbow Foundation I unfortunately can't go through all incentives, charity events and people who supported us in great enough detail to do them all justice. To our board members, volunteers and supporters, please know you have our love and eternal gratitude. There is a great deal of information about our charity beginnings and what we have achieved over the years on our website.

I would like to mention points that I feel had significant impact on our outlook towards gap year travel and offered different ways forward for our charity. There are also important elements to help people better understand travel and travel safety.

Travel is in our DNA, we are pre-programmed to want to explore, for me I could feel my hunter-gatherer instinct. In modern times we travel for pleasure. In English culture the goals are simple, a break from work, get a good suntan, have a few drinks and relax on a beach. This mentality has been cemented into our psyche gaining popularity during the 1960s and 70s when cheap package holidays opened up sun-drenched European holiday destinations to an eager British market. Although travelling is a much older and nobler concept. It was originally driven by the search for life enrichment, education and gathering of artefacts to enhance life post-travel.

Some great civilisations of the past understood the benefits of travel and expanding the mind, it was one of the main ways isolated communities gained more knowledge and ultimately strength. In the second century BC, the Egyptians were rebuilding their pharaonic state, developing it in new and mesmerising ways. They looked objectively and decided which areas were worth rebuilding and which areas needed to be replaced. The pharaohs sent expeditions crossing the Sahara and sailing down to Ethiopia, they were looking for knowledge and new ways of thinking they could incorporate into their society. The Egyptians also travelled for practical reasons using the River Nile to transport goods, building materials and livestock. They understood that certain products were better cultivated in certain areas.

The Romans travelled with armies to expand the empire but also for pleasure, although the modes of transport were far cruder than today, leaders and wealthy citizens were known to travel great distances in search of knowledge and valuable artefacts. The routes were dangerous, so people travelled with armed guards to ensure their safety. On their return journeys, they would be travelling with valuable treasures, which would often make them targets for opportunists and thieves.

In the seventeenth and eighteenth centuries people would embark on what was known as the 'Grand Tour'. This was not only for male travellers; women could also undertake a 'Grand Tour' but would usually need to find a sponsor. The aim was education and the broadening of horizons, both physically and mentally. They were in search of great art, culture and the meaning of life. Travelling from destination-to-destination was classed as the most dangerous part of a travelling experience. It was also very time-consuming, what would take us an hour now by air could have taken several weeks. This meant that tours could last anything from six months to a few years.

I believe this mindset has transcended through the civilisations and defines the way some people choose to travel. Today we can see amazing landscapes, art and architecture from the other side of the world on TV or computer screens. For some people it's enough to quench their need to explore, for others it opens a floodgate and starts a lifelong obsession with travel.

I love the romantic idea that we were travelling in search of knowledge, wisdom and to find answers to the bigger questions in life. I wanted the charity to convey this love for travel, taking people back to the roots of why we chose to travel in the first place.

Once people have an idea in their mind, decided on an adventure and got on the plane it's difficult to turn back. If they are not fully committed and planned an adventure for a significant period of time, then it can be costly to return early if they find out it's not for them. Before any travelling adventure it's pertinent ask yourself:

What — What adventure you would like to do?

Where — Where would you like to travel?

When — What time of year are you travelling?

How — How are you going to get there?

Who — Who are you travelling with?

Why — Most importantly, why do you want to go?

We held our first Charity Ball at York Racecourse. I helped where I could but, in the past, I was always on the kitchen side when it came to events, it was an eye-opening experience to see everything that went into putting on a large-scale event. David's background was in retail and senior management. When he was working, he was responsible for over 200 staff so was very used to high level organisation. Our other board members were all highly regarded professionals within their own specialities. They covered all angles, worked tirelessly and thought of everything. Working together we were able to host a fantastic event which smashed everyone's expectations.

Our inaugural Annual Golf Day was held at Allerthorpe Park Golf Club, twenty teams of four registered. I had never played golf before or even stepped foot on a golf course, it was a great experience. The weather was good, but we had a few spots of rain which created the most beautiful rainbow across the sky; we all felt Caroline was with us looking down with approval. We had to say a few words during dinner and prize-giving, I was extremely nervous but pulled myself together. I could feel the support in the room, everyone looked back at me with sadness for what had happened but also satisfaction that they were doing something to help. I quite enjoyed public speaking, if I could control the butterflies in my stomach.

We got caught up in what we were doing, a great distraction for a worthwhile cause. For Mum, it had become her new life's work, she put everything into trying to help people. She wanted to help keep people safe, everything was done out of pure love. This was evident whenever she gave interviews or talked about the charity's work, goals and aspirations. She was working tirelessly and as a result was nominated for a number of awards.

'Charity in the running

A charity set up in memory of murdered backpacker Caroline Stuttle is in the running for an award. Caroline's Rainbow Foundation was set up by

Marjorie Stuttle and her son, Richard following the death of the 19-year-old in Bundaberg, Australia, in April last year.

The teenager, from York, had been on a gap year holiday, travelling with a friend before taking up her place at university. Her body was found under a bridge in the Queensland town and an Australian man has since been charged with murder and is awaiting trial.

The foundation is one of only four charities that has been selected for the UK Charity Awards shortlist. Mrs Stuttle said yesterday: "We're absolutely thrilled to be shortlisted because everyone has worked so hard with the charity. We've had so much help from people.'"

Mum had also been nominated for the Hearts of Yorkshire Awards. People who spoke to her knew immediately that she was genuine and was doing it for Caroline. We attended the awards day; Sir Michael Parkinson was the honoured guest. Mum had a photo with him, we were all so very proud of her. I found it an incredibly humbling experience; we were just ordinary people. I had the utmost respect for everyone who attended and received recognition that day, they all worked tirelessly and had raised thousands of pounds for charity, working incredibly hard to improve their communities.

'Yorkshire woman of the Year 2003. Marjorie Stuttle for Yorkshire woman of the Year?

Making some good come out of tragedy. BBC North Yorkshire's nomination for Yorkshire woman of the Year is courageous mother, Marjorie Stuttle. BBC North Yorkshire have nominated Marjorie Stuttle as their Yorkshire woman of the year.

One of the saddest stories of the last year was the murder of Yorkshire backpacker Caroline Stuttle in Australia. Her mother, Marjorie, is still coming to terms with the loss of her daughter. But in the wake of it all she's set up a charity to help backpackers abroad keep out of trouble, it's called Caroline's Rainbow Foundation.

"My life's aim is that if I can save one life and stop somebody from suffering like I do then that is a goal to have. Having the charity gives me a bit of light in my black life."

Marjorie Stuttle is BBC North Yorkshire's nomination for Yorkshire woman of the Year.'

We got asked during most interviews how we coped, people would say we were so brave. I have talked with Mum about this over the years and the truth is we had no choice. It wasn't up to us; we had felt compelled to do it.

We were still working on the idea of leaving a pot of money in embassies for people who found themselves in trouble. Logistically, it was proving to be an absolute nightmare and was throwing up difficult questions. How would people access the funds? How would we decide who was genuine and who was going to make the final decision? We were full of good intentions, but very naive in the logistics about how things would work. It didn't matter which way we looked at it and who we spoke to it was looking like a non-starter. We unfortunately had to abandon the idea.

Our board of directors were an amazing pool of knowledge and expertise; we discussed in further detail the best way to focus our time and resources. How could we prevent what happened to Caroline from happening to someone else? We finally decided that prevention was better than the cure. If we could educate people about the risks and dangers before they departed, they would be better prepared for any situation that may arise.

Students were our primary audience as they generally had little independent travel experience. Most had been away for family holidays or group excursions, but travelling alone or with friends was completely new. They had to learn what to do if things went wrong, how to sort out their own problems and learn how to spot potentially dangerous situations. We could reach the most people by getting travel safety material into schools and colleges before students departed for their adventures. The idea formed; we would produce a short tutorial film which would run through different safety-related scenarios. This would be accompanied by a teaching pack. Teachers would be able to show the film to their students pausing after each scenario to discuss. Making it interactive would ensure that students better understood important aspects of travel safety. Once completed, the film would be distributed free of charge to schools, colleges and other educational bodies around the UK.

Working with an external company, we decided the film would be called the 'Time of Your Life'. It would include different scenarios that would be relatable to anyone going travelling. We still wanted to promote travel in a positive light; brainstorming a lot of ideas, two different scenarios came to light that we felt would create talking points for students to start thinking about their safety.

The first situation would stress the importance of research, local knowledge and knowing where you are going. Planning your route and being aware of areas that are known to have higher crime rates. Recognising potentially dangerous situations and having the ability to defuse them.

The second situation related to going out and having a good time, people having their drinks spiked was in the spotlight. There would be a situation where drinks were left unattended and backpackers belongings were stolen. We wanted to highlight when people become distracted by having a good time and miss what was actually happening.

Both scenarios were very serious and had to be handled carefully, we had to find a balance between highlighting the risks and keeping a positive outlook towards travel.

Our website was starting to build up a comprehensive inventory of safety tips, helpful hints and travel information. We contacted other travel companies, who were happy to provide a page of safety information relating to their specialist area. We produced flyers and other hard copy materials with safety tips and dos and don'ts for travelling. Our aim was to raise awareness of the risks of travel and to promote travel as worthwhile in gaining life experience, which was beneficial when applying for future career roles.

When I was twenty-two years old, myself and three friends, who were all keen skateboarders decided to go interrailing. We all purchased a train ticket valid for a month which allowed us to travel on most trains around Europe. We wanted to visit cities and skateparks that we had only seen on videos. Our route wound its way through eight countries during the month, it was going to be our greatest adventure to date.

Overall, the trip was amazing, we got to visit some amazing internationally-known skateboarding spots, as well as see countries we had always dreamt of. Highlights for me were the beautiful architecture of Amsterdam and the amazing skate spots in Rotterdam. Copenhagen was also incredible, and I really loved the Danish outlook on life. I fell in love with the mountains when we went to Chamonix. Berlin had the most amazing energy, such a vibrant city.

Thinking back from our charity perspective, we were four lads carrying skateboards. Firstly, we could have been perceived as if we were carrying a weapon. At the time skateboarding didn't have the same recognition it has today. Skateboarders looked like they were just hanging around causing trouble, which usually wasn't the case, they would just be skating. We got lumped in the same category as misguided youths. Secondly, on the other side, local gangs could feel threatened and may want to stamp their authority showing they were the kings of their patch.

I remember we were staying in Lyon and hanging out in a hostel. A big guy and his mates were also hanging around. Speaking French, he was calling us all the names under the sun, we couldn't understand what he was saying but knew he was making fun of us. It wasn't nice, we were ill-prepared and just had to smile and try to laugh it off. Afterwards, it made us feel horrible and put a stain on our time in Lyon. That experience stuck with me for years.

What it actually meant for us as skateboarders. We had friends wherever we went, we had a common bond with like-minded people, skateboarders would go out of their way to help each other. We were part of a community. If we needed anything, we knew we could ask fellow skateboarders and they would genuinely try to help. This spirit can be found in many places where you find like-minded people with common interests. I found the exact same community in the French Alps during my winter seasons. In an unknown environment meeting people who share the same passions can make you feel more comfortable and at home.

Throughout our interrailing experience we only made one real error which could have ended in something worse. We made a detour stopping at Dresden to see the solar eclipse. The following day we jumped on a train and found ourselves in Frankfurt. We thought it would be easy to find accommodation when we arrived, but we weren't aware of an annual festival that was in full swing. The city was packed and nearly every bed was occupied. The couple of rooms we found would have completely blown our budget. There were no trains departing until the next day, we had to make a decision. Conserving funds, we decided we would sleep in the station, it wasn't going to be comfortable. We lashed our bags to the benches, held our belongings tightly and tried to get some sleep. It certainly wasn't an enjoyable experience, with only a couple of hours sleep, the next day we were shattered. We tried our best to take a look around the city, but decided to travel on to our next destination, find a hostel and comfortable bed. Lesson learned.

The impact this had on our trip was three-fold, time spent travelling is priceless, we had to pretty much write off the next day. Our lasting memory of Frankfurt was tarnished, which had nothing to do with the city itself. Finally, but most importantly, we put ourselves at unnecessary risk. Everything was OK, but we could have quite easily found ourselves in a difficult situation. Ever since then I have always tried to check what's happening in a city before I visit; if I am travelling from place-to-place I always try to book my accommodation in advance.

Another thing that struck me when we were travelling was the number of different currencies we needed, this was before the Euro came into effect. Eight countries meant eight different currencies. We had taken some local currency with us for countries we knew we would be spending more than a couple of days in, we also had travellers' cheques that we changed in each place. This meant that we had to carry all funds with us at all times. It took time to find exchange points, and we were at the mercy of whatever the exchange rate was when we needed cash. When we moved on, we had local currency left over, we worked it pretty well, but I still have some leftover change in a pot at home today. When travelling on a budget every penny, mark and centime counts.

What were the best ways for travellers to carry their money? The history of banking can be traced back to India around 2000 BC, where traders would make loans to farmers who travelled to and from a city. I discovered that the earliest form of travellers' cheque was created by the Poor Knights of Christ and the Temple of Solomon, who later became known as the Knights Templar. Their mission was primarily to escort pilgrims across the Holy Land at the time of the Crusades in the twelfth century. As the knights took a vow of poverty but were generally from a noble background, they donated a lot of their wealth to the Order. This meant that the Knights Templar had land and wealth distributed all across Europe. Wealthy travellers could deposit their funds at one of the Templar's strongholds in exchange for a letter of credit, the travellers deposit could be redeemed at another stronghold closer to their destination. This system became commonplace and has been used across the centuries ever since. In the UK, in the seventeenth century people could deposit their money with goldsmiths for safety and be issued with a credit note for payment on demand.

Travellers' cheques were first issued by American Express and first used in Europe successfully in Leipzig, Germany in 1891 by William Fargo who was the son of James C Fargo, president of the American Express Company. Travellers' cheques offered additional security, each cheque had a unique serial number and could be exchanged for cash in most countries at major banks.

Not having to carry all your currency with you minimised risk, deterring opportunists from bag snatching, stealing your luggage or worse. Today travellers' cheques are still available but are no longer widely used by the majority of travellers. There are many prepaid credit cards and apps available to help you travel safely with money and find the best exchange rates. It is also always advisable to let your bank know before you leave the country and your phone provider if you use online banking or a payment system connected to your phone. This ensures that your cards will not be stopped when you are abroad and prevents any issues that might occur. For me personally, I always like to carry some cash just in case of emergencies.

The more I talked to people, the more I realised that everyone had a travelling story that related to their safety or where they had found themselves in a difficult situation they had to solve. I thought that these would be a great learning tool for people, far better and far more engaging than a list of bullet points. Research showed that people retain more information if they can put it in context or have an emotional response linked to the story. We asked people for travel stories, experiences they had which other travellers might learn from. I met Oyvind Eide, he was an international student studying in the UK. He was happy to share one of his experiences.

'An airport is a place many people don't enjoy being in. A place many consider connected to stress. There are many things that might go wrong in an airport: the flight may be delayed or cancelled, or they may ship your bags off to somewhere else. I always make sure to put the most important things in my hand luggage, just in case something like that was to occur.

'Thankfully there are many places to de-stress. Places like bookstores, restaurants, clothes stores, hell they might even have a massage parlour. If given time to kill and money to spend, there should always be something to do at an airport.

'I find myself occasionally purchasing items duty free upon re-entry into my country: a few gifts for my family help to smooth over the fact that I haven't been answering all of their calls, and that I haven't called them as often as I promised.

'I'm an international student from Norway, living and studying in England. During the school holidays I go home to see my family and friends. The events in this story didn't take place in a Norwegian airport or at an English airport, but in Copenhagen.

'I had just been home for Christmas with my family in my hometown of Bergen. I showed up at least an hour early, with a printout of my boarding card and flight plan. I like to be as prepared as possible when it comes to air travel. In the past, I have had trouble regarding lost luggage and sudden delays or changes to the route. I feel my pocket to check for my passport and find it securely in its place. I use it to check in my luggage and make sure to put it back in the same pocket.

'You might think I'm overly cautious, but I would rather be more meticulous than risk losing any of my important documents. If I were to suddenly find myself in England without my passport, I wouldn't be able to enter the country. The reason why I'm telling you this is so you can understand how seriously I consider international travel and even though I believe myself to be as careful and as good at planning my journey as possible: there is always something that can go wrong.

'My flight plan was changed a week or so before my flight, and what should have been a simple flight from Bergen to Manchester was changed. I now had to change flights at Copenhagen. I was understandably frustrated by this, suddenly the trip was four hours longer when taking into account the time I had to spend waiting in Copenhagen.

'I arrive at the airport in Copenhagen. First order of business: which gate? I tracked down one of the boards and find it hadn't been decided yet. Reaching the gate area, I find another sign which tells me the same. I figure this is the central hub for the gates as there are signs pointing in opposing directions, giving directions to clusters of gates.

'Now begins the boring part. I'm going to be here for a couple of hours, and I need something to do while I'm waiting for my gate to be confirmed. I decide to check out the shops and restaurants. I see an overcrowded generic restaurant. Next is a bookstore, selling magazines and the newest, popular books. I stop to have a look and consider buying one, before remembering there are plenty of books I need to read already. Buying one just for the trip from Denmark to England would be a waste.

'Next is a sports pub, with t-shirts of some local Danish football team signed and framed on the wall. Televisions line the walls showing some football match between reds and yellows. I'm not too interested in football. I wonder briefly if I should try having a drink but think better of it, after reminding myself of being prone to car and seasickness in the past. Being intoxicated usually doesn't improve conditions.

'What follows are a few unremarkable shops that sell clothes, (lo and behold) a massage parlour and finally a shop specialising in ceramic elephants. Yes, ceramic elephants. Now this I have to see. After admiring or rather staring blankly at most of the uniquely painted elephants I consider buying one before thinking better of it. Storing one of those in my hand luggage would be a pain, as it would probably break easily or take up too much space.

'While this might seem as a commercial of sorts for the airport in Copenhagen, it isn't intended as such. Rather, make a note of my interest in the various things for sale and my considering buying them. I could have spent some of my money here, but I didn't. I do what amounts to a couple of laps around the area, making sure to stretch my legs for the next flight.

'I see my gate displayed on the board. I confirm it with my flight number and check I have my cell phone, passport, boarding pass, everything. I find the route I must take to my gate and resign myself to wait for another two hours.

'Feeling slightly hungry and very bored (despite the several 'gigabytes' of music on my music player) I decide to find a place to eat. The first restaurant seems a bit too crowded and loud for my liking. I spot a stairway going up a floor to what seems like a steak and grill restaurant. I decide to go have a look and find it to be quite nice. Not too crowded and not too loud. From what I can see it seems to be a bit more expensive than I would normally be into, but I convince myself to eat there anyway. I tell myself I might as well eat some proper food now before I go back to England and start subsisting on noodles and cheap meals. I sit down, order some food and watch the planes come in from the large window. The meal itself is all right. The beef is good, but the chips are a bit underwhelming. I enjoy my dinner and listen to my music while staring out the window for a good sixty minutes. With about fifty minutes 'till boarding time I decide to go ahead and pay my bill.

'I don't have any Danish cash, so I pull out my debit card and insert it into the waiter's machine. I input my pin and after a few seconds the machine displays the word DECLINED in all capital letters. The waiter: a tall, darker-looking gentleman, most likely of Latin-European descent, informs me they have had troubles with some of their machines and quickly goes to fetch me another. I shrug and think, well, these things happen, and continue staring out the window, twirling the card with my fingers.

'Three machines later and three DECLINED later, I start thinking something might be wrong. I resolve to fix the issue and grab for my credit card, thinking perhaps their machines will enjoy this card instead. Nope. DECLINED, DECLINED, DECLINED and DECLINED.

"At this point I'm getting nervous and stressed. I wonder if there is something wrong with their card readers. It must be because I used more than one card.

'The waiter remains polite and shares my aggravation when none of the cards work for any of the apparently limitless amounts of card-reading machines they have. He asks if he should bring more. I ask to leave to try my luck at an ATM or bank instead. I leave behind my backpack and jacket with passport and take only my wallet with me. As I rush down the stairs, I have a look at my wristwatch and find that time is running out.

'About thirty-five minutes until boarding and I also have to go to the gate. Thoughts are racing through my head as I follow the directions the waiter gave me to the nearby bank office: What is going on? Why aren't my cards working? Am I out of money? I don't have time for this! I reach the desk and explain to the lady that I'm having trouble with my cards and ask if she could help me withdraw some money.

'We give it a go: DECLINED.

'I realise I'm officially out of options. I have no more cards to use, no cash on me and my plane is leaving soon. 'What happens now? Do I get arrested? Do I have to sign some papers and send the bill to my parents? Do I lose my flight? How does this work?' I stand there thinking, sweating and feeling too stressed out to measure, until the lady behind the counter says, 'Maybe your bank has locked the use of your cards outside your home country.'

'I grab my cards back and hurriedly ask, 'Where can I get Internet here?'

"She tells me to go speak to the people at the information desk and gives me directions. The gears in my head are turning now and I realise how incredibly lucky I am.

'Many of us get a bad feeling when we're about to travel. The feeling where you know you have forgotten something, but you have no idea what. I remember having this feeling as I arrived at the airport in my hometown, but I did a quick mental check of my belongings and found that nothing was missing.

'I had actually forgotten to change my settings in my e-bank. My e-bank has a safety-measure that says if your cards get stolen and somebody tries to use them in a different country they won't work without special permission. My settings were to allow use in Norway and England, but the setting for the rest of Europe is always off by default.

'I track down the information desk, asking for directions twice more to make sure I'm on the right path. They give me a flyer with all the information I need to sign up for the free Wi-Fi, and I rushed back to the restaurant. I find my way back to my table, and the waiter approaches me. 'Don't miss your flight,' he says. This is nice and calms me a little. I inform him I will be able to pay in a few minutes. I pull my laptop out of my backpack and quickly go through the steps for getting into the wireless internet. I notice I have below ten minutes left on the battery, but I work quickly and eventually get access to the Internet.

'This is why I consider myself lucky: my e-bank requires a separate code to be entered along with my information and this code changes every day. You are given a small device which you can carry with you anywhere that gives you the day's code. I had this device in my backpack. I could have put it in my suitcase, but I didn't. I left it in a room by itself in my backpack. If I didn't have it here with me, I would probably have to take up a job washing dishes until I could pay for the meal.

'I manage to log in with my details and code and change the setting to include Denmark. I call over the waiter and ask if we can try paying again. He brings me to another machine (and another one just in case) and I insert my card. As I type my pin, I still feel doubt: What if there's a delay on the setting? What if I have to wait for an hour for it to take effect? What do I do then? I hit 'ENTER'. Every time before it came up DECLINED it would take at least five seconds before it was done deciding whether I had paid or not. This time it took only a split-second before the screen on the machine told me: ACCEPTED.

'I did a fist pump while saying, "Yessssss" as if I had just scored the winning goal in the last game of the season (basketball, not football) and quickly grabbed my stuff. The waiter asked me what had been wrong, and I hurriedly explained what had happened while making my way out of the restaurant. I had a plane to catch.

"The way over to the gate was pretty long, but I showed up just as boarding was starting and I arrived in Manchester without incident.

'The moral I took away from this story was your gut feeling is mostly right, and even though you can't be prepared for everything, there are definitely some things you should check every time you leave the country. Things such as having your wallet, passport, phone, your suitcase, and notifying your bank of where you are. I like checking in online, so I always bring a printout of the boarding card. I always check the weight of my luggage, making sure it's not over the limit. I also make sure I know where I put my baggage claim tag. Missing even one of these could be a great inconvenience, if not catastrophic.

'From now on, I think I will be sure to try buying a book or a bottle of water, or maybe even a ceramic elephant before I go eat at the most expensive restaurant in the place. You never know, you might not be able to pay for it.'

Chapter 11
An uncertain adventure

In November of 2003, I left the UK heading for Australia. Although excited to travel, I also knew it was not going to be an easy adventure. I had imagined watching the New Year's Eve fireworks at the Opera House in Sydney, swimming in the sea in Byron Bay and watching the sunrise over Uluru. Over the last year we had done a lot of media interviews and we had become friends with a radio presenter from the BBC. Elly Fiorentini was travelling to Australia for the Rugby World Cup and we decided to fly together.

This next adventure would be life-changing. I kept a daily diary, which I have written every day since.

The following three chapters detail my time travelling around Australia and New Zealand. I wanted to include my diary and some pen and ink sketches of my paintings to offer a real-life account of my experiences as a backpacker.

To everyone who was part of my travels along the way, thank you, you made each moment extra special. I love you all.

17/11/2003
5 a.m. start, on the road for 5:30 a.m. Mum and David were kind enough to drive Elly and I to Manchester Airport; traffic was bad and the rain was pouring down. It was definitely a good day to be leaving the UK.

At 10 a.m. we were sat on the plane ready for departure heading for brighter skies. Elly was spending a week or so in Australia, she was excited for the Rugby World Cup Final and to catch up with friends.

Thirteen hours later, lots of chatting and a few movies, we arrived in Singapore. 5 a.m. local time you could feel the humidity in the air, it was going to be a lot hotter before the layover was over. Showered and breakfast, our body clocks were already confused but feeling refreshed we took to the skies once more.

18/11/2003

Singapore to Sydney is a seven-hour flight, during most of which there was turbulence which made us both a little uneasy, Elly more so as she was not the bravest flyer.

We were due to land at 8 p.m. local time, I had completely lost track of what the time was in the UK. One of my best friends Matty was already in Australia; with only a few hours remaining of the flight, I was starting to get excited. For the first time I only had the trip to think of, all the planning and work in the lead up to this moment was done.

Looking out of the window reminded me of Caroline, I felt a gut-wrenching pull on my stomach and had to restrain myself from crying. Hopefully, I would get to finish what she started nearly two years ago. We descended over Sydney; I remembered the amazing view.

We were now firmly on Australian soil. Matty was there; after a few drinks in the hotel, it was like we had never been apart. After a very welcoming soft bed and good night's sleep, our Australian adventure would officially start tomorrow.

19/11/2003

After a leisurely morning and a good breakfast, I donned my backpack which I would be carrying for the next year or so and headed down to The Globe Backpackers on Darlinghurst Road in Kings Cross. Dropped my bag in a four-person dorm, grabbed my sunglasses and we were out.

Stopping at The Fountain Restaurant we had coffee in the sun and chatted, I caught up with Matty's adventures so far. We spent the rest of the afternoon chilling in the sunshine and I got my paints out and started a watercolour painting in the park, it was hot! Time to relax, just perfect.

Evening was drawing in and it was still hot. Nobody goes out before 10 p.m., so after meeting far too many people in the hostel to remember, we cooked a spot of dinner, it helped as both of us were trained chefs. A group of us headed out to a bar just around the corner, reminded me of 1992, the same music as nightclubs in York.

We moved to a more relaxed place, my jetlag was kicking in and brain no longer working. After Matty and I kicked everyone's arses at pool, we went back for a final chill in the hostel and called it a night at 4:30 a.m., welcome to Sydney!

It took me a few days to get over my jetlag and settle in, I didn't feel the same pressure as last time. There was no media hounding me. The first chance I got we walked to the Opera House and stood where Caroline would have. I was actually living her experiences now; I am a backpacker. With my active imagination I wondered what she would have thought. I knew her all too well and would smile thinking she would have enjoyed this, she would have noticed that. Deep inside I knew that these were the final months of her life, I tried to enjoy each moment as she would have done. It was incredibly upsetting at times, a complex mix of emotion. I was here for very important reasons. I was here for Caroline, not just to finish her journey but also to attend the trial for her murder. It was overwhelming, I couldn't think too far ahead, it had been a year of extreme intensity. I was also in Australia to escape; a part of me was still unwilling to accept Caroline's death.

28/11/2003

Out for breakfast and over to the Internet café to get a couple of hours emails done before anyone was up. The weather was amazing, people were getting together to go to Bondi, we headed out en masse and took the bus ride to the beach. Shorts, t-shirts, bikinis, sarongs and flip-flops, or thongs as the Australians called them, were all that were required, and we could all work on getting a great suntan. I must have been the whitest person on the beach. Chatting, I was starting to get to know people.

Had time in the afternoon to do some painting.

We watched a beautiful sunset and colours change from blues to greens, yellows, oranges and reds in the cloudless sky.

Back at The Globe we took up our places in the Blue Room which was a communal area in the hostel with big windows looking over Kings Cross. There was every stereotype possible, but no one looked out of place.

I started to recognise backpackers from a distance, most were a good bunch. We met Jourg, a blind traveller also staying in the hostel, he was an utter inspiration. He had a love for travel and meeting different people, he travelled with his coffee machine and liked nothing more than a coffee and a smoke for breakfast. I admired his attitude and the way he just got up and set out to explore the world. He experienced a very different Kings Cross and Sydney to us. Over time, I am sure we will become good friends.

My thoughts came back to Caroline and Caroline's Rainbow Foundation, I was also here to understand what it meant to be a backpacker, the reality of travelling. I hoped people will never have to experience what happened to us, I know Caroline was having an amazing time. She was doing what she wanted to do, no one in life can ask more than that.

29/11/2003

Out to the Internet café; I was aware how important it was to keep in touch. When I got back, a group of people were getting ready to go down to Bronte

Beach for a BBQ; Matty and I joined the party.

We picked our spot with one of the pay-as-you-go BBQ's just back from the beach, a great idea used by locals and backpackers alike. Good burger and a couple of beers, we had a laugh. We took a walk along the beautiful cove, everyone and everything was beautiful, the girls had no inhibitions.

Had a dip, the water was pleasant and waves were crashing. I had been wearing two chains, one with little chefs' knives that I had been given for my 18th birthday, and a St Christopher who was the patron saint of travellers. The other with the gold cross that Dad had given me when we saw Caroline for the last time. For some reason I kept checking the chains as the waves crashed around us. The next time I checked the one with the cross had gone. I frantically looked for it, diving down and picking up handfuls of sand but nothing. The waves had taken one of the last physical connections I had with Caroline. Devastated was an absolute understatement! Later on, when I had calmed down, I thought it must have meant to be. A memory of Caroline should be free to travel the waves and not to be tied around my neck, it felt like I had the release of scattering ashes and letting go.

Over the next month I became acclimatised to the Australian way of life, Sydney became one of my favourite cities. The people I met at the hostel were all there out of choice and like attracts like. I met amazing people, we celebrated Christmas with a traditional turkey and all the trimmings in the hostel, Matty and I took control, it was an amazing atmosphere. After lunch heading down to Bondi Beach. A beautiful way to finish the day watching the sunset from the iconic beach. We were all completely in love with everyone in our group, incredible people with many very special moments.

It was a big change after the last few years in the French Alps, up to my waist in snow. In a short time, we had all created a special bond, friendships that in the UK would have taken years to form. After Christmas Matty left Sydney heading to Byron Bay; he wanted to spend New Year with a girl and friends he had met before I arrived. I completely understood but didn't go with him.

31/12/2003

New Year's Eve. Up, showered and out to Bondi Beach. Met up with our group. We could all feel the excitement in the air. Lunch at Bondi Café, followed by a wander along the beach which was always a treat checking out different groups of people and of course the bikini-clad girls. Early evening back at The Globe, Maddie and the rest of the guys were in the Blue Room, after a beer we all headed out to Neilson's Point, which boasted amazing views of Sydney. People were already taking their spots for the early firework display, everyone was happy, laughing and joking, it was amazing to be part of it. We had a couple of hours before it started at 9 p.m.

What a spectacle! Fantastic view across the harbour, the Opera House, Harbour Bridge and city skyline made a wonderful backdrop. I had of course seen the fireworks on TV but now I was actually here!

We all had a great vibe going. People were everywhere and the atmosphere was electric. The city was lit up and reflections of the neon lights on the water made it magical, I knew these memories would never leave us.

Midnight rolled around and everyone was buzzing, the show started. It was one of the most unbelievable sights I had ever seen; the most intense fifteen minutes of lights, music and fireworks I had ever seen. The display certainly lived up to its reputation as one of the best in the world. We were all going crazy and running around wishing everyone a Happy New Year. I thought of Caroline and lost myself in the crowds for a while.

The plan now was to head down to Bondi Beach for the sunrise. It took a while; we got the ferry back across the harbour and by the time we made it to the beach it was 3:30 a.m. Still a few hours before we would see the sun, we walked along the beach, paddled, chatted and had a chill. Everyone from the hostel had made it, the beach was packed. Just before the sunrise, we picked our spot and cuddled up. We welcomed a new beginning as the sun rose, yellows, oranges and reds, it was a beautiful moment. A fantastic way to start 2004.

1/1/2004

New Year's Day. 8 a.m. and we were all still going; my friend Liz and I decided to go for breakfast. We said our goodbyes to the rest of the group and wandered along the beach stopping to enjoy each other's company. A place nearby did a good fry-up.

The majority of people had left now and moving about was easier, we headed back to the city and the Botanical Gardens. Snoozing in the sunshine, it was a beautiful day and lovely start to the year.

Mid-afternoon sweaty and tired, walking back towards Kings Cross stopping at the Marina for a pie and peas, a well-needed treat. It turned out to be a perfect day, the atmosphere back at the hostel was relaxed and contented.

I knew this year was going to have its ups and downs; there were some parts I was not looking forward to, but they needed to be done not just for me, but for Caroline, our family and Caroline's Rainbow Foundation. I also knew there would also be some amazing, magical moments that would make this one of the best years of my life.

After all the celebrations the beginning of 2004 hit me hard, over the first week of January I travelled around as much of Sydney as possible. The realisation of what I would actually have to deal with became a cemented reality in my mind. In the hostel there was an underlying restlessness, everyone was thinking about moving on. Our magical time was over and we would shortly be saying our goodbyes.

I twisted my ankle skateboarding which meant I had to sit with my foot on ice for a few days. It pushed back my leaving date. After a week, I packed up and prepared to leave the hostel, it felt like I was leaving my family again.

8/1/2004

Well, my last day at The Globe for a while. What a crazy time, just what I needed, complete escape.

I popped over to Kraves for breakfast which had become a favourite — I will miss this place. I really enjoyed watching the world go by in Kings Cross. Paul, a Canadian guy, and I decided to wander down to Rushcutters Bay. Over the last month we had become really good friends, we chatted, both agreeing we could stay in Sydney long term, I had never said that about anywhere before.

Jaap was also leaving today, we were both on the late bus. He was from the Netherlands; we had played a lot of chess. Sat in the Blue Room we were trying to sum up our experiences over the last couple of months. The Globe was our oasis in the heart of Sydney's red-light district; I'd met some of the most wonderful people and shared some magical times. Although I had only known people for a short time, it felt like we were friends forever.

Sat on the bus leaving Sydney. We drove past the Opera House and across the Harbour Bridge. The bright lights disappeared, and the road opened up heading towards Newcastle, it was a twelve-hour drive north to Byron Bay. I had a lot of time to think, to contemplate. I had found Sydney one of the busiest, yet most peaceful cities I have ever visited. I will miss the place so much, but I know I would definitely be back.

Byron Bay was known as one of the most spiritual places in Australia; Caroline loved it, she said I would fit right in. It would only be a flying visit this time as I had to be in Bundaberg for an initial hearing in the murder case.

9/1/2004

After a few hours of broken sleep, we still had four hours to go. I will only have a day in Byron; I was due in Bundaberg on the 11th January. There was so much to see on the East Coast, it's where most backpackers spend the majority of their time.

We stopped for a break. The landscape was changing, it reminded me of Strensall Common back home. High clouds covered the sun, but it was still bright. Through Yorkshire eyes it looked like an icy winter's morning, but it was pure white sand patches around the trees and not frost.

Our bus was winding its way along the coastline, everything looked so young compared to the UK. I was getting excited to catch up with Matty and see new parts of Australia, but I knew this next week was going to be tough.

As we pulled up at the bus station, the sun shone hotter than I had ever felt before. I grabbed my bags. Emma and Anna, who I knew from The Globe were getting on the bus heading to Brisbane. Amazing to see them, brief hugs and kisses before they were on their way.

I sat in the sun and fresh air, soaking up everything around me and immediately felt an affinity with the place. I had seen pictures of Caroline here learning to surf, her postcards said I would love the place. I walked down to the beach and stood with my feet in the same sand that Caroline felt between her toes. I looked out over the same view. My heart was about to burst, I was so happy; she was right, I fell completely in love.

Matty turned up an hour or so later, he was definitely on Byron time. They had been staying in Ross' van, Steve, Matty and his girlfriend Lorraine. He sacrificed a New Year's in Sydney for Byron, which wasn't a bad choice.

Life immediately felt so much easier, we popped down to the beach for the afternoon. We swam, there was this strange seaweed that got all over you. Managed to get an hour's painting, lovely view of the beach with a lighthouse in the background.

Lorraine was leaving in the evening, so we left Matty and her to have some time together, Ross kindly drove us over to Nimbin. It was for me really, about eighty kilometres out of Byron. I had not been before, only heard stories and what others had told me. We arrived, there was the museum where I had seen the photo of Caroline standing in front of the camper van. I could imagine her here again; she would have thought very different things to me.

We wandered down the street, dealers asking every two minutes if we wanted to buy weed. I was happy to purchase. The shops were dedicated to the buying, growing and smoking. Over the years, I have had many battles with my family about smoking cannabis. I agree too much is detrimental, but one thing I always point out is that we smoked to enhance our experience. For example, we would hike to a viewing point, look over an amazing landscape, smoke a joint and take the time to feel and appreciate where we were.

We went for a drink in one of the bars, and in walked Darme, another of The Globe crew. For such a big country it was really very small! She now lived ten minutes up the road, we caught up.

I was booked in at The Art Factory. It was about ten minutes' drive from the centre of Byron, it was like a little adventure complex. The dorms were huge tents with short trails to the main complex. I liked it. It was old country design with modern hippy amenities, if that even makes sense. Very expensive at $30 per night. Matty and I finally had time for a good catch up. We were on three stack high bunk beds, on the top bunk there were big spider webs. We were definitely out of the city now.

10/1/2004

Met up with Steve and Ross in the morning and the four of us went to the lighthouse and cooked up breakfast on one of the BBQs.

We spent the day on the beach, suntanning and chilling out. I fitted in now, my skin was a lovely shade of brown and my hair was sun bleached. Further up the beach than yesterday and no seaweed. The current was really strong, but great fun.

Ross was driving up to Brisbane, it was the direction we needed so we grabbed a ride.

We drove along the Gold Coast and stopped at Surfers Paradise, very commercial. I thought exactly the same as Caroline. Had a walk down to the beach, ninety-six kilometres of beach. Caroline had walked here too. Just back from the beach was a line of hotels and skyscrapers, a few blocks back from that was into bush lands. An incredible sight.

As we arrived in Brisbane, it was getting dark and the city was lighting up, it looked really impressive. Finding the train station and I booked a train, heading up to Bundaberg tomorrow.

11/1/2004

I was up early. Nervous now, I didn't really know what to expect from the coming week. I had escaped reality for the last month and today it all hit home again.

I was thinking about people's lives after travel, getting back into a normal nine-to-five, then having the same job for thirty years. Travelling makes you appreciate the little things in life, the smallest moments are important. The trick, I think, is not to forget this mindset when I get home.

I feel it takes a complete break from reality to realise what's important, there are bits I miss from home but what I have found here I love.

On the train and started making notes for Caroline's Rainbow Foundation, I would call Mum tonight. The train systems work a lot better than in the UK, although they have different sized tracks from New South Wales to Queensland, we had to change trains. The procedure was a lot like flying, there was a little safety talk you watched on a small TV. Matty and I discussed the next part of our adventures and exploring Queensland. I was looking forward to seeing Kate, David and Claire from the B&B, they had been so good to us before.

David met us from the train and drove us back, great to see their place again. We had coffee and caught up for an hour or two. Although we had been through horrific times it was good to be somewhere familiar. It was more on my terms now, I can enjoy some of Caroline's happy memories and not only the utter heartache I felt on my last visit.

12/1/2004

Awake by 9 a.m. and into the pool for a swim. Kate sorted us out a big breakfast which set us up for the day.

I had a meeting with Mal Forman at 2 p.m. he was one of the town's officials. David gave us a lift into Bundaberg early and I took Matty for a walk over the bridge. It stirred up a lot of emotions, I was so pleased Matty was with me. I knew he felt the emotion too.

Under the bridge there was still a white cross with Caroline's date on and flowers which had been recently laid. It brought a tear to my eye knowing that people still cared, we sent our thoughts out for Caroline.

We met Mal at the Civic Centre, lovely to see him again and have a catch up. The Mayor Kay McDuff was on leave for a week, back at the weekend, I would be able to see her before we left. We arranged a press conference on Wednesday at the Botanical Gardens.

The court date was tomorrow at 9:30 a.m. I felt a wave of panic and a little afraid.

We missed the last bus to Bargara which was at 4 p.m. Walking around the corner, we passed a lady and jokingly asked, "Are you going to Bargara?"

"Yes, do you need a lift?" she replied.

We jumped in, lovely lady called Dale. She was from New Zealand and had lived here for nearly a decade, no plans to go home. We were comfortable hitching but if we were two girls travelling, I am not sure I would feel the same.

We went down to the beach for an early evening swim. I was shattered, the day had mentally taken its toll. I had to prepare myself, it was only going to get worse.

13/1/2004

I woke early. Initial hearing today, we left for the Bundaberg courthouse.

My heart was racing now, feeling nervous and uneasy. As I walked around the corner the media spotted me, cameras were flashing and videos rolling. I took a deep breath and walked past as calmly as possible. Inside I met up with Detective Dave Batt and some of the other police officers, I remembered most of them from our last visit.

In the courtroom were a dozen people, Judge Peter Dutney entered, and we all stood. The session was underway. The first couple of hours the court was introduced to Mr Peter Feeney for the prosecution, I had met him earlier and Mr Dennis Lynch for the defence. Each made statements and discussed the case. It was hard to listen to.

The session broke, I went outside for a cigarette, the media were on me for a quote. I said a few words and would say more at the press conference tomorrow. I also did a couple of short pieces for local TV, and an interview for a reporter from BBC Radio York and another for *The Telegraph*, they were based in Sydney.

Back in session, it was all bearing down on me. Ian Previte was brought into the courtroom. It's hard to describe my feelings. I was aching all over, my head was running wild and adrenaline pumped around my body, making me feel nauseous. It was a nervous excitement and huge anger with an overwhelming feeling of a broken heart, the overarching feeling was deeper sadness than I thought my soul could bear.

I had trouble focusing on what was said, I tried to control what was going on inside. The court broke for lunch and I had a chance to reflect on what had just happened. I had been in the same room as the man, who had allegedly murdered my sister.

The final session of the afternoon, both sides were going through the list of witnesses. The medical examiner was called, he showed pictures of the autopsy. I didn't expect it, Caroline's body laid out on a cold metal slab. After a few minutes, I couldn't take it, tears welled. I had to go outside for a few minutes of fresh air and another cigarette. The media had all gone. I took some deep breaths; it was all so incredibly sad.

14/1/2004

Press conference today. I didn't sleep well, nightmares again, understandable, there was a lot going on in my head. I had messages from friends offering their thoughts, really thoughtful and meant a lot.

The hearing back underway, nothing too terrible today. At lunchtime, we went to see Mal and had lunch in the Botanical Gardens; we walked down to where the tree was planted for Caroline, I was pleasantly surprised by how much it had grown. It had almost doubled in size, to me it had definitely captured the spirit of Caroline. Although there were a lot of media, they were all very respectful and I felt comfortable. Following a few questions, they allowed me to say what I wanted. I thanked everyone involved and sent thoughts from our family back in the UK.

Pastor Errol from the local parish came down to show his support. We had briefly met on our last visit; I was pleased to see him again. He asked if I would like to say a few words in his service on Sunday, of course I happily agreed. Mal drove us back to the courthouse to see what was happening, there were two witnesses to be recalled. The court will reconvene on the January 28. This will change plans slightly, but I had to be here.

Got calls from people wanting interviews. We walked back to the bridge for photos. BBC Radio York called for another interview. I considered it all positive to talk about Caroline, what had happened and what we were doing with the Foundation.

Another long day drained me; I was ready for bed.

15/1/2004

The worst two days were over and although it was hard on my heart and soul, I was here to represent our family.

Matty had decided to do a diving course, he went off for the day. Got a call from Ross, they were in town. Went to see about getting them into one of the campsites. It was all a little close to the bone. I hung out with Ross and Steve for a while, we had a swim, the waves were relentless, and it started raining. A new sensation, swimming in the rain. The water was warmer than the rain. It felt almost magical.

I gave Claire a call and we all met up for a couple of drinks in the town, it was nice to have friends around me, normality after a crazy couple of days. She was doing well with university and her job. Claire said, "If you ever forget what you look like just look in the paper." She was right, I was in every local paper. We laughed.

Back down to the beach, the air was clear after the rain. I had another busy day planned for tomorrow and was looking forward to going to Childers, meeting Mayor Bill Trevor.

16/1/2004

Matty out early for his diving course. Nancy picked me up at 9 a.m.

It was an hour's drive to Childers which was a small town similar to Bundaberg. I met Bill Trevor, he was a lovely gentleman, on first impressions he was a caring sensitive man who I could tell had been through a lot and understood grief. We were met by a couple of other people and the conversation moved to Caroline's Rainbow Foundation, what we were going to do and how we could potentially work together.

Bill gave me the full story of Childers and the Palace Backpackers fire. It was a horrific story which moved me to tears, I could feel them all. On the June 23rd 2000, a known arsonist Robert Long started a fire in the Palace Backpackers. The backpackers woke around 12:30 p.m. to thick black smoke, seventy people managed to make it out, but fifteen people weren't so lucky. Nine women and six men lost their lives. It had completely rocked the town just as Caroline's murder had in Bundaberg.

In 2002, they opened the memorial and art gallery. I found walking around extremely emotional, I could understand a little of what each family and the townsfolk had gone through. It hit me a lot harder than I thought, my emotions were all over the place.

Walking the main street, Bill greeted everyone he passed, I met his mother and father which was an honour. It seemed to be a very friendly place, just like Bundaberg.

The Palace Backpackers was in the middle of the main street, upstairs one side was an art gallery and the other was the memorial, a well-known Australian artist had done a very sensitive piece of work. A large-scale oil painting of all fifteen people who lost their lives in the fire, the backdrop was a tropical Childers' landscape. Next to the painting was a huge piece of stained glass with each backpacker growing up through the years. I could feel myself welling up.

We had a good conversation and discussed what we would propose to the council later in the month for getting a memorial for Caroline in Bundaberg.

We went for lunch and I met a couple of artists who were doing some work for the town, it was lovely to talk art. After lunch we completed the tour, it was a lovely day. Nancy gave me a lift back to Bundaberg. On the way we passed the avocado fields which were impressive, the biggest in the world. There were also trees planted for the backpackers who worked there. We saw some kangaroos, my first in the wild. We took a scenic drive back to the B&B.

I met up with Matty, Steve and Ross and felt like I had a really good day which was a pleasant surprise. We decided to round the day off by going to Mon Repos, a turtle sanctuary. 6:20 p.m. and there was already a queue. There were two groups, the guides offered a host of information which was fascinating: three types of turtle's nest around the area every year.

Waiting patiently, finally it was our turn to go down to the beach. A nest had hatched the night before, it takes between two and five days for all the eggs to hatch and the turtles have to dig their way out. The team dug out and found half a dozen babies that were still trying to escape the nest, it was incredible. About twenty eggs hadn't hatched, but over ninety baby turtles had made their way down to the ocean, all had been recorded by the team. We set up a series of torches to light the track. As the turtle's usually head towards the light from the moon on the shimmering water. We watched the baby turtles scramble their way down to the ocean fighting for their lives, it was incredible. Only one in a thousand makes it to adulthood, so the odds are certainly not in their favour.

17/1/2004

The weather had turned, we woke to the rain crashing on the roof. I knew there would be no diving today for Matty. On the plus side, we got to go and see Ross and Steve, they were leaving today. We planned to catch up with them again in New Zealand.

Sunshine and blue skies in the afternoon, Matty and I wandered down to the river and started a little painting. Spending a few days in Bundaberg my preconceptions had all but gone, I felt relaxed and could see why Kate and David had chosen to live here and bring up their family.

It's hard to believe what happened to Caroline, nearly everyone I met had been lovely and wanted nothing but to help where they could.

There were a couple of storm clouds remaining in the sky which made for the most beautiful and colourful sunset. Deep reds and oranges. I appreciated the moment.

18/1/2004

Down to the beach at Bargara for the day. I found it really relaxing, the sun was hot, breeze cooling and the ocean calm. Nothing better!

When we got back, I had a message from Errol to meet at his church, quick shower and we got a lift down.

Errol was greeting people as they came in, he met us and escorted us to the front row, where we took our seats. The church was a lovely building, a large room with a big stage at the front and a balcony behind. They had a full band set up, which included Errol's son and daughter who both played instruments. It was all very upbeat, after a few announcements everyone sang a few hymns, it created a lovely atmosphere, and everyone felt connected.

I was invited to speak, as I made it up to the lectern, I could feel my nerves overwhelming me. I looked everyone in the eye, around eighty people all looking up at me in anticipation. I could feel my voice wavering, my heart beating faster and faster. I had spoken to cameras and the media before, but this was completely different. I was shaking, my mind went blank. I opened my mouth and nothing, my head was trying to tell me what to say but what came out was somewhat incoherent. I stumbled through a few sentences.

"We are helping young people to travel safely,' I stuttered, "Err… we are creating a DVD to show in schools and colleges to help them understand the risks when travelling. Errr… we don't want what happened to Caroline happening to some other person and their family."

It felt extremely awkward. I struggled through, managing to just get the main points out about the charity. (It probably wasn't quite as bad as I remembered.) Errol stepped in and everyone clapped, I was sure it was more out of sympathy than for speaking eloquence.

I sat in the congregation feeling very disappointed but trying not to show it. Errol thanked me. He summarised the charity and the help we needed. The sermon continued I was more emotional than I thought. I could feel passion in the way he spoke and saw the way the congregation all got behind him. It was inspiring and something I would like to be able to do someday. He asked at the end if anyone would like to stand up and say a prayer welcoming God into their lives. I was caught in the moment and stood up. Matty didn't stand. I felt that something was missing and with the loss of Caroline it just felt right in the moment.

At the end of the service there was a collection, the church added to it and we raised $1000. I was overwhelmed by their kindness and was completely humbled by the experience.

Everyone started to make their way outside and introduced themselves, offering their sympathy. A gentleman called Wayne told me how the Lord had changed his life, he popped a note into my top pocket saying that he had been told to give this to me. I thanked him very much.

Errol and I called Dad back in the UK and we both spoke to him, I ran through what had happened during the service, it was good to speak to him and catch up. One of the other pastors took Matty and I for dinner with his wife and family, it was a lovely meal and finished the evening perfectly.

When we got back to the B&B, I remembered the note in my top pocket, pulling it out it was $100. I couldn't believe the generosity of the parish and what had just happened. I thought about me stuttering and not knowing what to say; I said it will never happen again! We had a lot of work to do, I was inspired, and I felt supported by the people around us. Slept well, felt peaceful and for once had happy dreams.

We had a week's respite and decided to leave Bundaberg knowing I had to be back on the twenty-seventh for the final day of the hearing on the twenty-eighth. I was happy to be out of the public eye. I felt emotionally a bit unstable, it highlighted to me that I had not dealt with everything. I spent many hours walking along beaches thinking how could I get through this, how could I ever come to terms with Caroline's death? I put on a brave face but welcomed some time alone and escape. Matty and I were both keen to do a trip to Fraser Island, total escape from man's world and back to nature.

20/1/2004

We met the Fraser Island trip organiser at the office in Harvey Bay. There were a few 4x4s going out, eight people in each with tents to camp each evening. Two nights on the island, we were super excited and met the rest of the people in our group. A few different nationalities, all backpackers.

We had the rest of the day to have a wander. Finding a skatepark and had a push about, it was good fun. There was a guy selling weed, we thought it was perfect timing and would enhance our trip to Fraser Island, why not.

Matty and I volunteered to do the food shop, we would be cooking over open fires, it was going to be amazing.

21/1/2004

Awake with the birds, so excited about the trip. Everyone met at the office, Jake who was an ex-island guide gave us a pretty harsh talk about everything that could go wrong. I listened intently, everything that happened to Caroline was still fresh in my mind.

Loading up and we were on the 9:30 a.m. ferry, I could feel everyone was a bit nervous. On the island, we loaded our gear, first stop was Lake Mckenzie. I had seen pictures on postcards and knew it was going to be special. We walked through shrubs and out onto the whitest sand beach and clearest water lake I had ever seen, my eyes couldn't believe it. Not even in my dreams had I seen such a paradise. It was enclosed by a blanket of green shrubs and trees. Until I stood with my feet in the sand, my mind didn't believe places like this existed. We had a swim which united us all as a group. We were in absolute awe. Matty and I had a smoke, which put us in another world in another world. It was heaven.

None of us wanted to leave but we had a schedule to keep. Back at the

4x4, Daz was driving, the sand was soft and deep, he had to punch it. We were lucky and made it out on to the main beach, it was classed as a national highway seventy-five kilometres long and ran the full length of one side of the island. Twenty kilometres down the highway and we arrived at the SS Maheno shipwreck. An ocean liner that operated in the Tasman Sea up until 1935. It was used by the New Zealand Navy in the First World War. The ship was washed ashore by a cyclone in 1935 and has been slowly sinking into the beach ever since. I had time for a quick sketch. The coloured rusted steel looked incredible against the sandy beach with blue sky backdrop and lapping ocean.

We pushed on to the camping spot. Matty and I took charge, our chef skills coming into play, we got the fire going and put in the potatoes and cobs to roast. The group walked up to the point to watch the sunset, we could see Champagne Pools in one direction and Indian Head in the other. Looking forward to visiting both places tomorrow.

It was the most beautiful sunset, just the peace I needed. I felt relaxed. Back at the camp and we got the food cooking, everyone was stuffed and nothing much went to waste. We had to get rid of the leftovers as Fraser Island is the only place on earth that still had pure-bred dingos and we were told they could be cheeky. Got chatting with Daz and his girlfriend, Sarah. Nice couple.

After dinner we seemed to pair off, Matty and I got chatting to Kyra and Francesca, both from Switzerland. I had spotted them on the bus out of Bundaberg, strange how we finally met properly and could share some time together. We were in harmony, the perfect time and place. It was an experience we were supposed to share.

Kyra and I chatted about everything and nothing while the fire burnt. We had heard about the glowing plankton in the water, down at the water's edge we started rubbing the sand. It worked and our hands started to glow, it was incredible. We played and rubbed the sand on each other, our bodies were glowing. We were close and shared a moment. Hand-in-hand we walked back along the beach, passing other campfires and groups of people. There was no artificial light, picking our spot we sat looking up at the stars. I had never in my life seen so many, it was magical. Laid out looking up we watched satellites orbiting the earth and both spotted a shooting star. We were definitely in paradise.

22/1/2004

Up for breakfast, bacon butties and coffee went down well. Kyra and I shared smiles across the camp. It was my turn to drive, not far to go. Parking up we had a forty-minute walk to the north end of the island and Champagne Pools; Kyra and I paddled. No swimming though, as just off the coast was one of the world's largest breeding grounds for tiger sharks. We walked along the boardwalk to the rock formation of the pools, there was a fantastic view of Indian Head in the distance. The rocks kept the sharks out, as the water crashed over the sharp rocks it created millions of tiny bubbles which was like bathing in a glass of champagne. Wonderful sensation. The rocks were sharp, everyone got a scrape of two. It was a small price to pay.

Had to be on the road by 12 p.m. to miss the tide, we managed to squeeze in a walk to the top of Indian Head, everyone ran out of water. Views were well worth it and helped us forget. Our vantage point looked over the Champagne Pools, the other direction was the seventy-five-kilometre beach and the highway, back from the beach were sand dunes, behind them trees and shrubs of every shade of green. This island was incredible. We saw a couple of manta rays in the water but no sharks.

Back in the 4x4, it got stuck in the sand, we had to dig it out, didn't take long. Punched it and we were back underway. Past the SS Maheno again and on our way to Eli Creek, it was a very cold freshwater creek. We walked up the boardwalk, jumping in the current took you back down to the beach again. The water was so clean and fresh, I had never tasted anything like it.

Next stop was Rainbow Gorge, where we would be spending the night. The 4x4 had to be off the beach by five p.m. we just made it but must have driven past the turning four times trying to find our way. We picked a good camping spot one sand dune back from the beach. I sat with Matty, poured a beer and had a smoke for the people who were no longer with us. How strange we were now in Rainbow Gorge, it felt fitting, emotional. I took a walk just before we went to watch the sunset, my thoughts were with Caroline and I was sure she was with me, we were having the most amazing experience. This is one of the reasons I was in Australia, I had certainly fallen for Fraser Island.

Kyra and I chatted, her outlook on life was very similar to mine, like attracts like. She asked me about my best and worst times, it didn't feel right to mention Caroline.

Spaghetti Bolognese for dinner. The camp went silent, all we could hear was the crashing waves and the crackle of the fire.

We laid back and looked up at the stars, I was just as overwhelmed as last night, we cuddled up with each other and watched the fire burn. Kyra's sister had bought her a star for her birthday. She asked again about my worst times, I don't know why, something compelled her. I told her about Caroline and everything that happened. In that moment, I felt like Caroline was with us, talking about her had brought her into the moment. There was something special between us and an electricity in the air. This place was paradise in every way.

23/1/2004

First stop Lake Wabby. A forty-minute walk through the forest down to the lake's edge. Sitting on the edge catfish nibbled on our toes, eating the dead skin. Funny sensation that made us laugh. Walking back, we saw huge spiders' webs, they made me feel a bit creeped out. The trees seemed to be alive with clicks and buzzing sounds, the closer we looked the more we could see. Watched a cricket fighting for its life with a load of ants swarming all over it; we thought it was paradise, but it was a battleground, life and death for everything that lived here. Our final stop was Lake Mckenzie for an hour. We swam and soaked up paradise, it was beautiful. None of the group wanted to leave but we had to make the ferry.

Back on the mainland and we were all buzzing, it had been an amazing experience. Everyone met up for a drink and dinner, we knew we had shared one of Australia's purest gems.

24/1/2004

Our little bubble was about to pop. The girls were leaving, our Fraser Island group were continuing on their Australian adventure.

Kyra and I said goodbye, hopefully we would see each other again in Byron Bay.

I walked around for the rest of the day with a glow and a cheeky smile on my face, what an amazing experience. Caroline was definitely with me. Everyone was in the right place at the right time to enjoy a magical, few days.

Matty and I talked about it, life after death, he knew I had more reason than most to believe. We discussed religion and what we experienced at pastor Errol's church, the sense of connection and community resonated with me.

I took some time by myself, went skating and walked along the beach. My heart was exploding in all directions, the pain of missing Caroline, the love of the amazing places and wonderful people I had the privilege of meeting. I tried to let it all flow through me, I could laugh, cry, shout and scream all at the same time.

Called Mum and Dad and told them about the last few days, completely different call to the one they got last week.

Got a text from Kyra, she had been on our Caroline's Rainbow Foundation website and said it had really moved her.

25/1/2004

Back to Bundaberg today. I had such an attachment to the place my heart already felt heavy and the weight was returning to my shoulders. We were offered a lift from Daz and Sarah, they had a camper van and were heading our way. I got a call from Mum and immediately knew that something was wrong. My thoughts turned straight to Grandma. Thankfully, she was OK. It was our Aunty Jean in Canada, Mum's half-sister. She'd had a heart attack and sadly died. My thoughts were with our cousins Grant, Kevin and Tracy. It was unbearably upsetting. I tried to comfort Mum; I knew what it was like to lose a sister. As if she hadn't been through enough. I had been feeling funny, I thought it was going back to Bundaberg, but Mum said I was feeling her pain too.

Matty and I took an evening stroll and watched the thunder and lightning of a tropical storm further down the coast, flashes of lightening every now and then. It was significant, we had a good chat about life and a bit of a heart-to-heart. We talked about coincidence and why you meet people, how certain people cross your path and at the right time. Is it all set out before us? The pendulum swing for good and bad has certainly swung both ways over the last week or two. We make choices on impulse, sometimes not sure why, but we just know it's the right thing to do. The more these things happened the more I was beginning to trust myself.

26/1/2004

I was remembering back to the times we had in Canada, our family holiday to see Aunty Jean. It was a good time and made me smile. Told Matty the funny story with Caroline when we were flying for a family holiday and we went to see the pilots in the cockpit. We both laughed.

Dad says we have been through the worst thing a family can ever face, it makes me afraid to have my own family, I thought I would be living in constant fear. People say you have never known love until you have had children, it's unconditional love for all eternity. I have a fear, maybe irrational but if I loved someone that deeply how could I survive if that person was taken away?

On the other hand, as in Alfred Lord Tennyson's poem, 'Tis better to have loved and lost than never to have loved at all'. I am sure Tennyson was a greater and wiser man than I will ever be, but at the moment I cannot dare to love anything that much, the unthinkable happening again would be completely unbearable.

27/1/2004

Bump back to reality this morning, it was the final couple of days of the hearing. I got a call from Mal. We had a meeting at the Mayor's office at 11:30 a.m. I was feeling a bit stressed, the time away had done me good. Had time to make some calls to get things in place, would meet Bill Trevor tomorrow.

Meeting with Kay McDuff and her team, great to see them again. They had nothing but praise for the work we were doing with Caroline's Rainbow Foundation, this meant a great deal. The funds they raised we agreed to save for a lasting memorial, I thought this was a lovely idea. I said that I was sure Mum would feel strong enough to come over one day and it would be nice to do something then. At the end of the meeting Kay said that we would always be welcome in Bundaberg, which touched me. Mal said we had become good friends. Their support meant an awful lot, I was deeply touched.

Met up with Matty, we tried to sort out the plans for the next few weeks. His Australian visa was nearly up, and we would head over to New Zealand for a month. Dad and Janet would also be there visiting Janet's son and his family.

We walked to the bridge; it was the last time I would visit for a while. It still invoked the same emotions, but I could now control them better, it was like everything, the more I did it the more I learnt. My perspective widened and I could see more of the area than I had before. It wasn't easy, I had some time talking to Caroline. Tomorrow was going to be a big day I didn't know what was going to happen.

28/1/2004

Terrible dreams about killing and war, I had woken a few times in the night sweat pouring out of me, soaking my pillow. I was beside myself, tried to put on a brave face. We were leaving tomorrow, I just had to keep that in mind. I think it was the not knowing. It was all getting to me; I'd never really experienced this kind of stress before.

At the courthouse at 9:15 a.m., there were not as many journalists as I would have thought. I saw a few faces I recognised, they wanted a few words, which of course I did.

Meg Owens met me; it was good to see her again. She said people from around the town had been donating and she had some auction prizes for Caroline's Rainbow Foundation. Extremely generous.

Previte was led into the courtroom, to see him made my blood boil, I could feel a poison and anger inside me. I was also overwhelmed with sadness, I felt I could just burst into tears again.

There were two prisoners recalled, I thought their answers were very sincere. The second guy looked straight at me and must have known who I was. As he was escorted out, we locked eye contact, I felt such pain and sadness.

The proceedings lasted a couple of hours, I was drained. As I made my way outside thanking people, the media were all over us. I was a little surprised. The police gave a statement, Ian Douglas Previte would be going to trial for murder and robbery. I followed saying we that we felt like the first part of our grief was coming to an end and we could start to gain some closure. I would be speaking with my family in the UK shortly and thanked everyone for all their hard work.

Caught up with the police and prosecutor, they thought the trial would commence next year. The Supreme Court met twice a year in April and September, a provisional date was submitted. They were pleased with the outcome and all felt a sense of relief that they had a strong enough case to go to trial.

Meg gave us the gifts for the auction, one was a one-hundred-year-old bottle of Bundaberg rum that could fetch a great sum. I gave my greatest thanks.

We went for lunch with a few officers, Meg told us a story. She was involved in a raid on a house a few weeks ago, on the mantelpiece in the living room was a picture of Caroline. She asked why, they said that she had touched their hearts and they felt terribly sorry for the family.

I called Bill, but things had come up and he couldn't meet. We went into Bundaberg, I popped in the art shop for some paper. The owner recognised me, and we had a chat.

Back at the B&B, caught up with Matty. It had been a mentally draining day, spoke to Mum and Dad. The UK were just waking up and finding out the news, my phone started ringing and I did interview after interview.

29/1/2004

On the bus by 7:30 a.m. I had a long day of travel ahead, Matty would meet me later, he had his diving course to finish and wanted to meet Lorraine. I was travelling for the full morning, it gave me a lot of time to think, I was filled with mixed emotion, sad to leave the B&B, Kate and David had been so good. Also, all the support we had from the police, Mayor's office and local people was overwhelming. It really meant a lot to me, their love made everything else a lot easier to cope with. I felt like Caroline would have been proud how I had dealt with everything, also proud of everyone who had worked so hard for her.

In Brisbane, I had a couple of hours to wait for my bus, I wasn't sure I was doing the right thing going to Byron again. I had a wander around the museum that I hadn't had time to check out before.

Back at the bus station, my bus number was 422, which was our house number. I smiled, thanks Caroline. I knew then I was doing the right thing, everything was going to work out fine. These little coincidences were starting to have great meaning.

Kyra and Francesca met me at the station, the three of us hung out.

30/1/2004

We slept well and were in no rush to get up, dozed for a while. The girls went shopping and I went to start a painting, looking north along the beach this time. It's still an amazing view but not as recognisable as the lighthouse.

The heavens opened which put an end to painting; I picked up some postcards and wrote home, I thought of Caroline, she would have done just the same. Met up with the girls for lunch, Francesca spotted the start of what turned out to be the biggest rainbow. It was amazing, we all knew the story and understood the significance.

Out for the evening, a walk on the beach, the air was clear and fresh. Went to the bar, who should we see but one of the guys from Fraser Island, these coincidences just keep happening.

31/1/2004
The last day of the month, January had flown by. It had been an emotional roller-coaster with some extremely difficult times and some absolutely perfect moments. The girls were leaving today, we had time to walk and chat.

Matty was arriving tonight, it had only been a couple of days, but I had missed him. Went to the skate shop and picked out a new board, crazy pop again! I went for a cruise, pushing down the cycle tracks; I hit a stone and went flying, cut my arm and hand open. Not too bad, shit happens. I was still happy to have a new board.

In the evening, we went to see a show from the Oz Fire Team; I had never heard of them, we got a seat in the front row. They blew me away, absolutely amazing. I felt like I was in the right place at the right time again.

1/2/2004
It was going to be hot. Matty and I hired a car for a couple of days and decided to check out the surrounding area. First stop Ballina, small place

but had an amazing skatepark, we got into a good session, I was liking my new board. Next stop was Lismore where there was a Sunday market, well worth checking out. We liked the vibe, got a couple of books and tapes for the car.

Back on the road and took a scenic drive to Nimbin, great to be on a road trip together. We both knew what was going to happen next, big smiles on our faces.

We got sorted in the campsite for the night and went for a wander, checked out the museum and had a coffee.

Back at the campsite we settled in for the night, couple of drinks, smokes, chatting rubbish and a few games of chess. All was well with the world, just what we both needed.

2/2/2004

Up early, another day for exploring. We drove the scenic route to Mount Warning which was an old extinct volcano. The landscape was not so different to the Yorkshire Dales, it was like someone had turned up the colour, everything was more vivid, brighter, made me want to paint.

We did the eight kilometre walk up the volcano, the views were amazing. Next stop was a local dam, it held two years of water for the surrounding area.

Back to Nimbin for the night, it looked like rain, we set up a tarp between the car and tent. Got chatting to a couple that were also camping and an old hippy who seemed to just be living on the campsite. Matty and I cooked up dinner and we all sat around for the evening. I loved the way these things happened.

3/2/2004

Everything was wet! We walked into Nimbin and treated ourselves to a big fry-up and pot of coffee.

Mid-afternoon we headed back to Byron, our little tour had been fun. Checked into a hostel, the same room as Kyra and I had shared.

We chatted about the rest of our plans before New Zealand; Matty wanted to go back to Sydney before leaving, we could get the overnight bus tomorrow. I knew Lorraine was in Sydney. I was happy to hang out and do what he wanted. Sydney would be good for me, I could do a bit of work and get some cash in, also try selling the little paintings I had done. I stood a good chance around the Sydney Opera House and out on Bondi Beach.

4/2/2004
Left Matty sleeping and headed up to the lighthouse. The sun was shining, it was beautiful, and I put in a sketch, had time to put some paint on, the picture just worked. I knew it would sell.

I finished off a couple of little pictures and got them mounted. I knew people in Sydney would recognise Byron, fingers crossed.

On the night bus we watched Calendar Girls. I thought back to the Hearts of Yorkshire Awards and meeting the real Calendar Girls. Incredible how different my life was now.

5/2/2004
What a wonderful view as we crossed the Harbour Bridge, Sydney looked fabulous, it's great to be back. We checked in at The Globe, couple of people passed out in the Blue Room from the night before. Nothing new! Vicki was up, it was great to see her and catch up.

We headed down to Bondi, another beach day. Matty hooked up with Lorraine, he looked happy. I left them to it and set up painting, a local guy wanted the one I was painting, said it would be done in a couple of days.

I headed back to our hostel. Steve and Lucas were still there and working construction, today they both had a near death experience and were celebrating life. They both nearly got electrocuted. We all raised a glass to how lucky we all were. The vibe wasn't the same as before, our New Year crew had pretty much moved on.

I spent the next week catching up with Sydney life, Matty was hanging out with Lorraine. I finished and sold a couple of pictures and picked up a couple of days cooking work for the chefs' agency. Spent time catching up and putting information together for Caroline's Rainbow Foundation.

12/2/2004
A couple checked into our room, Dan and Sophie, he was Welsh, she was French. I knew immediately that we would get on. I gave them the low down on the hostel and said we would meet up in the Blue Room later.

Visited the Sydney Museum of Contemporary Art; there was a Caravaggio exhibition on, it was amazing. The use of light and dark was wonderful and made you look closer into the painting. I loved his work along with JMW Turner and Rembrandt.

I was painting around Circular Quay, the Star Princess, a luxury cruise liner docked in the harbour, it was the right place to get exposure and meet people looking for a little reminder of their holiday. I sold pretty much everything I had painted. It was a great week and gave me the boost I needed. I got chatting to the ship's resident artist, he teaches painting a few hours a day and gets to see the world. It sounded like a great life to me, thoughts for the future.

It was good to see people back in the hostel, everyone was getting on well with Dan and Sophie. Vicki and Steve were on form, Paul and Emma were both amazing. Ross had come back. We had all become close and were enjoying the antics of the Blue Room.

20/2/2004

Very excited! Going to see Jewel tonight at the Sydney Opera House, her voice is amazing!

Matty and I had the day together, we hadn't hung out just the two of us for a while. Down to Bondi and some wave surfing, they were big, we splashed about and had a chill on the beach. Early afternoon everyone else turned up, Paul and I took our usual stroll along the beach and got an ice-cream. His visa was nearly up, he would be heading back to Canada. Him and Emma had been together for most of the time they were in Australia, she was staying another week. I thought they made the perfect couple.

Matty and I were super excited. I put a shirt on for a change and took a slow walk through the Botanical Gardens, as we arrived at the Sydney Opera House the light was just hitting the arcs, it was beautiful, we had a drink in the bar below looking over the Harbour Bridge. Caroline would have loved this. We toasted good times and people we missed.

The place was buzzing, we found our seats, just to the left of the stage, right at the front. Perfect. Her support act was great, guy from Brisbane, good tunes.

The lights dropped and a spotlight lit the stage, she came out looking absolutely stunning. Her performance was immaculate from start to finish, her voice utterly incredible. She did all the songs I knew and some new ones, told some funny stories and of course gave us some yodelling. I couldn't take my eyes off her. Even after the encore I didn't want it to end.

Slow walk back through Woolloomooloo, sat on the harbour and had a chill. Got a text from Kyra saying she was coming to Sydney for a few days, would be great to catch up.

A few more days painting around Circular Quay and the Botanical Gardens, little pictures of the Sydney Opera House and Harbour Bridge. The ship QE2 docked for a few days, it was perfect timing.

25/2/2004

Woke with a smile on my face, I was looking forward to seeing Kyra again. Matty was enjoying his last few days in Australia with Lorraine, we would be travelling in New Zealand together.

She looked beautiful, big smiles and cuddles. She was here for a couple of days. In the Botanical Gardens we drank coffee, catching up about the last few weeks.

Went to the IMAX, ended up seeing Cyberworld. It certainly was an experience, the best parts were the underwater scene, fish swimming and bubbles everywhere.

Lunch at the Harbourside Café, I became her unofficial tour guide. The weather was turning, black skies coming over. We walked over towards the Harbour Bridge, suddenly a huge rainbow appeared. It was amazing, neither of us had seen one since Byron. I knew it was Caroline looking over us with an approving smile.

Back through Hyde Park and across Circular Quay, her first real view of the Sydney Opera House.

26/2/2004

Lazy morning before heading down to Darling Harbour to watch a digeridoo show, she nearly convinced me to buy one. We looked at every didge in the shop, they say the right one will always find you. I was interested in the aboriginal culture although not seen much of it so far.

We happily wandered around central Sydney and I was pointing out the major sights. Visited the Chinese Gardens and found our way back to Hyde Park. We chatted freely, both having the same outlook on life and death, strangely similar since we were both from completely different backgrounds and cultures. The city was lighting up, lights along the park and St Mary's backdrop was beautiful.

27/2/2004

Determined to get up early and out to Paddy's Market. She only had a week left in Australia, so it was shopping time and the market was the perfect place.

We made our way to Darling Harbour. She wanted me to buy a didgeridoo, I didn't take much convincing and with expensive taste I found the perfect one. Just had to learn to play now.

We sat in the same spot I had two years ago, I told her the story of coming over for a week, going to Bundaberg and coming here. There weren't many people I had talked to about that time.

Kyra was staying in Manly for a few days with friends. I was leaving for New Zealand tomorrow. We hoped our paths would cross again sometime, maybe at the top of a Swiss mountain snowboarding. I saw her to the ferry and waved goodbye.

Back at The Globe and it was Dan's birthday, few drinks and a play on my new didge was in order. It was a good evening; everyone was sad we were leaving. I knew I would be back, but things would be different again.

28/2/2004

At the airport, we were leaving Australia. Matty was welling up, it had been an amazing year for him.

Auckland, nice place and a great vibe. Completely different to Australia. We hooked up with Ross and Steve, the four of us would be travelling together. Went out for a few beers to talk about the trip. Dad and Janet were here so I would stay with them for a week then the guys would swing by and pick me up.

Janet had family in New Plymouth, her son had moved over years before with his wife and they had started a family.

29/2/2004

It was Sunday, all shops closed. Matty and I grabbed our skateboards, great way to see more of the city. Went down to Queens Street, at the park there was a Circa demo, Chad Muska and the full team were here, amazing and absolutely perfect timing.

A relaxing evening just hanging out, looking forward to seeing Dad. I had really missed him and was looking forward to catching up.

1/3/2004

Flight leaving at 1:15 p.m. We hired a car and they dropped me at the airport with about five minutes to spare.

I got off the plane, Dad and Janet were waiting; it was amazing to see them, I had so much to tell them. I couldn't stop talking, just like Caroline.

They had booked me a room in the B&B they were staying in, it was the first night in three months I had been in a room by myself and it had an en-suite. Absolute luxury!

2/3/2004

I woke to the sun shining through the window, weather was amazing. Over breakfast Dad said they had been here a couple of weeks and they had just seen two years' worth of rain in a month. I said not to worry, I am in sync with the world at the moment. Sure enough, it was sunny and we went painting for the day.

Met Les and Louise, Les was Janet's son. Great to meet them and their kids, Joseph, Ethan and Neve. What a lovely lifestyle they had, we all went out for dinner and chatted the evening away.

3/3/2004

Sun was shining again. It was lovely for Dad and I to have some time, we had not seen each other much over the last few years. We went to the beach near Mount Taranaki to paint.

Picked a nice spot, the beach was black sand which came from the inactive volcano. We could see what were known as the Sugar Loaf Islands, a collection of five small islands just of the coast, they made a lovely painting.

4/3/2004

Where we were staying was close to a place called Waters Meet where two rivers came together. Walking around; I could feel a strong connection with the place. For some reason, I felt a very powerful energy. Dad and I started a painting, we talked about art and the Old Masters.

Every time I had visited London, I loved going into the National Gallery, an inspiring place. In the afternoon we drove to the base of Mount Taranaki, the views were incredible.

5/3/2004

Went around to see Les and his family, chatting about the lifestyle in New Zealand. He said it was a beautiful place to live, the land of opportunity. He wouldn't want to go back to the UK. It made me think, would I like to live here?

We went out for a few beers and games of pool, just the lads. His mates kept losing, I blamed it on my misspent youth working in kitchens. We worked split shifts, the only thing to do in the afternoon was go and play pool and snooker.

6/3/2004

Painting for the day down to Waters Meet; quiet and relaxed, we were both able to get lost in our own thoughts. Time passed quickly, we talked about Caroline and our time in Byron Bay.

In the evening, Janet and Dad said they would babysit. Les and Louise hadn't been for a night out in six months with their kids only being young. We went down to the pub and had a couple of beers.

8/3/2004

A visit to the glow-worm caves. It was a couple of hours' drive, along the coastline passing beautiful countryside along the way. It wasn't too dissimilar to the UK. We arrived at Waitomo Caves. Taking the forty-five-minute tour through the limestone caverns that had been hollowed out by running water over the centuries, the limestone itself formed over thirty million years ago; there were stalactites and stalagmites forming everywhere, the colours were amazing, due to the rich mineral content. The next part of the tour took us on a boat ride through the rest of the cave, looking up were thousands of blue lights. It reminded me of Fraser Island and the thousands of stars.

Back in New Plymouth, Dad and I took an evening walk down to Waters Meet, it was a full moon yesterday, the light shining off the water was incredible. We talked again about Caroline, both of us missed her terribly. It was so hard; I was at a loss as to how we could make it any better. Our hearts were broken, looking at the beauty of nature we both wondered where she was now, was she looking down on us? We talked about belief and what we thought happened when we died, does heaven exist?

9/3/2004

After speaking with Matty in the morning I was going to meet them in Rotorua, which wasn't far from us.

It was my last day with Dad, the time had gone really quickly. It had been a lovely taste of home. We grabbed our paints and headed out for the day, down to the lighthouse, it was a lovely subject. There was a village nearby and we stopped for lunch.

Painting for the rest of the day, it was lovely.

We had dinner and went out for a walk, it was a special time for me and Dad; we talked about the future and what we were going to do when I was back in the UK. We chatted about life as an artist.

10/3/2004

Early start. Dad dropped me at the station, I was sad, knowing that I wouldn't see them again for at least another eight months. The bus drove towards Hamilton and onwards to Rotorua; when I arrived Matty, Ross and Steve were waiting. They had already booked white-water rafting, I had no objections. Always in search of the next rush and the feeling that snowboarding and skateboarding gave.

In the briefing they told us we would be going through some rapids which would be lots of fun, they ended with a seven-metre waterfall. The likelihood was that we would capsize, it put us on edge a little, I was still super excited.

In the water and we were off, paddling like hell, water splashing everywhere and carving our way past rocks following the water flow.

Rounding the corner in front of us was a huge waterfall, seven-metre drop. "Paddle," shouted the instructor. We started paddling, straight over the edge, we hit the water below and the raft flipped, we were all thrown into the water. Pulling ourselves back into the raft we were all laughing, what a rush!

Back on the road, we were The Four Horsemen, chatting and catching up. Our destination: Tarpo, we wouldn't make it today. We found a sunset and hot mud pools; the ground was warm for camping. Cooking up and a couple of beers, it was good to be back on my travels although I did miss Dad.

12/3/2004

Up early and made the ferry in plenty of time. It was the start of our South Island adventure. I had heard a lot about it and was really looking forward to it.

We found a hostel and dumped our stuff, they had free bikes, so we took a tour around. There were wineries everywhere, I wanted to visit Cloudy Bay. I had seen much of their wine in the places I worked and thought it was excellent. Picked up a bottle of Pinot Noir and we all sat outside in the sun and enjoyed a glass. What could be better?

14/3/2004

Checking out the WOW place, The World of Wearable Art. I had no idea what to expect, they had beautiful costumes, the actual ring from Lord of the Rings and many classic cars.

At the hostel in the evening, no one was about. I took some time on the balcony to myself. These moments were rare when travelling, I looked up at the stars thinking I was happy to be here. New Zealand had been amazing so far.

There was a part of me that wasn't happy, I don't know if I'd taken a wrong turn somewhere or missed out on something, if so, I don't know if the chance will rise again. I remembered back to when Dad and I were talking. He talked about the good times and impeccable timing, sometimes you are just in the perfect place and moment. These moments though don't come around very often. Why? Surely if you make the right choices life can just bump along from high to high. Although, I know you must have the bad to appreciate good. I'm learning to listen more to myself, but sometimes can't hear what I am saying with the noise of daily life.

16/3/2004

We were heading towards Queenstown; in my research it was where all the extreme sports lovers hang out, they had skiing in the Remarkables in the winter and you could do all the extreme sports you wanted.

On the way we stopped at Hokitika, the place was famous for jade and were renowned for carving. I wanted something to add to my chain, since losing the cross I wanted something to connect me and Caroline.

Queenstown was a spectacular place to visit, they had the largest bungee jump in the world. I looked and it reminded me too much of the bridge and Caroline. It was the only thing I wouldn't do. I didn't want to be falling towards the ground, I had already lived that moment so many times in my nightmares.

19/3/2004

I woke to terrible dreams again; it was the same nightmare. It had come and gone during my travels.

We decided to get on the road again, heading for Milford Sounds. The drive was amazing, we were passing places that had been used in the filming of Lord of the Rings and it was even more incredible in real life. I was used to seeing mountains, spending winters in the Alps, I was always in awe.

We stopped at Mirror Pools for photographs which was exactly what it said on the tin. The reflections were perfect.

Parked up for the night, it was raining so camping wasn't much fun. My thoughts were with Caroline again, next month would be another anniversary. Two years since her death.

20/3/2004

Boat trip today to see the spectacular Milford Sounds, weather wasn't great, but the skies were clearing. The scenery was incredible, the mountains and waterfalls dwarfed the boat, it was one of the most amazing sights I had ever seen. The captain said to look in front of the boat, there were dolphins catching the waves. Amazing! There were also seals just chilling out on the rocks. I was overwhelmed, I loved the natural world. It warmed my heart. Caroline would have absolutely loved it, I remembered she had seen dolphins on one of her tours with Sarah.

21/3/2004

It was Mother's Day in the UK; I know Mum would be finding it hard. I gave her a call, good to chat. Grandma was there too so I got a chance to speak to her. It was lovely to have a moment in my head back at home. Mum didn't sound good. I knew exactly what was on her mind. It was on my mind too.

Driving back to Queenstown. We drove past Lake Wakatipu, it was around eighty kilometres long and the longest lake in New Zealand, I can't stress enough how amazing it is. We stopped to take in the view and get some photos.

22/3/2004

Steve was doing a bungee jump, Matty and I went up in the gondola. It reminded me of France usually heading up with my snowboard. The views from the top were amazing, taking me straight back to my winter seasons. We could see the Remarkables in the distance and I could see where the runs would be in the winter, it looked fun.

At the hostel I was looking through the leaflet guides and found a place called Caroline Bay. We would have to go tomorrow.

24/3/2004

Best night's sleep for a while. We headed to Caroline Bay; I could feel the emotion immediately. I took some time to have a walk along the beach and sent some thoughts out for my sister. I was living these experiences for her, trying to cram in as much as we could each day. I hoped she could see the world through my eyes and enjoy my travels with me.

Finally arrived in Christchurch. It was a great place and I got a good vibe. It was our last day, the Four Horsemen were disbanding. It had been a great time travelling together. So much fun. We went out for a few drinks, would be sad to leave each other, we had created a strong bond. Ross was leaving early tomorrow.

26/3/2004

It was Matty's and my last day together, we had been through a lot. Some amazing experiences and of course difficult times. Overall, Australia and New Zealand had been so much fun. Steve was also leaving in the morning, it would then be just me, back to solo travel.

27/3/2004

We had our final breakfast and they were both off to the airport. It was sad to say goodbye. I had a few days before I would be flying back to Sydney.

It had been a hectic month, caught up with emails and what was going on in the world. We had been in our own bubble for a while.

I hung around the hostel in the evening and got chatting with a girl called Kristy, she had a rainbow belt which made me smile, also a rainbow on her phone. She was a nurse from Melbourne. We were on the balcony, chatted the evening away and got on really well, strange how I had just met her when the guys had left. She was leaving in the morning but said if I was ever in Melbourne to look her up.

Experiencing Christchurch for the next few days, I started to write about travel for Caroline's Rainbow Foundation. The differences in mindset and the confidence needed to be a solo traveller. Even when you are travelling alone you are not really alone if you have the confidence to talk to people, there are many backpackers on the same journey.

30/3/2004
My final day in Christchurch, I was on a flight back to Sydney, 1359 miles. I was feeling emotional on the plane, I would be completely alone back in Australia and I knew I had some very difficult times ahead.

Booked in at The Globe, there might be a few people I knew still there. Back to Kings Cross and walking up the stairs to the hostel it felt like I was home. I was greeted by a couple of familiar faces, huge smiles, great to see them again.

31/3/2004
It was good to be back. I grabbed my paints and was looking forward to heading down to the beach. Steve and a few others weren't at work, so we had a small crew together. Bondi for the day, it was warm and not a cloud in the sky. Good to be back.

'Behind every wave is a hidden rainbow'.

1/4/2004

Dad's birthday; gave him a call. Told him all about the rest of my adventures in New Zealand and it was good to be back in Australia. I went down to the Opera House and did a painting where he had stood back in 2002.

A week in Sydney, I felt so comfortable around the city. It was a beautiful place to be. I had to continue my travels. Did some work for Caroline's Rainbow Foundation and sent my thoughts on solo travel. It was time to head west, Melbourne was big for the food culture and jazz scene; being a chef, I was looking forward to exploring. I booked a flight and a hostel and spent the next week getting to know my way around the city.

10/4/2004

Two years to the day since Caroline lost her life. It hurts more than ever. I headed into the city to Flinders Street station.

Decided to go skateboarding, it was a good way to clear my head.

I met up with Kristy after she had finished work, it was amazing to see her again. I felt comfortable talking about Caroline. It was a hard day for me, it was lovely to have her understanding. I offloaded a bit. There was a program on TV speaking about omens and mediums contacting the dead. It went on to show a Spiritualist church which piqued my interest again, I had been skirting around the topic for a while. We flicked over to a woman singing *Live and Let Die* and she was wearing a rainbow dress — make of that what you will! I was also reading *The Alchemist*, it was about change and letting go of the past, alchemising thoughts to change perceptions to enhance the present and future.

Kristy was working, we would catch up and hang out on her days off. We could take a drive along the Great Ocean Road. It would be lovely. I knew it was on Caroline's list.

15/4/2004
Driving out of Melbourne heading for the Great Ocean Road. I had seen pictures and it looked amazing. We drove past Apollo Bay, it was raining. I

had faith that it would brighten up. It was mid-afternoon when we parked and walked up to the view I had been waiting for. The rain had stopped, and the sky cleared. A few bands of clouds were high in the sky and the sun glistening off the lapping waves which surrounded the stacks of rock which made up the Twelve Apostles.

We walked and enjoyed the rest of the afternoon, at another of the viewing points and who should we see, but Steve and Vicki from The Globe. They were both leaving Australia soon and grabbing some last memories together. For such a big country I kept bumping into people, we were all on the same route. It was lovely to see them.

We saw Holy Rock from the movie.

16/4/2004
Continuing down the Great Ocean Road, passing beautiful cove after cove. Each was special in its own right. We stopped at Bells Beach where they filmed Point Break, no choice but to re-enact the final scene — 'I can't handle a cage man'. Seeing these places with Kristy was perfect, it was a pleasure to be in her company.

17/4/2004

Back in Melbourne and I was on with the Foundation's work; talking to a few reporters. Following on from the two-year anniversary, they were interested in the positive side and how we were dealing with everything.

Spoke with Matty back in the UK, he wasn't happy to be back. It's easy to forget real life and earning a living back home, he was in the kitchens paying off credit cards. I knew I would have all that to come.

18/4/2004

It was Vicki's last day in Australia, I went down to St Kilda to meet her. It was a lovely part of Melbourne, where all the cool kids hung out. It had such a nice vibe, by the beach, lots of windsurfing. We found a spot along the Esplanade near the market and had lunch, reminiscing about the days at The Globe and all of the good times we'd all had together. It felt like it was the end of an era. Painted for the rest of the day.

Everyone from The Globe had become so close. It was intense, the same as winter seasons; if you didn't see each other every day it felt strange. Bonds that take years to form at home can reach a similar level here in a couple of months. I believed in the next level of coincidence; we were all there at the right time because that's where we were meant to be. Christmas and New Year were some of the best times I'd ever had.

We were making friendships for life. I know they say you make friends for life at university, I never went to university, but consider travelling part of my further education.

Caroline was on my mind a lot, it was strange travelling alone, I only had myself to please. There were no rules, I could do exactly what I wanted. I had the realisation that I wasn't travelling alone. I would never be alone; Caroline would always be with me in spirit.

Reading the *Psychic Explorer*, it was interesting and got my mind thinking back to what Dad and I were talking about the Arthur Findlay College. When painting I would spend hours looking out at the same view, different thoughts and feelings would pass through my mind. I found it interesting to follow these trains of thought. I could see different things in my paintings, they very much reflected what I was feeling.

I was reading about listening to yourself and your intuition, the more you understand about yourself the more you knew whether you were picking up your feelings or if it was other people. I would always know when I would think of Caroline, I could feel it deep inside. It was different, I could feel her childhood excitement when we used to snorkel together and follow the fish or the energy when we had snowball fights and got absolutely soaked. Each feeling was slightly different.

I sensed Caroline around me, she was still part of me, and our bond extended further than just our physical body; we were connected by mind, through unconscious thought. I had seen rainbows when I needed hope, she made herself felt with a shudder down my spine or a warmth on the back of my neck. I believed she was sharing moments of this journey with me.

I spent the rest of the month finding out more about Melbourne, the food, the bars and the general vibe. Kristy and I hung out when we could and always laughed. I was talking to other backpackers, asking why, when and how they had chosen to travel? I was beginning to understand the mindset as to why people had chosen to leave the comfort and security of home to see the world. Caroline's Rainbow Foundation was in the news. I did more interviews about travelling in Australia and how the charity was working to keep backpackers safe.

I painted most days and was selling small landscape watercolours. All too soon I felt it was time to move on but will always leave a piece of my heart in Melbourne.

29/5/2004

The alarm went off a couple of hours early, plenty of time to make the flight to Perth; it would have been a lovely drive, but just taken far too long. I would be meeting up with Dan and Sophie, who I had met months earlier in Sydney. Kev who was also a regular at The Globe would be there too.

The plane descended into Perth, from the window I could see the Bay of Islands. Perth was apparently the most isolated city in the world. The hostel I had booked was pretty much in the centre of the city, dropped my bags and grabbed my skateboard. I spent a couple of hours wandering around the city, it had a nice vibe.

Back and showered, went to meet Dan and Sophie, great to see them again. We had gotten on well from day one. I was introduced to Megan and Beth who they were staying with, we had a laugh and a few drinks. It was a lovely introduction to Perth.

30/5/2004

After coffee and breakfast, I was meeting up with everyone and we were going out to Fremantle. Beth was off work; we all jumped in her car and drove along the coastline, she became the tour guide as she had been in Perth for a while. The skyline was beautiful, I noted a dozen places to paint.

We arrived in Fremantle; the St Kilda of Perth. We wandered the esplanade and the indoor market. I knew Caroline would have loved all the stalls and shopping. I had told Dan and Sophie about what had happened, but the others didn't know.

After a yummy lamb and mint pie from Fosters, which is only in Perth we walked down the harbour. There was a microbrewery called Little Creatures, places like this were becoming popular. I loved the atmosphere and the decor was cool, the brewing equipment was all on display. We tried a couple of beers, all different and really tasty.

I spent a couple of weeks exploring and painting around the city, I liked the feeling of the place. It was different to other cities I had visited in Australia. As they were isolated, they had developed their own culture and unique way of life.

12/6/2004

Sent postcards home, I was missing my family. I had been away for a long time now, every now and then it would get to me.

I picked a spot and set up painting.

A Korean girl came over and started chatting, I always met a lot of people when I was painting. She was on her travels and exploring the West Coast of Australia, she was saying that a lot of Koreans choose Australia. It had a good reputation for travel.

It started spitting, had to pack up. Walking towards the CBD, I saw the biggest double rainbow, it was amazing and must have lasted for about five minutes. I had an overwhelming feeling of peace.

Decided to go for a skate in the evening and headed down to the skatepark, it was a good session. A few kids came down, no skateboards just wanted to mess around. They only confirmed my disappointment in people, the younger generation don't have the values or respect that we grew up with. I could sense something brewing and sure enough they started causing trouble. They were looking through people's bags, looking through my bag! I went over and pushed the guy out of the way. He wanted a fight and there was a standoff. I knew I had the upper hand, he just didn't want to lose face in front of his friends, I stood my ground. After a few minutes it calmed, and he backed off. There were more skateboarders around which gave me confidence. I thought of the Foundation and what I should have done. Sometimes you have to stand up for yourself. I had assessed the situation and knew he wouldn't have tried anything. I was bigger and older and had a bunch of skateboarders who would have backed me up, he just wanted to come across as the big man. Was it the right decision?

Over the next week I carried on painting watercolours and was lucky enough to sell. It inspired me; small mounted original paintings seemed the way to go. I had registered with a chefs' agency, but they favoured Aussie chefs before any random backpacker.

Speaking with Mum, her and David were getting married. It was quite a shock, but if it was right for her, of course I would be happy. I made the decision to not fly back, it was going to be a small intimate service. They would be having a blessing and big party later in the year and I would fly home to celebrate with them.

17/6/2004

Mum and David tied the knot today with only family and close friends. It was strange to think she was getting married again, all I had known was her life with Dad. I am sure David would look after her, Caroline would have approved. I called home to wish them well and send my love, missed them. Interesting coincidence: today was the same date (17/6) that Grandma and Grandad got married.

Kev was in the city with his girlfriend, we met up for a beer, really good to see him. We were talking about moving on up the coast, I wanted to visit Broome; it was another place on Caroline's list. Researching the best way to get there, we favoured hiring a Winnebago. There were cheap options for relocations, the only downside was you had to do it in a very short timeframe, the companies had to get them where they needed to be for the next hire.

19/6/2004

I headed down for a skate, I knew the locals at the park. Skateboarding was our common interest; it was a brotherhood. For a lot of my travels, I had carried a skateboard, which for me had three major benefits. Firstly, getting around cities very quickly. Secondly, people were less likely to start a fight or mess with you, I think we had a bad reputation! Thirdly, and more importantly for me, you automatically had a circle of friends; if any skateboarders visited our local park, we would have a chat and make them welcome. It was the same here, we had a common bond, they would do what they could to help. If you were any good at skating it was all the better. I felt lucky to have this, it was like being back working the snowboard seasons. Like-minded people with the same love and passion I had.

20/6/2004

I woke with the sun beaming through the curtains, my birthday. I opened the cards Mum had sent, really thoughtful of her. Into the city and picked up some supplies, I was leaving with Kev and Anise tomorrow for our road trip up north, destination Broome. Perth had been amazing, but I was looking forward to my next adventure.

Feeling a little bit down, it was a strange birthday. I got some lovely messages from people which cheered me up. My mind was all over the place, another birthday without Caroline.

Dan and Sophie were about, Beth and Megan came home. I was told in no uncertain terms to go in the other room. When I came back in, they had a cake with twenty-seven candles! Party balloons and poppers. Absolutely amazing, I felt incredibly happy! We celebrated, few drinks, smokes and many laughs, I felt on top of the world again. They had really made my birthday special. I love them all.

21/6/2004

Sad to leave but going on an absolute high. It was the first day of our road trip. I met up with Kev and Anise, we picked up the Winnebago. There was a tight deadline to get the vehicle to Broome. After an eternity filling in forms and doing vehicle checks we were given the keys. What a machine, more luxury than I had seen in ages, it had everything. Called in on Dan and the crew to say our goodbyes, as always wished them well and catch up soon for the next adventure.

After a few problems getting out of the city we were on our way, perfectly straight roads in front of us and over 1200 miles to cover. We drove for the full day stopping at a couple of beaches and coves along the way. We finally pitched up in a campsite for the night, I took a stroll along the beach. Today was the first day of another year, I was living the dream, travelling Australia, meeting amazing people and enjoying once in a lifetime experiences.

A lot of road to cover, all we could see was a completely straight road stretching into the distance, red dirt either side scattered with a selection of rocks and cactus. It felt like we were journeying on the surface of another planet.

23/6/2004

Many more miles to cover today. Kev was driving and kept looking at the petrol gauge, it was going down fast. We suddenly lost power, out of petrol! Shit! Anise and I started walking, it can't be far, can it? 10 minutes later and we could see the petrol station just off the road at the next junction, we were bloody lucky! Back on the road, lesson learnt.

We passed plenty of roadkill in various states of decomposition, mainly kangaroos and some of them were huge animals; they would certainly cause some damage to the vehicle. A sign read Tropic of Capricorn it was getting warmer even though it was the middle of winter, we were back in shorts and t-shirts.

We finally reached Coral Bay and pitched up for the night. Sorted out our next stop tomorrow and some snorkelling with manta rays, really looking forward to it. We went for a walk along the beach and had a swim, it was lovely to be back in the water. We watched the sunset and Anise cooked up a wonderful dinner.

24/6/2004

The sun was just peaking over the trees filling the fresh morning with a wonderful glow. I started a little painting, just wanted to capture the moment. The colours were beautiful and bright.

Anise and I headed down to the dive site. We descended the line, immediately there were more fish and colours than I had ever seen before. We passed a shark cleaning ground, but luckily for us none were about. We carried on to the Ningaloo Reef; it was stunning, corals and fish everywhere. We descended further to around twelve metres. The fish didn't seem bothered about us at all, they were just going about their daily business. It was a wonderful dive, all too soon we were back up to the surface.

Back in the boat and on the move to go snorkelling with manta rays; they can be as big as nine metres. I was scared, but really looking forward to it. The captain spotted them, and we were soon in the water. We saw three of them a few metres below us in a courtship dance, looping around and around each other, it was unbelievable. They must have been three metres across.

Our final swim of the day, crew started to throw feed into the sea. The fish swarmed around us in seconds. There was everything from huge snapper to small butterfly fish. I saw a turtle and decided to follow it for a while, it glided along a few metres under the surface.

I was just drying off, one of the crew shouted, "Whale!" There were two humpback whales further out to sea, I never thought I would get the chance to see them.

Anise and I got off the boat with the biggest smiles on our faces, what an amazing experience!

Time to get back on the road, Coral Bay was a lovely little place. Relaxed and in perfect harmony with nature. We had to get going and cover some ground, driving until dark before pitching up for the night.

25/6/2004

We had a mammoth drive today, that was the deal with the relocation. It was my turn behind the wheel, up ahead I spotted two large birds of prey picking at a carcass. We had been warned that they took a while to get off the ground due to their size and wingspan. I slammed all on and they took off in front of us, it was an amazing sight. They flew straight towards us, over the windscreen and disappeared.

We drove on to eighty-mile beach, passing a couple of road trains along the way, they were immense! Not much other traffic at all. The sun was going down and the sky was lit up with amazing colours, we settled in for the night and chilled.

26/6/2004

Up early and it was the final leg of our trip. 250 miles to go, easy! We each took turns driving. Arriving in Broome we drove straight down to Cable Beach. One of the top five beaches in the world. It was amazing, some wonderful rock formations on the beach and soft white sand between our toes. Made it! We returned the Winnebago to the drop point and handed over the keys, it had been a cracking trip.

Found a hostel and checked in, got chatting to a Swiss girl who was in my room. It was lovely to meet so many people from so many different places, we all had the common love for travel and had actually got off our arses and done it!

27/6/2004

It was Matty's birthday, I sent him a message. He had asked me to get him a didgeridoo, I went down into the town and there was a local market on. I saw the perfect didgeridoo, how fitting that I would buy it on his birthday. Kev and I both played and headed down to the beach for a relaxing afternoon in the sun. Gave Matty a call.

It was lovely to relax, the beach was beautiful, being on the West Coast we were in for a real treat, sunset over the ocean. It was spectacular, the changing colours in the sky as the sun moved closer to the horizon. We spotted a line of camels walking down the beach, what? Of all the things I would never have expected that.

Back to the pub and got chatting to a few other backpackers who were staying in our hostel. They seemed a nice bunch, a lovely place to slow down and relax into a more chilled out world.

In total, I spent a around three weeks in Broome. I got to know people, chilled, we were on 'Broome Time'. Our days very much revolved around the beach and watching the sunset each day. I had a strong connection with a few people and was able to talk about Caroline.

A few people who I had met back in Sydney arrived, it still amazed me how we could meet up time and again in such an overwhelmingly large country. Our group was expanding. Every day we would hang out, go off and do our own thing, mine was painting of course.

We all knew we would all meet up on the beach, late afternoon sun and another inspiring sunset.

5/7/2004

After breakfast, I walked up to the Japanese graveyard, I put a sketch in. The graves dated back to the late 1800s, most of the graves were carved from the local stone. I could feel the energy in the place.

I went down to the beach to meet everyone. The sun was just going down, the colours in the sky were changing quickly, from blues and yellows into oranges and reds, then into the greens and deep blues. It was one of the most magical sunsets I have ever seen. My heart was aching, I couldn't grasp the beauty of it all.

There was a 'gathering' of backpackers, if that's what they are called. We had met Amy and Freda in Broome, they brought the group together, both had the most amazing energy and the ability to make everyone feel happy. Sally and Claire were amazing, full of energy. Oz and Lorraine, I had met before, Mel was new to the group and loved watching the sunset as much as I did. We had many beach days, laughed and joked all the way.

We were all excited and having the time of our lives. This is what travelling was about, like-minded people coming together enjoying a shared experience. There was no pressure, everyone got along and we were all here because we wanted to be. The beach is a huge part of Australian life, some people liked to be busy when they travelled. Seeing as much as they could, visiting all the tourist attractions. I did too, but I was also happy to spend time on the beach, talking to people and soaking up the day. To me, it was just as important and Broome was the perfect place to do it.

9/7/2004

It was our last full day as a group, people were starting to move on. All good things must come to an end. Broome had been epic!

Our little tribe headed down the beach, we were all happy although we knew some were leaving.

Chatting with Amy, we had a lovely connection and were completely in tune. She was a beautiful person to be around. We started talking about Caroline, it turns out she was in Bundaberg at the same time that Caroline was murdered, she knew the story all too well. We shared a few emotional moments, incredibly special.

Watched the sun fall behind the ocean and the explosion of rainbow

179

colours in the sky, it was intense. Lush! Back into town and to the pub, we were going to make sure everyone had a good send off.

Over the following ten days, people were moving on, Australia had so many places to visit. It was almost impossible to travel around the whole country in only twelve months, which was the standard visa length. Although backpackers could do some fruit picking or similar work to extend their visa and it was easy to see why many did.

A couple of days before we were due to leave, Dan and Sophie had done the road trip from Perth. It was great to see them again, if only briefly.

19/7/2004

Still dark outside when my alarm went off, it was cold as we walked down to watch the sunrise. We could see the glow behind the mangroves, the sand flats were glistening, it was the beginning of a new day and the next chapter of our adventure. Sad to say goodbye.

We got a lift to the airport, destination Darwin. I didn't really want to leave but moving on was a part of travelling. We had met some incredible people and had some wonderful experiences.

Darwin was super-hot, yet still winter. I think the summers would be unbearable. Kev and I got a taxi to the hostel and went for a wander around, we were not getting the same vibe as in Broome. We were both on a bit of a downer.

The sun set a little later, around 7 p.m. We got a couple of hours on the beach. The Vic was a famous backpacker bar and we caught up with a couple of people from our Broome tribe who had left a few days before, it made us feel at home again.

20/7/2004

A little worse for wear. Amy had arrived with Freda and we went to meet them. Hit up a local backpacker bar for lunch. Who should we bump into but more of The Globe crew from Sydney, you just couldn't write it. We ended up going out for a few drinks again, Darwin was tiring us out! I wasn't used to partying and drinking so much any more.

22/7/2004

I hooked up with a few people and we went down to the beach for the day. It was super-hot, we decided to go around the market. I saw EmDee setting up his didgeridoos, he had a run of four that he could play, I had heard of him and looked forward to his set. He played some speed didge, over 240 beats per minute. Absolutely incredible. I managed to have a quick chat with him, he had been playing for over thirteen years, his music came from the heart.

23/7/2004

Music was happening in Darwin; it definitely had that vibe. There was a concert in the open-air amphitheatre, and we managed to get tickets. It was all the artists that had become the soundtrack of our adventures.

Pete Murray was warming up, we picked our spot and settled in. There was a crew of us, it was a great atmosphere. Missy Higgins started, she was great. I loved her voice, really chilled, but powerful. Pete Murray was on, some of his songs had blasted out in every hostel I had visited.

What a night! We wandered back to the hostel, Dan and Sophie had arrived and checked into the room next to ours. It felt like our little family was getting back together again.

24/7/2004

Cloudy today, had a walk down to the beach. It was great. Had a swim but had to watch out for crocodiles! Had some time to chat, I felt a special connection with people, I would miss them but knew I would see them again.

Jumped on the three-and-a-half-hour flight back to Melbourne.

I spent a week back in Melbourne calling in at a couple of old haunts, caught up with Kristy and friends. I visited the Grampians mountains, they were fantastic, it was an inspiring place. Breath-taking views.

Booked a bus back to Sydney. I hadn't gone to Mum and David's wedding, but promised I would be there for their blessing. It was important. It would also be a welcome flying visit home for a few weeks.

Back to the UK

The blessing was beautiful, I had time to see Grandma, Mum and David. I told them nearly everything I had been up to, parts I knew Caroline had seen and places she would have loved. A part of my heart was devastated that I had made it home to tell my stories and I never got to sit next to Mum and listen to Caroline's adventures.

I travelled over to Scarborough for a couple of days to catch up with Dad. He was coming out for the trial, but only the second week. He said it's all he could take. I understood, but I knew I needed to be there from start to finish.

I caught up with friends. Matt Hills said he was coming back to Australia with me, I was excited. We had done a lot of travelling over the years including a road trip around the UK in a campervan and the interrailing trip around Europe.

I knew the next leg of my travels was going to be tough, I had the trial to contend with. I tried to mentally prepare imagining a little of what it might be like, although I could never really be prepared for what lay ahead.

18/9/2004

It was my final full English breakfast in the UK for a while. Tensions were running high. My bags were packed, I was ready to go! Mum and David drove me to York station where I was meeting Hills, we were getting the train to Manchester and flying to Brisbane via Singapore.

On the flight and I had plenty of time to think, it was less than ten days before the trial started. I knew it was going to be horrific, but what could I really do? Hills was a good friend and we talked openly.

20/9/2004

Somewhere along the way we had lost a day as we touched down in Brisbane. Weather was great, it felt so good to be back. We checked in to the Palace Embassy Backpackers. Dumped our bags and headed out, skateboards in hand. We found out that there was a Zero demo happening, so we went to check it out but the heavens opened.

Back at the hostel, we had a couple of beers and talked. Hills was excited about everything. We decided to have a little road trip before I had to leave for Bundaberg.

21/9/2004

We hired a car and set off, first stop Surfer's Paradise. I remembered Caroline's conversation with Mum and what she had said in her letters and postcards again. We had a walk along the beach, it was so good to feel the sun on my face. Arriving in Byron Bay we got a hostel for the evening.

Love it here, so happy to be back.

22/9/2004

I woke with a smile, it felt good to breathe Byron air again, just what was needed. Caroline was right. Something had drawn me back; I do love it here and felt an infinity with the place.

We took a drive, called in on Nimbin again and made our way back to Byron late afternoon. Up to the lighthouse and watched the sunset, it was beautiful. I remembered when I was here with Kyra. Hills and I chatted, he shared the same love of nature and freedom found in the natural world.

23/9/2004

We had to get the car back to Brisbane, it was a leisurely drive. Kev had flown in from Cairns, it was good to see him again. We caught up about the last month. He was making his way down the East Coast, he said Cape Tribulation and the Great Barrier Reef were amazing. We planned to go up north after the trial.

Jet lag was kicking in, we had to battle through.

24/9/2004

Up early, Kev and I cooked up breakfast just like old times. He was leaving today for a boat trip which would take a few days. We had a wander in the morning and chatted.

25/9/2004

Checked emails, the media interest was huge for what we were about to go through. I made a lot of calls arranging meetings for the coming week.

Happy that the work was done and feeling back on form, I wanted one last day of escape. We got the metro out to a big skatepark some guys had told us about. Great skate, Hills and I always have bounced off each other.

Back at the hostel, we went out for a couple of beers and relaxed for the evening. My head was distracted, all I could think of was Caroline and what the hell was going to happen over the next few weeks.

26/9/2004

Didn't sleep well. Time had run out, I now had a long bus ride to Bundaberg, plenty of time to think. I knew this was going to be hard.

Backpacking had been a completely different experience than I imagined up until this point. There was a part of me that felt like I was at home, comfortable and confident. I had fallen in love with the country. I was enjoying the freedom and the fact I could just blend in with the crowds, no special treatment or looks of sympathy. The death of my sister was like I had a secret, something that set me aside and made me feel different. Although, the secret of my sister's murder couldn't be less of a secret.

There was a part of me that didn't want to face life as who I now was. It wasn't that I wanted to be someone else, but I wanted to be me without the breakup of our family and loss of my sister. Travelling had given me escape, but it made me realise two things. One, I actually didn't want to be anyone else, the friends I had made liked me for me and the special times we had shared together. Two, escape was good, but it was only in preparation for dealing with life and facing up to hard times that come along. Another quote that resonated, 'What doesn't kill you, makes you stronger.'

I sat alone on the journey full of mixed emotions, angry and frustrated, confused and nervous. I always liked to be busy, creative and have a goal to achieve. The trial was not going to be easy and this time there was nothing I could do, I just had to be there, sitting and listening to everything happening around me. It was all out of my hands, I hated feeling powerless.

I always knew this part of my life and travels was coming, it was the burning ship on the horizon that I knew I had to board. There was no breathing apparatus, no lifeboats, no other souls aboard. I just had to sit in the flames, endure and hope to finally emerge from the ashes.

Chapter 12
The trial in Bundaberg

The police and British Consulate had kept us well informed over the last two years, but nothing could have prepared me for the few weeks that lay ahead. I had thought about it a great deal, part of me welcomed the closure, another part was absolutely dreading it. I really had no idea what to expect.

My travels over the last eight months had been to live for Caroline, I found out more about myself and experienced the beautiful country of Australia. I had not mentioned Caroline to most of the people I had met, if it had come up in conversation and I was asked if I had a sister I would just say yes and try to leave it at that. I wanted them to see me for me and not a tainted awkward view filled with sympathy.

I arrived in Bundaberg and was welcomed by the police and councillors, it was good to see everyone. Unfortunately, again, it was under the most horrendous circumstances. Checking into the B&B, great to see Kate, David and Claire. It was familiar and became my sanctuary once more.

Mum was still in the UK and had decided not to come out, it was going to be too painful, she was in a very delicate place with the pain still hitting hard. It was something I was unable to imagine. No parent should ever outlive their child. I now had to stand up for our family, I had to make Caroline proud.

27/9/2004 — Day 1

Text from Dad offering support. Mum texted saying her thoughts were with me. It was early, I had time to take a long shower and contemplate the day ahead. Megan Hunt has been fantastic support since Caroline died, she picked me up and we headed straight to the courthouse, the media were already outside. Megan and I went straight in, I gave a forced smile at a few faces I recognised. After the body search, we went up to the courtroom, my heart was racing.

The accused, Ian Douglas Previte stood in the dock, wearing a white shirt, he had short-cropped hair, trying to look smart. Nothing like the photos I had seen in the papers. I saw through the facade, there was no way he could cover up his past.

I sat with Megan. Judge Peter Dutney entered. First was to pick the jury, it was a small courtroom. Fifty people came in, after some deliberation twelve were picked. The judge went on to explain the proceedings, good for me to hear as I didn't really understand how everything worked. My heart was still pounding, and I was experiencing waves of nausea.

After lunch I went down to the bridge with Megan for a press conference. First, I looked at all the tributes placed on the spot where Caroline's body was found. Someone had left a picture of Caroline with her friends on the last day of school, I picked it up and looked closely. I don't know who left it, but it must have been someone who knew her from the UK. I took a deep breath and felt overwhelmed; in the background I could hear camera shutters clicking. I gathered my thoughts and walked up to the cameras and smiled, they were respectful, but asked the questions they needed to. I can't remember what I said, it seemed to be over quickly.

The afternoon session. I sat in the front row of the balcony, Ian Douglas Previte entered his plea. Not guilty. Opening statements were given from both sides. Mr Peter Feeney for the prosecution and Mr Dennis Lynch for the defence.

A pathologist Dr Ashby was called; on a big screen there were pictures of Caroline's body shown under the mortuary lights. She gave a detailed account; it turned my stomach and I could feel sadness deep in my very core. As the pictures flashed up, I could feel the reporters and others on the balcony look at me trying to see my reaction. I felt devastated and there was no way I could contain my emotions. It seemed an incredibly long afternoon.

The first day was finally over. Megan had been fantastic and supported me all day, I couldn't have asked for more. She dropped me back to the B&B. I caught myself on TV, entering the courthouse and the interview I had done under the bridge. There were also pictures shown of Caroline and Previte. It was too much for me to live it again.

I grabbed my paints and escaped down to the beach. Set up my easel and started to splash some colours on the paper, it helped me relax. Met a photographer called Pete Willis, he took some photos of my paintings. As I was getting my photo taken, a gentleman and his two children walked over to us on the rocks. His kids came over and said, "My Dad says you need a hug." One after the other the kids gave me a big hug. I felt the emotion welling up inside, their Dad shook my hand and offered some words of comfort. He then carried on along the beach with his kids running out in front. It was a very special moment and really meant a lot to me.

Megan and I talked, she was a great listener and said she was really proud of me how I handled myself and my confidence in front of the cameras. It was very kind of her, she knew I was carrying the full weight of everything on my shoulders. I thanked her for all her support.

The day was done, I needed some time alone and took a stroll along the beach. I watched the shimmering water and thought of Caroline. It was really difficult, and I felt like there was a mountain ahead of me.

I started the walk back to the B&B, Kristy called, it was lovely to hear from her and we chatted for a while. I felt more connected again. Chatting with Kate, didn't know that Queensland didn't have daylight savings time, still gets dark at 7:30 p.m. even in the summer. Spoke with Mum and Dad, all had gone as good as it could have.

Thinking about tomorrow and what was going to happen, more interviews and on show. Would have a chat with Megan about working with Caroline's Rainbow Foundation.

Tried to get some sleep.

28/9/2004 — Day 2

I read the news online first thing before breakfast, the News Mail had just published an article.

'Caroline Stuttle murder trial opened

"COME and meet me" were the final words Caroline Ann Stuttle uttered moments before her death, a jury heard yesterday.

The final minutes of the British backpacker's life were played out in the Bundaberg Supreme Court at the beginning of one of Australia's most publicised murder trials.

Ian Douglas Previte, 32, stood in the dock —— his long hair now close-cropped and face clean-shaven — and calmly told the court he was not guilty of the robbery and murder of the 19-year-old.

187

The small court room was already cramped with Australian and British media when the jury of seven men and five women was selected.

Crown prosecutor Peter Feeney then recounted the events that followed when Ms Stuttle went to call her boyfriend from a telephone near the Bundaberg Post Office at 8 p.m.

"It was a clear and moonless night and Caroline was wearing a light blue hooded jumper over a white T-shirt, corduroy pants and she was carrying a bag with the strap over her shoulder," Mr Feeney said.

After telephoning her boyfriend Ms Stuttle began to walk back across the bridge about 9 p.m.

"Previte was sitting on a bench on the east side of the bridge just out of sight and he saw her walk by alone," Mr Feeney told the court.

"About nine minutes later Caroline called her friend Sarah and said, 'Come and meet me' in a hurried voice."

Mr Feeney told the jury the evidence would show Previte intended to rob Ms Stuttle and murder her by forcing her over the rail of the bridge.

"This is all going to be proven by a lot of witnesses who each have a little bit to tell," Mr Feeney said.

"It will come down to timing — to where people were and the aspects of what Previte has said which are facts that would only be known by the killer."

Mr Feeney told the jury they would hear police interviews and secret tapes of Previte telling prisoners he was responsible for Ms Stuttle's death.

Evidence from forensic pathologist Dr Rosemary Ashby suggested Ms Stuttle had been assaulted before she fell from the bridge.

Dr Ashby said severe skull fractures and a severed spinal column from the impact of the fall ultimately led to her death, but there was evidence of an assault.'

After breakfast, Megan arrived to pick me up. We headed straight to the courthouse. Ian Nelson had been called and was taking the stand before lunch. He did really well, I could tell he was nervous, Caroline would have been very proud of him. Lee Longworth took the stand, he knew Sarah and Caroline and was staying in the same campsite.

We went to the Riverside Café for lunch, Ian told me he had been offered an exclusive with a UK paper. He was going to do it and offered to donate the fee to Caroline's Rainbow Foundation. It was really kind of him and I respected him greatly.

Back in the courtroom in the afternoon. The focus was now on the police verifying important points of the case, to me it seemed all very meticulous and detailed as I would have expected. It was hard going through the last moments of Caroline's life. The more everyone talked the clearer the picture in my mind, it felt like they were going through it over and over again. It was a long day.

I was happy to leave the courtroom and head back to the B&B. I had a call from Hills, he was doing well and enjoying the Brisbane. We talked about skateboarding and what we would be doing after I left Bundaberg. Amy called, and offered her thoughts, we had a good chat. Rocka who I knew from the Alps called telling me about everything that had been happening. She was having a fantastic time. It was wonderful to hear from my friends, it really made the difference and gave me a glimmer of normality.

In the evening, I was thinking about the day in court, it brought back the memories from 2002. I felt like I was reliving the telephone call in Meribel. I felt strangely happy, it was weirdly comforting to bring back all those memories and feel the extreme heartache. It felt like I was really remembering the loss of Caroline. I lived it once for myself, once for our family and friends, now I was reliving it again for everyone who knew our story and wanted justice.

29/9/2004 — Day 3

Woke to a text from Mum, she was thinking of me. Megan came to pick me up and we went to meet Richard Crinnion, Ian and Lee for breakfast. I was meeting Sarah later. Down to court, there was no media outside today, they already had their photos and story.

Hearing evidence from more witnesses, Janet Thompson was the lady who heard Caroline's scream, she gave evidence. It was the ungodly scream that had haunted my nightmares for the last couple of years, as she spoke a shudder ran down my spine. I felt very drained by the end of the session, mentally shattered and in pieces.

Met up with Sarah and her boyfriend, Megan looked after us all. It was good to see a familiar face, she looked drained and scared. We went down the beach for some photos.

Dave Batt, one of the lead detectives on the case, came to pick us up, he had the day's papers with him. I hadn't seen them yet, there were still pictures of us but just not on the front page. He was going to a leaving party for one of the officers, I didn't feel up to it, so he dropped me off at the B&B. I had a quiet evening, trouble sleeping, nightmares had started again.

30/9/2004 — Day 4

Caught up with the news in the UK they were behind with the time difference, *The Guardian* had picked up the story.

Dave Batt came to pick me up and we went straight to the courthouse. More witnesses. The prosecution was working to establish what happened and corroborate the timeline. It was hard to hear. All I thought was, I know she is dead. I felt alone again, the weight was still very much on my shoulders and pressing hard.

Checked my emails during lunch, I had a lot from friends, some made me smile. I replied to many, but not all. People sending their thoughts was comforting.

Back in court for the afternoon and I was feeling stressed, angry and frustrated. Unable to do anything, everything was completely out of my control. All I could do was sit and listen, reliving her last few hours again and again. I felt a part of me dying in the courtroom as every hour ticked by.

Met up with Megan, Dave Batt, Ian, Richard and others in the evening. We all went for a bite to eat. Dave took us to the pub for a couple of pints. Keith the landlord gave us a set of mugs. It was very kind of him. We proceeded to drink out of them for the rest of the night, it was a well needed bit of release.

Dave and I had some time to talk, I knew it had been a hard road for him. It had put a lot of pressure on his homelife and family, he spent a lot of time on the case. I told him how much I appreciated what he had done, what the whole team had done. Our family were in their debt and it was a debt I knew we could never fully repay.

1/10/2004 — Day 5

Feeling a little bit worse for wear this morning, but it was good to laugh and release a little of the pressure. Dave collected me and we picked up Ian and Richard.

It was one of the days I had been dreading. Sarah was called to the stand. She looked composed, but I could feel she was terrified. She did amazingly well, Caroline would have been so proud of her.

She ran through what happened and answered each question concisely. As she talked, I thought of the panic she must have been feeling when she couldn't find Caroline. I was thankful that she didn't find Caroline's body. Feeling her pain in every word, I wept. We were all so proud of her, such a brave young woman.

Next, we listened to the confession tape evidence, it was difficult to hear. Sick, just hearing his voice made me feel angry and disgusted.

The judge closed the morning session and the week was finished. Friday afternoons off, thank the good lord.

Sarah and I went for lunch, it was good to see her properly. She was incredibly relieved. We went for a walk and talked about Caroline, I told her how proud she would have been. She had a photoshoot with a paper in the afternoon.

I took some time on the beach and had a swim in the sea, it was the first time in what felt like ages. I watched the sunset, felt a little more relaxed and started to unwind. It was nice to think I wouldn't have to be back in court until Monday. A warm wind was blowing hard, thousands of grains of sand flew past stinging my ankles. It looked spooky, like spirits or ghosts dancing across the beach.

2/10/2004

No one was picking me up this morning. Kate kindly cooked me brunch and gave me a lift down to the beach to meet up with Sarah, Richard, Ian and the others. Everyone had had a stressful week and was pleased to be able to relax for a day. It felt like another world, hanging out, playing frisbee and chatting in the sunshine.

I wandered up the beach and found a nice spot to paint, lost myself for a couple of hours and all was as well as it could be with the world. We walked up to Bargara and had dinner, good company and great conversation.

3/10/2004

Sunday. After breakfast I got a lift down to Nelson's beach. Traditionally Sunday was a day for skateboarding. I had a well-needed push, you must be completely present and think of nothing else when skating otherwise you ended up on the floor.

I remembered swimming here with Ross and Isabella in the pouring rain, it was absolutely amazing. Not a cloud in the sky today.

Sarah, Ben and Lee came down, we sat on the beach having a blast on their didgeridoo. I was getting pretty good! They were lovely people; we had all just experienced something horrific. Sometimes it's easy to forget the normality of people around you. I talked about Caroline's Rainbow Foundation and what we were doing, they all offered to help where they could. It meant a lot to me.

When the sun had fallen beyond the horizon, we went for dinner, Villa Italia. Chatted over a bottle of wine, it turns out Lee knows some people I know from home. He had been skateboarding with Hills and a friend of his. Such a small world!

We all enjoyed a conversation about coincidence and intuition. Ultimately, we all agreed, there is no such thing as coincidence. Our pathway through life is about recognising moments when they happen and acting upon them when you feel your intuition telling you to do so.

Said goodbye to Sarah and Ben, they were heading off tomorrow. I hope to catch up with them again soon.

Reality check, the weekend is over, back in court tomorrow.

4/10/2004 — Day 6

I didn't need to be in court first thing, Dave Batt picked me up. The jury were getting taken down to the bridge and over to the campsite to walk the route Caroline did before her death. I met up with Lee to say goodbye, he was leaving for Harvey Bay to go whale watching.

Back in the courthouse for the afternoon session. We were watching video evidence of the police interviews, Previte looked like shit. It was disturbing, he confessed to everything. Good news! After sitting through the tapes and hearing the cases from Mr Feeney and Mr Lynch my head was all over the place, I was getting a headache.

Leaving the courthouse, I was pleased with how the day went, but felt

192

completely drained and shattered.

The jury had an evening session. They went down to the Burnett Bridge after dark to experience the exact conditions that Caroline had faced. I was tearful just thinking about it, it was strange the different things that triggered my emotions.

I was dropped off down the beach and did a quick sketch. At the beach bar I sat writing and catching up with my thoughts. A gentleman came over, eighty-eight years old, strong, thick white hair and a deep suntan. We got chatting, he had written a diary every day since he was nineteen, at sixteen years old he couldn't read or write. Now he had a passion for it, catching the moment in words was his speciality. He told me, some people go through the world not seeing or feeling anything, for others the opposite, it's everything. He told me I was the latter. Our conversation inspired me. I remembered a report I had at school. I must have been around 14 years old. My reasoning power and understanding was around two years older than my actual age, but my reading and writing was about three years younger than I was. I also had dyslexia, but it was never properly diagnosed. I am going to keep writing every day.

5/10/2004 — Day 7

Colin, who was Megan's husband, came to pick me up and took me early to the airport, Dad and Janet were arriving. We had a big hug. I was dropped off at the courthouse and they went back to the B&B to get sorted. It had been a really hard week. It had taken its toll, I felt I had aged many years. It was a relief to have some support.

They were going through more video evidence, interviews and statements from the police. There were a few photos of Caroline again, which were disturbing. I was pleased Dad wasn't in the courtroom to see them. The defence argued badgering of the witness, everything was denied.

We went down to the River Cruz Café for lunch. Met up with Megan, the police team and some of the people from the media. I knew them all now. We did an interview and had some photos. Dad was the focus and a father's story about losing his daughter.

The afternoon session, there were no more graphic images. He didn't need to see any of that. I thought back to when he had to identify Caroline's body, that was enough. I could see Dad going through the same emotions that I had the week before. At the end of the day, he was completely drained. The long flight and courtroom were both physically tiring and mentality destroying. When we got back to the B&B he crashed out.

Megan, Colin and I went for dinner down on the beach, we had a beer and chat. I felt more support now, but I had to be there for Dad, he was now on the same rollercoaster I had already done a lap of.

There was a storm brewing over Bundaberg, I stood outside watching the stars and dramatic clouds, the sky lit up followed by a deep rumble a few seconds later. It was an amazing sight.

6/10/2004

Woke to not a cloud in the sky. Megan arrived, told us that court was off today as one of the jury members was ill. It was unexpected relief and gave Dad a little more time to acclimatise. Megan arranged a trip to Childers for the afternoon to catch up with Bill Trevor.

We wanted to use the morning, so we headed down to the Botanical Gardens to see the tree they had planted for Caroline. It was starting to bud as summer was on the way. Dad and I started a painting, it was good to paint together again.

We drove over to Childers, lovely to see Bill, he looked larger than life and full of energy just as I remembered him. He showed us the memorial at the hostel which was now completely finished. I thought it was a beautiful tribute to the backpackers who lost their lives in the fire. We had a good catch up, Bill told us some of the things he had been through with the fire and the families. We could completely relate; it was an incredibly moving experience. I felt a great emotional connection with all of them and Bill.

Spoke with Mum and filled her in on the news, she was happier now I had support.

Megan got a call. There was a seventeen-year-old girl travelling around Australia with her boyfriend. Her brother back home in the UK had just committed suicide. It's easy to get caught up in our own world, there are lots of other families going through tragedies every day. My heart poured out for their family.

7/10/2004

Court was cancelled again as the juror was still ill. Megan and Colin were driving back to Brisbane today, she had a lot of other work to deal with. It was sad to say goodbye, Megan had been there for me since day one. I felt a very strong connection with her. Colin and I had also become good pals. I would look forward to working with them and Caroline's Rainbow Foundation in the future.

Checked my emails and caught up with some bits for the charity, everything was going well. Mum and David were working hard. Dad and I went down to the river to paint the southern end of the Burnett Bridge. I didn't like it, horrible subject, made me feel terrible.

We were meeting the Mayor Kay McDuff, Mal Forman and a couple of other councillors for dinner. Everyone chatted around the table, Bundaberg was doing well, and everyone was working hard to make it a great town. I did like the place despite what had happened to Caroline. Dad upset me a little, going too far with what he was saying. I could understand, he had just arrived and was upset, but I had been here from the start. I just let it go. Overall, it was a lovely evening.

Back at the B&B I got a call from Sally. On her way back to Kings Cross in Sydney, she was staying at The Globe. Had a good chat and she lifted my spirits.

8/10/2004

We were ready for court. After breakfast, I got a call from Dave Batt, the juror was still ill. They would restart again on Monday whether the juror was better or not. I was not prepared for this, it threw me a little, I wanted to get on with everything.

Dad and I had a long chat in the afternoon, it was good for us to have some time together. We shared some feelings, both of us were depressed and understood when we said — we were just trying to get through each day. We remembered the last time we were here and our emotions, time had moved on, but it felt like parts of us hadn't and might never.

I chatted with Mum, she was ok, but I could feel the sadness in her voice. I reassured her that it was for the best that she hadn't come over. Dad and I were here to represent the family, everyone understood. I knew Mum, she would be beating herself up about it, thinking she should be here for Caroline and for me. The things I had seen would have completely destroyed her.

9/10/2004

We had a good day planned. It was unexpected time and not to be wasted. We picked up a hire car, Dad, Janet and I set off on the road to Agnes Waters, it was a small beach town with a similar vibe to Byron Bay. We walked over a bridge, Dad and I looked at each other and I felt a little shudder. We didn't say anything but felt the same. Walking through some trees we came to a beautiful beach, lovely and quiet. A perfect little oasis.

Continuing our journey, we came to the town of 1770. Drove through the town and out to the point for a great view. To our right jagged rocks zigzagged into the distance. Left was a deep channel and sand flats. Amazing sight. To think this was the first part of Australia that Captain Cook saw when landing here.

We grabbed a juice at one of the shops in town; just back from the beach, found a quiet spot and set about painting.

It was nice to get out of Bundaberg; although it was a lovely place, I still felt a heavy weight on my shoulders when I was there. Our paintings flowed and I felt myself loosening up, if the painting was free and going well, then I knew I was ok. It was the perfect therapy.

We left before sunset, driving back the road wound along the coastline. Suddenly, I had to brake hard, there was a huge snake in front of us. It was one of the biggest I have ever seen. Unbelievable! We waited for it to cross the road in its own time. Nature could always surprise you.

We stopped in the Botanical Gardens in Bundaberg and got a few more photos of Caroline's tree.

Made a few phone calls after dinner, it was good to touch base with friends. I felt recharged and human again remembering some of the other reasons I was in Australia.

10/10/2004

Sunday, a day of rest but I was raring to go. Kate dropped us in the town centre to have a wander around an International Food Festival that was happening. There were amazing smells coming from the stands, we tasted a lot of different foods. I was in my element.

The Mayor gave a welcoming address and handed the keys of the city to Chantel Wolfenden. She was an eighteen-year-old Paralympian, who had won six medals in Athens. One gold, one silver and four bronze. It was humbling and brought a tear to my eye. I had the privilege of meeting her, such energy and an amazing smile. We chatted for a few minutes, I felt her positive outlook on life. She was an inspiration. It was all about attitude which resonated deeply.

We went up to the Hummock in between Bargara and Bundaberg, it was the perfect place to watch the sunset. I lost myself in thought, it had been a good weekend all considered.

11/10/2004 — Day 8

Back in court. Dave Batt came to pick us up, there were a few media people about snapping photos as we went in.

First up, there was a handwriting expert who analysed what was written on the park bench, 'I throw the girl off the bridge, I am sorry'.

The park bench evidence was inconclusive. The afternoon session was more promising. Two men who knew Previte and were locked up with him took to the stand. I thought they were brave to come forward, they could be endangering their own lives. They gave evidence and both said he had confessed to them on more than one occasion. I thought both did a good job. After court concluded for the day, Mr Feeney said that the men wanted to have a word with me.

I was tired, my head buzzing with everything that had happened and thinking back to the previous week. I talked in detail with Dad about all the things that happened. Called Mum and told her what was going on. I checked the news online and fell asleep with the TV on. Woke up a few times in the night, nightmares again.

12/10/2004 — Day 9

The sun was beaming through the shades, I slept longer than usual. Mental exhaustion. Breakfast was welcome, I was getting used to having it cooked for me.

We were into the final few days of the case and the media were out in force, there was a large gathering outside.

The morning session was more about the handwriting on the bench. This time the testimony held up well and was more conclusive.

During the lunch break, Dave Batt took me down to the police station to speak with Jason and Bruce, the two men who testified yesterday. Their testimonies had moved me, I thought they were both telling the truth and appreciated talking to them. They were both in for minor crimes, they said murder was a step too far and they were appalled with what Previte had done.

In the afternoon session, there were a string of witnesses. Mr Lynch and the defence carried on making excuses for each person who took the stand. They tried to pick apart what everyone was saying. I knew it was their job, but it was starting to get to me. How could someone defend these people for a living?

The BBC called. As the trial was now in its final days, they wanted to do a big story on how everything was going. Of course, I agreed and arranged telephone interviews.

13/10/2004 — Day 10

It was going to be a busy day. The defence called their first witnesses, men who had either confessed or knew details about the case. They were going for reasonable doubt, both Ross Graham and James Campbell had confessed to others that they had committed the murder. Mr Feeney and the prosecution were good and picked holes in their stories. It was difficult to hear. To be honest, it did make me question whether we had the right guy, and that was exactly the outcome the defence wanted. My feelings were all over the place. The law states innocent until proven guilty, nothing was certain.

The afternoon was a hard session, there were some photos of Caroline put up on the big screen. Dad had to leave, Janet went to console him. I stayed, it was important.

Mr Fenney gave his closing statement and tied up all the loose ends. He was telling the truth and I believed him. The Judge closed the court to reconvene at 10 a.m. the following day for the defence's closing statement.

Dad and I went down to the bridge and did an interview with 7 News, it went well, but we were both drained. Dad had found the day difficult. After we headed to the Botanical Gardens for an interview and photos with News Mail.

On the way back to the B&B we passed an accident, no one hurt thank God. Accidents happen all the time, just a reminder that life can be so fragile. Why someone would choose to deliberately destroy life is beyond me.

14/10/2004 — Day 11

We were back first thing. I didn't know how many days the trial would go on or how much more I could take. I read the latest UK news.

It was the turn of the defence; the gallery was packed. It had been busy throughout, but today seemed more claustrophobic. Mr Dennis Lynch spoke for the defence. He talked for two hours giving some very valid points that could quite easily have put doubts in the mind of the jury. I was only an observer, there was nothing I could do, and my opinion was irrelevant. The police were sure they had the right man.

Judge Peter Dutney had the final words of the day, he spoke strongly and succinctly. He went through each argument first from the prosecution, then the defence. Everyone listened intently, for me it was good to hear. He finished leaving a few points for tomorrow. We were heading into another day!

Hungry, but none of us felt like eating. The mood was sombre and we didn't know what was going to happen. It didn't seem like an open and shut case.

15/10/2004 — Day 12

Hadn't slept well and felt a lot of nervous energy. We had no idea how today was going to end. Dave Batt dropped us outside the courthouse, we had to push through the cameras and reporters.

Judge Peter Dutney entered, we bowed our heads, the mood was very different. He addressed the jury. His statement was fair and reflected both sides as you would expect, he finished with, "It is now up to you the jury to make the final decision in this case."

Outside we waited, nothing we could do. I escaped around the corner for a cigarette. The media collared me for statements and interviews, nothing new to say really it was more about how we were feeling. I thanked everyone for their hard work and trusted in the Court's decision.

We went to the Botanical Gardens and just had to wait. It was up to the jury now, it could be hours or days, we just didn't know.

Mayor Kay McDuff came down and had coffee. She was a wonderful person, so busy but still had time for us. She showed us round the Chinese Gardens before having to leave for a meeting. A couple of reporters turned up for photographs and comments. Dave Batt called; the jury had reached a verdict. We raced back not daring to hope what the decision was.

Previte stood up. The jury read their decision. On the charge of robbery, GUILTY. On the charge of murder, GUILTY. Life imprisonment, he would serve a minimum of fifteen years with no chance of parole.

Slumping back in my seat I felt a huge sense of relief wash over me. I felt heavy and completely shattered. I looked over to the box. I strangely felt pity for the shell of a man I saw standing there. On April 10, 2002, he'd thrown his life away and given our family a life sentence.

It was like a weight had been lifted from our shoulders. Dad and I sighed, it was over. I turned my phone on, it was ringing almost immediately. First Richard Crinnion to say well done and offer his thoughts. Mum got through, I told her it was over. Call after call, BBC, ITV followed by all the other media outlets I knew in the UK. I repeated my thoughts and sense of relief — it will never bring Caroline back, but we were pleased this chapter could now be closed.

We made it outside to flashes and microphones in our faces, I was conscious of smiling. I didn't want to look happy. We said everything we needed to and thanked everyone for their support over the last few weeks and the police for their tireless work over the last two years.

We could finally breathe; I took a deeper breath than I had for the last two and a half years. I couldn't believe it was over! I started to fill with emotion. I didn't really know what it meant, I was overwhelmed with sadness, although didn't cry. A part of me still doesn't believe that Caroline is dead, and I will never see her again in my lifetime. I pulled myself together.

We went to the MIR, the police and prosecution were all there, we said a huge thank you! They had all worked so hard on the case and were extremely happy with the result. We listened to *Nothing Man* by Burnside. The whole team used to play it every morning before they started work.

Pastor Errol came down on his motorbike, a beautiful Triumph RS. Great to see him again. He offered his thoughts and sympathies.

Dad and Janet got a lift back to the B&B, I decided to stay out and have a few drinks with the team to show our appreciation. I managed to talk to most people, after a time I made a sly exit. My mind went through everything that had happened. It didn't matter how much I knew, there would always be questions. Some things Caroline had taken to her grave and I would never know. Now wasn't the time and I would have to let them go. It had been an almost unbearable, few weeks, but now it was all finally over!

16/10/2004

I would have felt good, but a bit of a hangover from last night. Leaving today but had a couple more interviews to do, met up with the reporters and photographers. I was more than happy to do them, felt far more comfortable.

As we drove out of Bundaberg, I didn't know whether I would ever be back. Dad and Janet had a few days before they were flying back to the UK. We were heading for one of Caroline's favourite places. Looking forward to a few days relaxing, no courtroom, no media or interviews, no pressure.

Some things in life have a way of eating away at your very soul. Ian Douglas Previte was sentenced to fifteen years imprisonment with no chance of parole. We had the best result we could have hoped for, although the rest of his life in prison still wouldn't have been enough for me.

We could live with the verdict; the jury had found him guilty and the Judge had given the maximum sentence in accordance with the law. It felt like we had bandaged an open wound and it was starting to heal. We wouldn't waste any more energy thinking about Ian Douglas Previte, well for fifteen years anyway. He had wasted enough of our time and destroyed enough of our life. He certainly wasn't worth it.

There were still questions in my head. Anything to do with the case was finished, the jury, police and Australian legal system were all convinced, he was guilty.

Sometimes the simplest questions hurt the most. Was Caroline happy? I know she was travelling, she had done well at school and college, she had lots of friends, but I never remember asking her if she was happy. I really wanted to know the answer, even on our final conversation I remember her saying she was having the best time, things were great, and she was doing so much. I know she had been through a lot in her life, but was she happy with who she was and her short 19 years?

Chapter 13
An uncertain adventure continued

Where do I go from here? The last couple of years had been building up to the last few weeks. I hadn't really considered what life would be like after the trial. We had done what was needed and could finally close this chapter. We had justice for Caroline.

The people of Bundaberg had been fantastic and supported us every step of the way. We left Bundaberg heading to Brisbane.

I went to the Victoria and met up with Hills, Kev and Vanessa. It was lovely to see them, after a few awkward conversations skirting around what happened, we were soon back talking about travel and what they had been up to.

The following day Dad, Janet, Hills and I hired a car and drove to Byron Bay. It was the right place to go, the perfect place for a bit of respite.

As I drove the now almost familiar route, my shoulders relaxed and the constant tension that had been there for over two years started to subside.

18/10/2004

It was raining hard. Byron was crying. We were staying in a lovely B&B, a change from my usual backpackers. By afternoon, the rain subsided, we walked into the town, the beach was welcoming. Standing with my feet in the sand I sent out thoughts for Caroline. She was with us, I visualised her stood next to me, looking out towards the lighthouse. She was smiling, she was happy. She was proud of us.

In the afternoon we went to the Crystal Castle, I was interested and ended up getting a book on crystals. Something that had withstood that much time and pressure must contain a lot of energy. Diamonds after all were held in the highest regard.

We enjoyed dinner, lovely fresh swordfish, vegetables and butter sauce. It was the quality of ingredients kissed by the sun that made the difference, a lot of produce in the UK was either imported or ripened in transit. Here, things were kept fresh and simple.

19/10/2004

Another day of rain, I knew Dad was frustrated, we both just wanted to be out painting. In the afternoon it brightened up, we grabbed our paints and headed down to the beach. Lovely landscapes looking towards the lighthouse, I could stay here a lifetime and never feel like I had painted everything.

We spent a few days relaxing, talking and recharging with appreciation of the place. Dad and I had time to talk and paint, it took me back to my childhood when we used to paint together and go walking in the Yorkshire Dales. We both had happy memories; Byron Bay was our new happy place in Australia.

22/10/2004

We thought back over everything that had happened, but now from a slightly different perspective. Reluctantly we packed the car and I drove back to Brisbane.

In the afternoon, we had a meeting with the Consulate General and her team; Megan met us at the Foreign Office building. From the 26th floor, the views were amazing. Megan handled the introductions; we had the opportunity to talk about Caroline's Rainbow Foundation and all the work we were doing. I felt privileged they made the time for us; we offered our thanks for all their support. Dad gave them a framed painting and I promised to keep in touch.

We had time for an early evening painting session and set up our easels.

The light was perfect, it was a positive day.

23/10/2004

Dad's final day in Australia, I was sad they were leaving. We had a couple of hours painting together.

Over lunch we talked about the emotional roller-coaster we had all been on. No one expected it but we had dealt with everything as best we could.

At the airport, said I love you, and watched them until they were out of sight.

In the evening I felt like a disappointment. So much I hadn't said, so much more I could have done. It was strange to feel this way, but my brain had created a route that said each time I leave someone it might be for the last time. I felt pressure being the only one left; I could see how devastated Mum and Dad were living every day without Caroline.

Back at the hostel and I got chatting with Vicky, everyone else had crashed out. We talked and talked. I must have needed to offload, bless her for listening. We chatted on the balcony until the sun started to rise.

Over the following week, I wasn't feeling great, it felt like the biggest comedown in the world. My emotions, anxiety and stress had been so high, so much happening on all fronts, I felt hyper on every level. I had been in demand during the trial, not in a good way but people looked after me. I had also been through intense family time. Now, I had to take charge again but and I felt alone with absolutely nothing.

26/10/2004

Bad night's sleep. I felt like the world was a blur around me. Not had many replies from the barrage of emails I had sent out for the Foundation, I know people are busy.

I thought back to the *Celestine Prophecy* that I had read a while ago; I had enjoyed it but wasn't taking note. I needed to centre myself and find my rhythm again with the world. I couldn't process everything that had happened, or I had suppressed everything so much it was now trying to burst out of me, I couldn't control it.

Edwina was arriving today from the UK; we had been friends since childhood and swam together at our local swimming club. I pulled myself together and went to meet her at the train station. I introduced her to Hills and the rest of the crew, spent the afternoon chatting.

27/10/2004

I was meeting Megan for coffee later, had a little painting for her as a thank you, past a florist on the way and picked up some beautiful flowers. It was lovely to talk about all the positives and potential we had for the future, there was so much we could do.

In the evening, everyone was going out, Edwina and Kev seemed to be getting on well and they went out for a few drinks. Hills and I chilled on the rooftop terrace and battled on the chess board.

We spent the next few days in Brisbane, I was happy to be leaving. It was not one of my favourite cities. A plan had come together; Rainbow Beach next stop, we got on the bus and arrived late.

30/10/2004

I woke early and went straight down the beach; it really was a rainbow beach. The sand created a rainbow with all the different colours of the grains, once again mother nature had done the impossible. I felt free again looking out to sea.

After Rainbow Beach we travelled further up the coast, felt like I was back on my travels again. Edwina and Hills with me, I could go off painting and they were happy to hang out together. We stopped at Hervey Bay then Airlie Beach.

2/11/2004

Up with the birds, it was a glorious day. I spent the morning finishing a couple of paintings; a lady got chatting, interested in buying. Tomorrow it would be finished.

I got a call from Bundaberg, Previte was going to put an appeal in about the case. It was expected but it hit me like a ton of bricks. I was unstable. Here we go again, it sent me into a bit of a spiral.

Later got another call, it was Nat; I hadn't heard from him in ages, we used to work together at The Grange Hotel in York. Said he was in Airlie Beach, was he kidding! Fifteen minutes later we were sat having a beer. Just ridiculous how these things happen. The evening got a bit messy and took some unexpected turns, no need to go into detail. Nat, Hills and I know what happened.

3/11/2004

Super excited, we were going sailing on the Whitsundays; this was a dream and I knew it was on Caroline's list. The three of us walked down to see the boat. Seven of us in total, plus two crew, it was going to be amazing.

We sailed out, it felt wonderful, I could hear music playing in the wind and sails.

First stop, a spot of snorkelling. Edwina and I were straight in, it was just like back at swimming club, but with amazing fish everywhere and beautiful corals.

I got stung by a blue bottle jellyfish, had to pick the tentacles off my hand, poured vinegar on. It felt just like pins and needles, no problem.

Next stop Whitsunday Island and Whitehaven Beach, we had a couple of hours hanging out on the pure white sands which stretched for seven kilometres. It felt like we were looking out over heaven, no other way to describe it. I remembered back to Caroline coming out to see me in the Alps, we talked about this place. It was even more incredible than we imagined, I was heartbroken she never got to be here. The water babies swimming and snorkelling together in paradise.

The boat anchored for the night, the crew cooked up dinner and we had a few beers, got the giggles about how we were in absolute paradise, it was just amazing. Both Edwina and Hills knew Caroline well, I was able to talk freely, she would have absolutely loved this.

The boat gently rocked us to sleep.

4/11/2004

Awake early, sun beaming through the skylight. Strong coffee and fresh fruit for breakfast, the flavours were amazing. Back on to the island and had a further explore, we took the path to the lookout. The views were just unreal, my jaw was on the floor as we stood and marvelled at what Mother Nature had created. The sheer diversity of things to behold, changing blues, turquoises and greens of the ocean. The rich dark greens of the shrubs and trees, pure white sands contrasting it all. Everything looked luminous as the sun beamed in the cloudless sky.

We sailed round to another cove and there was the chance to dive. There were three of us, Inga, Cas and me; we suited up and we were in, descended to around fifteen metres and took a leisurely circuit around a large coral bed. So many fish, angels, parrots, coral fish, and a couple of small sea slugs which I had never seen before. Incredible!

The boat sailed to Blue Pearl Bay and anchored for the night. We were in again for some snorkelling; I loved seeing all the fish, beautiful corals — stunning colours.

Hills and I went for a walk around the bay, picked a spot. Neither of us said a word, just the occasional sigh.

Back on the boat for dinner, the sun was setting, and the water was dead calm. After dinner Inga and I laid back and looked at the stars, chatting away; we both saw a couple of shooting stars, it was beautifully relaxing.

5/11/2004

Already our final day, none of us wanted to go back to the mainland. After breakfast we sailed to the Langford Reef and island, we suited up. Cas had been bitten and was itching, so stayed on the beach. Inga and I buddied up and took a swim around the corals, just mind-blowing. We took a long walk across the sandflat to the island; we both laid out on the sand, our bodies absorbing the sunshine.

After lunch the wind was picking up and we set sail back to the mainland. We all had a wonderful few days, none of us could have asked for more.

As Airlie Beach came into view, we saw the devastation man had created along the coastline, concrete structures and buildings all along the beachfront. They weren't ugly buildings, they were just buildings. We had not seen anything other than the natural world for a few days' corners and straight lines, all looked very strange.

Back on dry land, people everywhere, noise and traffic. We ducked and dived keeping out the way heading back to our hostel.

Caught up with the rest of our sailing crew in the evening, we were all still feeling in shock to be back on the mainland. A magical, few days, we all agreed.

The following morning, we said goodbye, or maybe just see you later. We had shared some perfect moments, it had been incredible. The three of us boarded the bus, a long journey ahead of us. It was late evening when we arrived in Mission Beach. Dunk Island was just off from the beach, we spent a few days exploring.

I got a text from Sally saying she was going to be in Cape Tribulation, and it would be great to catch up if we were about.

Deep inside I still wasn't feeling well, I could feel my inner self struggling. Doing these amazing things and visiting amazing places masked the sadness I felt. I was seeing the world for Caroline, but deep down it was partly an excuse not to deal with my own bereavement.

8/11/2004

Awake with an air of excitement, I was going to be jumping out of a plane today. Edwina and Hills were going to Dunk Island again. Down on the beach I had a chill and met up with instructor Rob. I would be jumping with another English guy called Dave. Both of us looked terrified but excited.

The pilot pulled back on the stick and we climb into the sky, Dave and I had nervous smiles. At 12,000 feet the door opened and Dave along with his instructor disappeared. It was very real now, my heart was pounding. 14,000 feet and the door opened, we shuffled to the edge. Three, two, one and we were plummeting back to earth. I couldn't take a breath for the first few seconds. Once I had air back in my lungs I was in ecstasy, 1 minute of freefall, 200 kilometres per hour falling straight towards our planet, just amazing. The shoot opened and we did a few power turns, then relax and enjoyed the view, just wonderful; I could see the island and all the way along the East Coast.

As soon as we touched down, I wanted to go again.

Caught up with Edwina and Hills, chatting away, what did you do today? 'I jumped out of a plane two miles off the ground, how about you?'

After a couple more days and painting in Mission Beach we made it to Cairns. Back on the emails to see what was happening with Caroline's Rainbow Foundation.

I had spoken with Megan and been able to extend my visa. I was flying back to Sydney soon, we were filming for *The Time of Your Life* DVD. There were a few days to visit Cape Tribulation before I had to leave. Hiring a car, we made the long drive up to the Cape.

11/11/2004

A lovely drive, we were definitely entering a rainforest, I had never seen anything like it. Checking into PK's youth hostel and had a walk around the complex. Sally was sat by the pool. Dude! Amazing to see her.

She showed us down to the beach, following a pathway through the tropical trees and undergrowth, along a boardwalk and out onto white sands. Beautiful blue water and tropical palms. The perfect spot to paint.

It was lovely to catching up, we had done completely different routes up the East Coast. Lots of stories to tell.

12/11/2004

Just like old times, we started the day with a coffee and a smoke. The four of us spent the morning sunning ourselves on the beach. After lunch we jumped in the car and headed up to the tree walks. What a place, the rainforest was totally mind-blowing. We walked up the boardwalk and stairs to the top of the canopy. A gently swaying sea of green surrounded us extending all the way to the ocean. We could hear bird calls in every direction. The thought of the millions of different creatures below our feet left us speechless.

It was close to dusk, dinner was waiting and we were ready for it. Great times. Sally and I had the same sense of humour, bit twisted. Edwina and Hills were getting on really well. We all walked down to the beach, lit by the moon we could hear the trees rustling and water gently lapping on the white sand beach.

The next few days we hung out in the rainforest, up for the sunrise and spending time in nature. All too soon I had to say goodbye, I was meeting the film crew. On the sixteenth, I drove back to Cairns and boarded a flight to Sydney. I was excited to see how the film was progressing, I had been keeping up to speed over email.

The crew had filmed the two scenarios and it had gone well. Prevention is better than cure. We had an opportunity to speak to people before they went travelling, empowering them with the knowledge they needed to recognise and avoid potentially dangerous situations.

My piece would come at the end of the film and I had a few bits to say about what happened to Caroline and the story of Caroline's Rainbow Foundation. With the cameras set up in the Botanical Gardens, it took a few takes to get it right, the crew and director were very patient with me.

The Time of Your Life was to be introduced by Blair McDonough, who played Stuart Parker in *Neighbours*. The scenarios covered, having your drinks spiked in a bar and getting mugged for your wallet and belongings in unfamiliar streets. The idea was that students could watch the scenarios, pause and discuss in groups with their teachers. I watched a rough cut and discussed what would be included in the teaching pack that would accompany the DVD.

20/11/2004

Sally was back in Sydney and it was her last day in Australia. It was too easy for us to fall back into the same routine. Coffee, smoke and a laugh in the morning, life in the Blue Room. Last visit to Bondi, she was emotional. Back in the city and we had a walk around the Botanical Gardens and look at the Sydney Opera House.

Final chill in the Blue Room watching the world of Kings Cross go by. Claire arrived and laughed at the two of us at the window; taxi arrived and they were on their way to the airport, next stop UK.

21/11/2004

Out painting again, had one to finish. The Sydney skyline was very familiar now.

Called home and had a chat with Mum and Dad, it was good to catch up. Mum filled me in, the film crew had made it back to the UK and they were starting editing. I was excited to see the results.

Back in the Blue Room I was chatting with Beth and Ian, a lovely couple. I was thinking about sponsorship and seeing if I could stay for a few years; not sure what I would do, cooking was the obvious choice, but I didn't really want to go back into the kitchens. Now it's fine but old chefs look knackered. It's a hard profession.

I booked my bed at The Globe for the next month, there was no point leaving Sydney now. I found myself some work in the kitchens for a nice guy, he was running a small restaurant, there were a few days a week up until Christmas.

25/11/2004

Another day in the Botanical Gardens painting, my head was whirling. I was reading about past lives and different beliefs, Hindus believed that your soul goes through a series of different lives one after the other called samsara, in each life there would be lessons to learn. Your next life would depend on the last, karma. I believed in karma, what you give out you get back.

I do believe that the human soul carries on after death. Was Caroline's death linked to one of her past lives? Had she learnt her lessons for this life in only 19 years?

26/11/2004

Glorious blue skies, I chatted to Claudia over breakfast; she was from Germany and had been travelling a while.

Headed to Bondi Beach, it was just like old times, got my paints out and started a small landscape of the rocks and beach.

Getting quite good at this view. It made sense to me, I felt at peace. I wanted to look, capture the view and atmosphere so completely I would never forget it. My feet in the sand and standing behind my easel, I felt I could soak up more of the place.

Went for lunch and bumped into Keith, Crissy and Conor, they had been surfing.

27/11/2004

Over a year now since I arrived in Australia and it had been quite a ride. This year had some incredible ups and downs but meeting new people and travelling around I have certainly changed and grown as a person. I hope I've also become a little wiser.

A group of us headed to Shark Island, I had not been before; on a speed boat and shot past the Sydney Opera House, it was worth it just for that. The island was only small, but views were incredible. Great city skyline.

Emma and I set the pace for the way back, it was a long walk. We stopped at Harry's for a chicken and cheese to keep us going.

Daz had given me a book called *The Devils Chaplin* by Richard Dawkins, I was interested and had not come across the author before. We got into a discussion, talking of God, war, 9/11 and other horrific events that have been fuelled by belief and religion. Ancient religious texts and their messages have been interpreted or misinterpreted by people to justify their own agenda. Nothing can really be proven or disproven now; I thought it more a moral and philosophical message. Miracles were another discussion, surely this is purely down to perception. If you don't understand how it works, then it could be perceived as a miracle. I see miracles every day in most of what nature has created, especially after the Whitsundays and diving on the reef. Interesting chat about time, how crystals are formed, their structure and the power they hold. It took me back to the Crystal Caves in Byron.

It was the end of November and people were starting to think about Christmas. I was working in the kitchens all next week.

2/12/2004

Beginning of December and no snow for the second year running. All the people I was with last Christmas had left the country, their travelling adventures over and they were back in reality. It wasn't quite time for me. There was a new group of people in the hostel, a completely different vibe but still the same essence.

I had a couple of pictures that I thought were good and went to get a few prints done, I thought I could sell them for a cheaper price. I mounted them and was really pleased.

Chatting with Claudia and we grabbed dinner and hung out, lovely conversations about everything and anything.

Edwina and Hills arrived at The Globe. When in Australia, Sydney was the only place for me to celebrate Christmas and New Year.

13/12/2004

Walked into the Blue Room for my morning coffee and Hills was sat at the window watching the world go by. Later on, Edwina joined, we caught up with each other's adventures. They had been working their way down the coast after Cape Tribulation and were also now officially a couple. Great news, I secretly thought something might happen. I had missed them.

Evening in the Blue Room, Rich and I had a mammoth game of chess. Hills was going to play the winner; epic battles were in full swing.

The hostel was buzzing with people, everyone getting excited and settling in for Christmas. We all soon became great friends. I was working in the kitchens and enjoying it. Painting and hanging out with everyone when I could.

21/12/2004

Day off today, it had been busy. Definitely a beach day, I hadn't been for a while. It was busy, set up my easel, the usual view and got cracking. The girls were about, we all caught up in the afternoon. There was no rush back, the sun wasn't setting until about eight p.m.

I remembered back to Paul and I taking our walks along the beach this time last year. Missed our chats.

It was late by the time we got back, I was left with time to unwind, then Lorcan walked through the door, I hadn't seen him for a while, I always enjoyed our chats. He had the same inquisitive mind and we could lose ourselves on various topics for hours.

22/12/2004

Down to the Blue Room for breakfast. Lorcan was enjoying his first morning coffee looking out over Kings Cross. Over the road at the Kings Motel, a forensic police van pulled up, five uniformed men got out. They disappeared upstairs, two of them carrying a stretcher. We carried on drinking our coffee. Shortly after, the five men reappeared carrying a heavy stretcher, loaded it into the van and pulled away. Just another day in the crazy world of Kings Cross.

I was working, finished on time and headed back through the Botanical Gardens. The evening air was refreshing, I am so lucky to still be in Sydney. Everyone was hanging out. Chess battles happening, the girls were all having a laugh it was such a great atmosphere. Back at work tomorrow.

24/12/2004

Christmas Eve and Edwina's birthday, I was getting a painting framed of her and Hills I had done on Dunk Island. It seemed to be their favourite place.

I went shopping for Christmas dinner, not the same this year as Matty wasn't here. I took charge of the kitchen, there was about fifty of us to feed. Went to the market, some great produce, sun-kissed made all the difference. John had his car and came to pick us up, loaded the boot with bags and bags of food.

Edwina was out with her friends for a few drinks, we went to join them, the atmosphere was electric around the city. Everyone was so excited about Christmas.

25/12/2004

Not a lot of sleep, it was around eight a.m. and I was in the kitchen with plenty to do. Around an hour later I got a load of enthusiastic helpers. It was great fun pulling everything together, we sat down to eat at one p.m. Christmas lunch with all the trimmings.

A mass outing to Coogee Beach, I hadn't been many times, but liked the vibe. The afternoon we all spent laughing and joking on the beach. Another crazy Christmas in shorts, t-shirt and thongs.

Back at the hostel and everyone tucked into the leftovers.

26/12/2004

Boxing Day and I was back at work, it was pretty busy.

Thailand had a natural disaster. Earthquake and tidal wave, it was unbelievable! A big tsunami had hit the coast. 1500 dead.

The atmosphere was sombre, it hit the backpackers' community hard. We were all in shock, many of us knew people who had recently left to spend Christmas in Thailand. Everyone was sending emails and trying to get in touch to make sure friends were OK. I met three people who were travelling together, great company and such a good laugh; they left last week, my heart sank. I didn't have any contact details, no way of knowing where they were or if they were OK.

People didn't know what to do with themselves. It was at the back of everyone's mind. Most people when visiting Australia would visit Thailand, either on the way out or the way back home. Any of us could have been there.

31/12/2004 — New Year's Eve

If it was going to be anything like last year, I knew I wouldn't be back in bed for a while. We went for an afternoon skate, would be our last of this year. We met up with a few people from the hostel in the park and played frisbee for a while.

A group of us headed down to the harbour bridge and met up with everyone. The sun was just going down over Sydney and the night's celebrations were about to begin. The atmosphere was amazing.

The kid's fireworks started at nine p.m., the show was incredible. Completely different to last year, I had a few moments to think about the crew I was with back then, great people and amazing times.

It was time for the main event, our group was filled with love and happiness, a New Year's Eve that would never be forgotten. The show was incredible!

4:30 a.m. it was still dark, we all met up on Bondi Beach. It wasn't long before the sky became lighter and the colours started to change. It was still a little cold but as soon as the sun appeared, we all warmed up and started New Year's Day with a smile.

I took a walk and sent out thoughts for Caroline, I missed her terribly. Mum, Dad and Grandma. I love them all.

1/1/2005 — New Year's Day

Breakfast, it was a beautiful morning and the first day of 2005. This was going to be a good year, I had no underlying sense of dread for a pending trial. There was no rush to leave the beach, getting back to the hostel was going to be a mission. The place was still packed.

Finally made it back to Kings Cross, I had to crash out for a couple of hours. People were very subdued, we played chess and sat around chatting. Nothing much happening. I got in touch with home, wished everyone a Happy New Year!

2/1/2005

Thinking back over the last year, I felt I had come alive, my emotions had gone to more extremes than ever before, my spirituality and sensitivity had grown. I understood more about people and who they were. I knew I needed time alone, painting and on the beach. It was my meditation. Although, I still no idea of my purpose in life. Caroline's Rainbow Foundation was one of our missions, helping people stay safe when travelling.

Met up with Edwina and Hills, we headed down to the Opera House and met up with some of Edwina's friends from home. They were out on holiday. It was great to chat about life back in the UK. It brought back the fact that I would be going home this year. In some ways I miss life in the UK, other ways I felt I could build a life in Australia.

I had a love for Sydney, it was my base in Australia and felt like home. I spent the next couple of weeks painting watercolours, I just wanted to be in the sunshine and focusing on my art. There were a couple of days kitchen work which I took but cooking wasn't where my heart was any more.

15/1/2005

Lots of our people had left, another group were starting to arrive in the hostel. It had a different feel. I was getting itchy feet and wanted to move.

I popped into the shop, picked up a bottle of water. Bumped into Gem and her sister Jo, along with another couple. I hadn't really spoken to them before but seen them around the hostel. They hadn't been in Sydney long, I walked down with them passed Woolloomooloo and into the Botanical Gardens, it was my favoured route. They went off shopping, I set up to paint for the afternoon.

Just packing up and I saw Gem on her way back, the others had gone for drinks. We sat on a bench and chatted for a while, watched the colours change in the sky and the sun set behind the city skyline. The gardens were home to around 20,000 grey-headed flying foxes; as the sun set each evening there was a mass exodus as they left their trees to feed, it was an amazing sight. Gem loved animals and I mean really loved animals!

Walking back along the harbour of Woolloomooloo, we spotted a pigeon in the water, it was struggling apparently, they can't swim. I went out on a rock to try to grab it but couldn't reach. Gem just jumped in, no regard for her own safety! She gave it so much love and attention, nursing it back to life. All life is incredibly important.

I lay in bed and thought it had been a good day. My intuition was trying to tell me something, I didn't know what, but something had changed.

16/1/2005

A group of us decided to make the walk from Bondi Beach around the coastline to Coogee, it was a lovely day but a little windy. There were not many on the beach and we started the walk.

Mum and David called, filling me in with all the things the Foundation was doing. Grandma was not well and had gone back into hospital, her mind couldn't cope with what had happened to Caroline. I felt devastated, what was I doing here? I should be at home with my family, they needed me.

18/1/2005

Got another call from Mum. I knew it wasn't good news. Grandma had fallen and broken her femur. It wasn't good, she was in the operating room as we spoke. As we talked, I felt my body becoming heavy, the weight of Mum's worries now sitting on my shoulders.

19/1/2005

I needed some time to myself and went for a walk towards the city, I sat in the café where Matty and I had sat all those months ago when I first arrived in Australia. It brought back all those memories spanning the last fourteen months.

Grandma was OK, out of surgery but she was weak. All I could do was pray for her.

20/1/2005

There were a few people about, it was Keith's last day. A group of us decided to go to the beach for a final blast. He had been travelling for nearly two years and didn't know how he was going to deal with life back in the UK. I think it's a common worry for returning backpackers.

I booked flights to New Zealand. My visa was running out in a few weeks. Flying on the February 14th. Time for a couple of adventures first.

21/1/2005

I went down to hire a car; the idea was a little road trip to the Blue Mountains. It wasn't too expensive when we split the cost. Gem, Jo and Si all jumped in and I drove us out of Sydney. Arriving in Katoomba, a small town, driving down to Echo Point we had the most amazing view of the Three Sisters; we all savoured the moment, it was lovely to be out of the city.

Edwina and Hills had been in the Blue Mountains for a couple of days, we caught up with them for a couple of drinks. We walked down to the falls, lit up by huge floodlights, it was an amazing sight.

22/1/2005

We decided to do the 'Grand Canyon' walk for the day. The guide booklet said good walking shoes, but I thought flip flops were better, I had worn little else for over a year. Turned out to be the right choice.

The views were incredible. We passed a natural waterfall and took the opportunity for a quick shower; it really was like being lost in paradise.

There were a few clouds and spots of rain coming in, it was still really warm. We walked on and up to the top of the ridge. The view was breathtaking, it was about forty feet down to the forest floor.

23/1/2005

Woke to the rain pouring down and headed to the Jenolan Caves; incredible, thousands of years to create intricate underground labyrinths. We did the diamond tours, thousands of crystals glistening off the water with well-placed dramatic lighting. The water pools were eerie, the water was so still it was hard to tell where the rock formations finished, and the water began.

Back to Sydney in the evening and caught up with everyone in The Globe. It had been a good couple of days.

24/1/2005

Up this morning, woken by the noise of Kings Cross. Skateboarding with Hills today, great to have some boys' time.

We walked back through the Botanical Gardens, stopping to watch the bats flying out for their evening feeding session. It would be our last day chilling together for a while. I had decided to head north for a couple of weeks with Gem and Jo.

My mind was on Grandma; Mum called, she had pulled through and was doing OK. Her body was healing. I felt for Mum and sent her my love and healing thoughts.

Caught up with Rich, Lorcan, Daz and the boys in the Blue Room, played some chess and had a few drinks.

25/1/2005

Rain pouring down this morning, felt the right time to leave. The night bus, backpacks on. I was looking forward to another adventure up the East Coast.

26/1/2005

After a forty-minute stop in Ballina I knew we were close; the bus wound its way past Lennox Head along the ocean road. Finally, off the bus, fresh air. As we walked down to the campsite my mind wandered back to my previous visits, magical times with Matty and Kyra, such good memories. Dad and I had some perfect moments. Caroline of course, I felt so lucky to be back.

Camping this visit, two minutes from the beach. I could hear the sea. We walked down to feel the sand between our toes. I did a painting of the lighthouse, it was a familiar scene,

We took an evening stroll, it was lovely, the lighthouse lit by moonlight. So many stars, it's easy to forget with all the light pollution of the city. It was just magical.

After a couple of days on the beach, and painting the now very familiar lighthouse, couple of the residents came to chat who remembered me painting last year. It was good to catch up, they commented on how my art had improved.

28/1/2005

We booked on Jim's Tour. He was exactly what you would expect, relaxed hippy dude, believed in peace and love. Uniting the human race. Easy to think it's possible when you're here.

After shopping in Lismore, we got back on the bus to Nimbin, Jim told us a few stories explaining how Nimbin came to be. I had read the guidebooks, but it was great to hear it from a local. Originally it was an escape for people who had been serving in Vietnam and needed some space, free-thinking people who enjoyed smoking weed. One story goes that the police arrested two people out of 600 and locked them up in the police station. The following day, 598 marched down to the police station, joints in hand and demanded their release. The police had no choice, Nimbin is still a free-thinking place today. No crime, no violence, just a place where like-minded people can hang out with no trouble.

Our next stop was Mirror Falls, it was beautiful. Our final stop was shopping before arriving back in Byron. It was a great tour, we thanked Jim and headed to the beach to watch the sunset.

Another week in Byron Bay, I was out painting most of each day. Lovely way of life. Stood painting for hours each day gave me a lot of time to think, what do I actually believe? What is our origin? Where are we from? How did we come to be here? Travelling gave me plenty of time to read and talk to people. I was given a couple of books, all had been through the hands of many travellers, passed down with a knowing smile and a comment, 'this book will change your life'. Some I read, others I just passed on.

I was interested in consciousness and how our minds evolved. I started to think about our mind, our feelings and emotions. We all have a knowing, it's more than confidence, some things I just knew to be truth, somethings I knew were going to happen. What I couldn't explain was how or why. Where was this information coming from?

I had time, back in the real world I was time poor. One of the beautiful things about travel is that you have plenty of time to fill as you see fit. Your time is your responsibility.

There were conversations where the hairs on the back of my neck would stand on end and I would have a realisation of something more. Something suddenly clicked and made sense on a different level.

I took long walks along the beautiful beaches, enjoying time to think, contemplate and consider what I actually thought. My opinions formed by taking little bits from different ideas, beliefs and religions, not one seemed to explain everything. It was like looking at a beautiful work of art, it could be boxed into any '-ism', realism, cubism, impressionism etc... on closer inspection it was far more, elements of every '-ism' could be found in every masterpiece.

Science or religion alone couldn't answer all questions for me. Both are extremely powerful, but I needed a blend of each to help me understand. According to science, a bumblebee can't fly yet it can; according to a certain religion the Earth is only 5000 years old, but it isn't.

I asked myself about morality, what is my moral code? how can people do what they do? How can Ian Previte live with himself after what he did?

We have laws to govern society, but it's the choice of the individual if they want to live in it. Ultimately, all you have to do is live with yourself. If I can live with myself then it doesn't matter whether people agree with what I have or have not done.

Henry Ford said, 'Quality means doing it right when no one is looking.' The point for me is that I am always watching myself, I do justify things that I know are wrong or unacceptable. Where then does destiny play a part? Does everything happen for a reason? One idea that came up time and again, everything happens for a reason and couldn't happen any other way, it all happens with a greater purpose. Our energy is interwoven in the rich tapestry of life on our planet, we all have a role to play and make up a part of the whole.

4/2/2005

My last full day in Byron, spent the morning painting, finishing one of the lighthouse. Got chatting to a guy from Sydney, he was here on holiday and bought the picture as a memory.

5/2/2005

Early start and still stars in the sky, we took a walk down to the beach to watch the sunrise; the silhouette of the lighthouse looked fantastic as the sky behind turned from deep blue, greens, oranges and yellows before the sun finally shone its warming light. It was the perfect end to our time in Byron.

On the bus, not too long before I was in Brisbane again. Memories of times I had spent here with Hills and Edwina. I checked into the same hostel as we had stayed before, I flopped into a soft bed.

7/2/2005

I had a meeting this afternoon, it wasn't often these days that I wasn't in flip-flops or skate shoes. It was nice to put trousers and a shirt on again. I walked over to the British Consulate, 26th Floor, and waited to see Megan. It was lovely to see her again and we caught up.

I had a meeting with Phil and Neil, wonderful people and willing to support us in any way they could. We discussed what could be done, stickers, flyers and safety advice for people visiting the city. I was excited.

I took an evening stroll; the mood was very different in Brisbane. Every place has its own unique vibration.

10/2/2005

Back in the air, 32,000 feet flying above a cotton wool ocean heading back down to Sydney.

Back to The Globe, familiar faces Amy and Nina were still hanging out. Rich was up for a game of chess as usual; it was like I had come home.

Called the kitchen at The Grange Hotel and had a chat with the boys. It was good to touch base, put a smile on my face.

11/2/2005

Meeting today following on from Brisbane, loads of energy and excitement. We discussed the DVD and everything we could do to raise awareness for backpackers and tourists visiting the country.

I walked back around Circular Quay and through the Botanical Gardens. I preferred the energy here. Somehow it suited me better.

12/2/2005

Wendy, one of our close family friends, was on her travels. I was the same age as her son and daughter, we used to hang out and play together as kids. She is an inspiration, retired from work and decided to go out and see the world. She was on a world trip until May. I went to meet her for coffee and a chat in the Hyde Park café, we had a walk around the city. It was good to catch up and talk about the good old days when we used to play out in the streets and at each other's houses.

I wandered back stopping at St Mary's Church, it was beautiful, and I would often pop in for ten minutes, share a thought. Now was one of those times, Caroline was in my thoughts as we were all together back then.

Caught up with Rich in the hostel, we chatted and played chess. We came at life from completely different ends of the spectrum, I was all about feeling, knowing and the spiritual side of things, he was science and hard fact. It made for stimulating conversation. Ultimately, we would both arrive at the same conclusion. It was just a different way of working things out.

13/2/1005

Seven a.m. and the bedroom door burst open with a group of party goers just getting in, a consequence of hostel living! I was awake and it was better to get out of the way. Got up and went down for coffee. I popped out to pick up some food and saw Hills just coming out of the station. We caught up and had a chill. I was leaving for New Zealand tomorrow and he was heading back to the UK.

We went skateboarding in the afternoon, always a fun session when we were together. We reminisced about some of our most amazing experiences. It had been a wonderful adventure. It would be the last time we did everything on this trip, our last skate, our last walk through the Botanical Gardens, our last game of chess. It was a happy day, although another chapter was ending.

14/2/2005

Hills and I had our final morning coffee and chill, next time would be back in the UK. I would miss our skateboarding and good times.

Flying didn't bother me much any more. I used to get so nervous. Did I have everything? Were my bags going to make it? Was I going to get stopped or not be allowed into the country? It all seemed a lot easier now, I always wore a shirt and tried to look a bit smarter, clean, tidy and showered. I was still clearly a backpacker, but I looked respectable.

At the airport, they wouldn't let me fly as I didn't have a ticket booked to leave the country, I thought I could do it when I was there. It just hadn't clicked in my head, previous flights I always booked both ways. I had no choice but to book one there and then, cost me more money. Silly mistake!

Looking forward to seeing Dad and Janet, they were on holiday in New Plymouth. It would be great to catch up again. Arriving in Wellington I had toothache, not good. Hammered some painkillers and tried to get some sleep.

15/2/2005

Woke with pain in my face, toothache was getting worse. I found a dentist and luckily, they had an appointment free. Cost $100 to get sorted, numb face. Well worth the money.

I walked down the waterfront; a pathway led up from Oriental Bay called the Southern Walkway. I followed it to the top of Mount Victoria. I could see the whole city. It had its beauty but there were a lot of towers and concrete.

Popped into a bar for a drink and to write my diary. Got chatting as usual, played pool with a couple of guys. German guy, who was here studying psychology, the other had been working here for a few months now and enjoying the lifestyle. Later got chatting to another guy, he was American, left at fifteen to move to France, picked up the language and met a Kiwi girl, followed her back here and was now working as a DJ. I loved these brief encounters, learning about people's lives, truth is nearly always stranger than fiction.

16/2/2005

The bus was pretty empty, I had space to spread out. It was amazing to see Dad, I had missed him. It was good to relax, I had a room in the lodge where they were staying, 401, same room number I had in Wellington.

So much to catch up on. I felt comfortable. We went down to Waters Meet; Dad was on form. Sometimes it felt like I was seventeen again, living back at the house when I was innocent, and life was easy.

Called Mum. She was OK and David was well, still worried about Grandma, who was slowly getting better. There was nothing I could do to help, I had just had a reality check, felt bad about enjoying myself when people were going through trauma in the real world. I remembered a friend saying, 'Don't be so hard on yourself, you're your own biggest critic.' Read for a while before falling asleep. Toothache was back.

17/2/2005

Dad and I went painting and sketching for the day. The hours flew by, the weather was good with a Mount Taranaki backdrop.

In the evening, we caught up with Janet's family and all went around for a BBQ, the lifestyle here was perfect. Les said life was so much better, property was great, the weather was better, people were friendly. For him everything beat the UK hands down. I could see why! We chatted until late.

My tooth was annoying again, would need to find another dentist!

18/2/2005

Managed to get in at the dentist, nothing worse when you are travelling. She cleaned out the tooth and put another temporary filling in. I had another appointment next week, fix it properly for $600 or pull it out for $100, no choice really!

Painting Mount Taranaki for the rest of the day. In the evening, Dad and I had time to chat. I told him about the Whitsundays, Fraser Island and Broome, all the beautiful places I had visited. I felt such a strong connection with the natural world, it felt untouched and a little haven from the rest of the planet that had been overrun by humans.

Over the next week, we all spent plenty of time together. Lots of painting and talking about what should happen now. How we were going to continue without Caroline. We had tears of happiness and tears of utter despair; ultimately, I felt it was all healing.

28/2/2005

Last day of the month, Dad had gone for a walk around Waters Meet. I went to join him. It was easier now, this was just a holiday, no stress or pressure. We had coffee and said our goodbyes, they had a long flight ahead. I would see them in a few months.

I went for a walk around New Plymouth, it felt strange to be back by myself again. I was going to stay with Les and Louise for a couple of days before making my way back to Wellington and flight back to Australia.

4/3/2005

My last day in New Zealand, Wellington wasn't the most picturesque city. I took a walk down to the boat shed and did a bit of sketching.

Flight booked to Brisbane with a change in Sydney. I was reading, one passage resonated with me. 'Be like the fountain that overflows, not like the cistern that merely maintains'. We were circling over Sydney; I felt a warmth in my heart. I loved the city and felt a draw to stay. I picked up my bags, there was a free shuttle to the domestic terminal. Five minutes before the flight was due to depart, I was hailing a taxi, 'Darlinghurst Road please!' I wanted to be back at The Globe.

Caught up with Rich, Nina and Amy. Tim would be around after work. There were loads of new people in the hostel now, I didn't want to get to know them this time. I was happy just to catch up with people I knew.

It was a strange thing to not to get on the flight, I had never done that before. I thought about it later, I needed people I knew around me.

5/3/2005

It was Sydney's Mardi Gras. I didn't know, it was pure chance. Felt like I should have known this was happening, more research required. Another lesson for Caroline's Rainbow Foundation. We all got together and headed into the city; the streets were buzzing. The crowds were six deep; we squeezed and shuffled our way through. Gay Pride was great, we caught the dykes on bikes. They were followed by huge floats, music blasting, half-dressed people dancing and going crazy. It felt like the whole city was partying.

There was so much litter, beer bottles and cigarette butts on the streets. In a few hours, it would all be cleared up and another day would begin with only memories left from the night before.

7/3/2005

Up and refreshed, said my goodbyes and headed for the airport. The flight landed in Brisbane, got on a bus and finally arrived in Hervey Bay, it was familiar.

Met up with Gem, it had been a few weeks and we had a lot to catch up on. Back in nature felt good. As the sun set, we watched a frog-mouthed owl hunt and saw it swoop twice for its prey.

9/3/2005

We booked a bus to Agnes Waters. It felt strange knowing the bus would take us through Bundaberg. I felt a pull on my heart. The thoughts of

Caroline's travels struck me. She had got this far and no further. As we pulled out of Bundaberg I began to cry, she never left this place. I knew this, but sometimes experiencing it from a different perspective brought it all back in a completely new way. It felt like a new movie, the same plot only told by a different director.

10/3/2005

The morning shone and we took a walk down to the beach. It was the start of a beautiful day, there were a few scattered clouds in the deep blue sky. We passed a few early morning dog walkers.

Gem was completing her diving course; we were looking forward diving together. I found an old makeshift bridge, which I thought would make a lovely painting.

12/3/2005

I left the room early and walked to the phone box, thick cloud cover today. I just made it before the heavens opened. Spoke with Mum and David, they were well. Still lots going on a home. Grandma was better but looking her age now. Mum was still worried.

Gem's sister Jo arrived; she had been travelling with some other friends for a while. It was good to see her. I liked the fact they were both independent.

13/3/2005

We hired little mopeds to cruise around the backroads of Agnes Waters and 1770. I had forgotten how much fun they were; I have been riding motorbikes since I was sixteen years old. I loved the feeling and freedom. We stopped a few times to see kangaroos and wallabies. It was great fun.

15/3/2005

It was Jo's last day in Australia. I disappeared to do some painting for the day and let the girls spend some time together. Someone interested in buying, I said to give me a couple of hours to get it finished.

The three of us hung out in the evening, it was a good laugh. Gem wouldn't see her sister again until back in the UK in a few months' time.

16/3/2005

It was our final day in Agnes Waters, it had been a great week and some much-needed chillout time.

We got the first bus to Finger Board Road, it was pitch black as we waited for the second bus. We could see so many stars, so clear and could see the Milky Way. The second bus wound our way to Rockhampton.

Unloading and Gem's small bag she had put in the hold was missing, someone must have picked it up at one of the previous stops. She was absolutely gutted. It had all her personal bits, diary, camera rolls and CDs. I was angry, how could someone do this? Nothing in it of real value, it was more sentimental. Another big lesson learnt, keep your personal things and small bags with you at all times. Big rucksacks are different, it would be strange if someone walked off with two. But a rucksack and small bag is normal.

17/3/2005

Called at the police station first thing to report the bag stolen. There was not much they could do. I remembered the name Rockhampton Police Station, it was mentioned in Caroline's trial.

Rockhampton is the beef capital of Australia, amazing flavour and tender steaks, we of course had to order a big T-Bone. Early pick up tomorrow, we were heading to a farm stay.

18/3/2005

We were met by Olive and driven the hour and a half to Mylena Farm Stay. Gem was in her element. Both of us excited, we arrived and were greeted by the most beautiful, picturesque farm. Coffee brewing on the fire and we flamed bread to make toast for breakfast.

We were going out trekking on horses later, I was scared. They had never been my thing, Caroline was better. We rode for a couple of hours, it was a good job Barnaby knew where he was going, I just hung on! It was great fun, but I did prefer an engine.

The afternoon was more my thing, we jumped on motorbikes and headed out. We rode as the sun was setting, it was amazing. Back at the farm, I could smell beef cooking on the BBQ, what a lifestyle! The perfect end to a great day.

19/3/2005

I had an hour painting before breakfast. We saddled up for a morning ride. It was fresh and I was a little more confident on Barnaby today.

Our next job was to brand the steers, ninety of them had arrived last night. They needed branding, horns cut and tagging. It wasn't a nice job, but this was part of a working farm.

We had some chill out time in the afternoon, which was great, had a swim, feet up and pretended I was Clint Eastwood. I could see Gem was in her element, her love for animals was unconditional.

20/3/2005

It was our final day on the farm stay, the sun lit up the fields and tame kangaroos wandered over for a stroke. We milked the cows, fresh milk was amazing.

Gem went horse riding, I decided to finish my painting of the farm. I was going to give it to Lynn and the team as a gift. They insisted on giving us a discount in return. Signed and mounted, it was a lovely memory of our time here.

We were sad to leave. Dropped back in Rockhampton, it felt as busy as Sydney, even though it was a sleepy town in comparison. The next day we got the bus to Airlie Beach, I felt a completely different person now. From there another long bus journey to Townsville. We had the opportunity to dive the SS Yongala wreck, the passenger ship sank off Cape Bowling Green on 23 March 1911.

24/3/2005

Up at five a.m. there was a group of us doing the dive, we sailed out to the wreck. I got chatting to a guy called Jack; turns out his Dad studied at the Royal College of Art at the same time as Dad and they knew each other. What are the chances? How did we end up on this boat, about to do this dive today?

Arriving at the dive site. It was the deepest dive I had done at twenty-seven metres. As we descended the line the water got darker, looking around I could see nothing but open water fading into black, the occasional shimmer of light cut through from the surface. Suddenly the bow of the ship came out of nowhere, my breathing quickened, it took a few moments to calm myself. We swam the length of the wreck, the sea life was amazing, it was teeming with fish. We had forty minutes to look around the old ship. I was amazed by the life we saw bass, gropers, sea snakes and a turtle. It was an absolute privilege to be able to see something so special, the wreck was hidden from most, only open to those who sailed past.

All too soon we had to head back to the surface with a couple of decompression stops along the way. Going from learning to dive in murky pools in the UK to this was amazing.

25/3/2005

Ferry over to Magnetic Island which was a little paradise. I looked back over to the spot I had painted the island from. Later I put myself in the picture looking back at myself painting the picture. Bit of a head trip. I liked putting cheeky little things in my art.

Got chatting to a few other artists who lived on the island, it was a beautiful lifestyle in a beautiful environment.

We spent a few memorable days on Magnetic Island, it was a beautiful escape. Australia prioritised the natural world and had a respect we sadly didn't in the UK. We walked around the island and chatted about the meaning of life, what was important and how we should live.

Ian Douglas Previte had appealed the verdict and his appeal was to be held on the 31/3/2005. I had spoken with police and there was no point me attending, they didn't think he stood much chance of getting the verdict overturned.

30/3/2005

I got a call from a reporter I knew at the News Mail, he was doing a story that was going out tomorrow. I did an interview over the phone, we were concerned but had full confidence in the police and justice system. I would never get over what he has done.

Just the thought of him getting released drove me insane. I know there was only a slim chance, but still a chance was more than I could bear.

31/3/2005

The day of the appeal, I hadn't slept. In the morning, my phone didn't stop ringing. I grabbed a coffee and a copy of the paper to read the article. I was distracted and inadvertently stepped on a syringe lying on the ground. Ohh shit! It had pierced the skin, could be in trouble here. What the hell, what a day and it wasn't even lunch time.

I prayed to a higher power, had to pull myself together. I started to walk to the hospital to get checked out, had a blood test, they would get in touch with the results. Received a call from Dave Batt, the appeal had happened, and a verdict would be given in a couple of weeks. He tried to reassure me that Previte stood little or no chance. It was all over for Caroline in a split second, standing on a syringe could have dramatically changed everything for me. A split second of carelessness or one bad decision and you could pay with your life.

1/4/2005

Dad's birthday. I thought it was not a good time with the appeal yesterday. He must be going through it. It was still the middle of the night in the UK.

I was still not in a good place; it seemed a tough day or two. I needed some painting therapy and knew it was the only way I could switch off. I could see my sadness in the work.

Called Dad, told him about what I had been up to, mainly the good bits. Tried to keep the mood positive. Chatted about painting and selling my work, he said he was proud. My card had arrived, he was pleased. We touched on the bad stuff, not much to say. Tried to not think about it all too much, Previte wouldn't get out of prison.

2/4/2005

Got a call from Rich, he had not heard from his travelling mate Daz for over two months, his family hadn't heard from him in over a week. I controlled myself, didn't want to spring into panic mode, although thinking the worst was my usual reaction until my rational mind jumped in. I told him all would be OK, had he tried everything to get in touch, call, message, email. I am sure Daz will be fine. Inside I was a little worried.

Settled in for the afternoon painting, a guy came over and got chatting; he said, "I've seen you painting over in Townsville." It was nice to be recognised for something positive.

Back in Townsville, Gem and I met a lovely couple called Tony and Debs, they needed some work clearing their garden. They were looking for a couple of backpackers to come and help.

6/4/2005

Another day and we finished filling the skip in Tony's garden, it was looking loads better. I wasn't on top form; suddenly my phone rang. Matty! Just what I needed. He was back working, still paying off his travelling debt. He filled me in with all the gossip. We chatted about our times in Byron, it seemed only weeks ago.

8/4/2005

I got a call from ABC News asking for a quote in regard to the news that a decision had been made regarding Previte's appeal. It had been declined. I had to act like I already knew. 'We felt like it was the right decision, but nothing would ever bring Caroline back.'

Minutes later Terry Baldin called telling me the decision was unanimous. There would be no chance of parole. Fifteen years minimum sentence. I breathed a sigh of relief.

The rest of the day my phone never stopped, interview after interview, I was happy to talk, far more positive than I'd ever been before.

In the evening, it started again with the BBC and the UK papers as they were just waking up to the news, I did live interviews for the radio. It was good to be able to mention Caroline's Rainbow Foundation.

Called Mum, great news about the appeal, but Gran had been taken into hospital, it would be her 94th birthday tomorrow. It was Caroline's anniversary on the 10th. Caught up with the news, the Pope John Paul II had died. He had been Pope since I was a baby. I am not that religious, but it felt like it meant something.

9/4/2005

Grandma's birthday, ninety-four years old. Things she had seen in her lifetime. Absolutely amazing. I was sorry I was not there with her. A part of me was afraid I wouldn't see her again, sent her some happy thoughts.

I had some small pictures ready and went over to Magnetic Island and the gallery there. Sasha loved them and put them in the window, she was sure they would sell.

10/4/2005

Three years to the day since Caroline died. My thoughts were immediately with her. What we had all been through over the last three years was horrific but also incredible. I felt more peace this year; we had justice as much as we could, and Caroline's Rainbow Foundation was building.

It was raining in the afternoon. I decided to go for a walk, all I could think was 'Some people walk in the rain, others just get wet.' It was all about outlook; many people can have the same experience but it's their mindset that decides whether it's positive or negative.

I thought of home today, family, friends and even York itself. It was not often I felt like this, I had been away for a long time and was missing my roots.

I had a message from the hospital, my blood test was clear. It was a huge relief. Over the next couple of weeks, we worked for Tony and Debs; they had an outside porch and BBQ area with a big white wall, they wanted a mural painting. I was happy to take on the project, I had never done anything this size before. We took a week or so to put in a landscape with ruins, using sand mixed in the paint for the textured ruins. Gem was happy painting animals, birds, snakes, butterflies and rabbits. I also put in Pompeii, a smoking volcano, Darth Vader and Luke Skywalker at Tony's request. Soon enough the job was done, and it was time to move on further up the coast.

23/4/2005

Our final day in Townsville, we went to see Tony and Debs to say our goodbyes, they had been great to us and their house was looking great. I caught up with some emails, got one from Rich, he had finally heard from Daz, thankfully he was OK. We got the on the bus, destination Cairns.

24/4/2005

We were excited about diving and looked at what was on offer before booking a couple of trips. It was going to be amazing, one of the highlights. We were in the didgeridoo shop, I was getting better and could do the circular breathing. I heard someone shout 'Rico', I turned, it was Morgan, amazing to see him again, hadn't seen him since Sydney. He had travelled up the coast to Rainbow Beach with Nina and Amy in their van then made their way to Cairns. Great to catch up.

25/4/2005

Good breakfast and we were ready for the dive. We walked down to the marina and past the lagoon, it started raining. Didn't matter too much but made us a little uneasy. There was a dozen of us heading out, Captain Mark and his crew Pauly and Brandon set sail.

We looked back towards Cairns and saw the biggest rainbow, which was in the sky for around 10 minutes.

It put a smile on both our faces, we knew it was going to be a great dive and everything would be OK. Checking the log Pauly recognised my name and we had a quick chat about Caroline and the Foundation's work. He said he would look after us. We reached the dive site, which was a nice, sheltered part of the reef. I dived with Gem and Brendan, great dive, beautiful corals, we saw large wrasse, loads of rainbow fish, parrot fish and snapper. I loved the feeling of being underwater, such great freedom.

Lunch and headed to the second dive site, Michaelmas Cay, only four of us this time. Suited up and we were in, more of a play dive, we got to have fun. We saw turtles, pipe fish, sea cucumbers and giant trevally. The trevally were super-fast, it was obvious we were in their domain.

The ride back wasn't fun, three metre swells; I saw my lunch again. When we got back Pauly gave us our money back, offered his condolences and said it was the least he could do. I said I would put the money in as a donation and thanked him for his support. People could be so kind.

27/4/2005

Bus journey then ferry up the Daintree River, we saw a couple of crocodiles. Another bus before arriving in Cape Tribulation. We checked in and the heavens opened, it was an intense tropical storm. Wonderfully dramatic, saw another rainbow.

28/4/2005

Up early and out for the day, it was good to be walking around the rainforest, it was refreshing; we couldn't be any more immersed in nature if we tried. We walked from Myall beach around to Cape Tribulation beach. Was this place real? Even though I had been before I still was rubbing my eyes, utter paradise. We went snorkelling and playing around in the water. Sunbathing, relaxing and checking out all the animals hiding around the place, it was just perfect.

29/4/2005

We were sad to be moving on, got the bus to Port Douglas. Walking down around the town, everything was pristine, and it looked like it was straight out of a story book. So expensive but well worth it. We sat and watched the sunset by the harbour. Reminded me of the South of France.

30/4/2005

Up early, after breakfast we headed into town and the Habitat Rainforest Sanctuary to check out all the animals. They had three sections: wetlands, grasslands and rainforest.

In the afternoon I grabbed my paints, Port Douglas was so picturesque, I could spend a lifetime painting here, I'm sure many artists did. Found a lovely church and picked my spot. Painting away, it looked like they were setting up for a wedding; a few of the guests came over, their friends were getting married later today and they would like to buy the painting. No problem, it would be finished tomorrow, I would even put them in as they walked out of the church. It would be a unique work.

1/5/2005

Can't believe it's May; in just over a month, I will be back in the UK. It seemed like the time has flown. Final day in Port Douglas, it was a shame as I liked the place and thought I could make a living as an artist here.

Beautiful day, down to the church to finish the picture, there was a market on. It wasn't long before I spotted the people I was talking to yesterday, they asked about the painting, a couple of hours and it will be finished. They said they had had a wonderful day and the couple are very happy, the painting would make a lovely gift. They were really happy, I signed it, on the back I wrote 'Congratulations, Marty & Jenny, married on the 30/4/2005.'

We stayed in Cairns for a week, I was out painting and managed to sell a couple more. We went white-water rafting which was great fun.

My money had finally run out and even with the pictures selling it was not enough, I was into my credit cards. Not long of the adventure left and it would be silly not to make the most of it for the rest of the trip. I knew when I got back, I could earn good money in the kitchens and it was summer in the UK, there would be as many hours as I wanted.

6/5/2005

On our way to the airport early, we were soon up to cruising altitude. It was nearly a three-hour flight to the middle of the country, it's easy to forget the scale of Australia. As we descended, we got an amazing view of Uluru, I had never realised how strange and out of place the rock looked, it was like something out of this world had landed in the bush. Incredible. After a short pitstop we were back on the plane to Alice Springs.

7/5/2005

Had a walk to find out more; there was a lot of aboriginal art, it seemed more authentic, not commercialised like in the big tourist cities. I was interested to learn more about the history and culture. We visited the Telegraph Station and learnt about where it all began one hundred years ago.

It hadn't rained here since June last year, nearly twelve months. It was the middle of winter and we were still in shorts and t-shirts.

8/5/2005

Up at 4:30 a.m. and we were on the road, destination the rock. A few hours into the drive and the bus started to drift across the middle lane, there was a campervan coming the other way. People started shouting and the bus jerked back across to the right side of the road. The bloody driver had fallen asleep. When we got to the next stop, we questioned him. He said it was a wind pocket but none of us believed him; as a group we demanded another driver. How fragile life can be, so many times each day our lives are out of our control. We are all in God's hands, some of us are just luckier than others.

The bus arrived at Kings Canyon, walking up a large step way the views were incredible. It was amazing, the canyon carried on behind us, red dust in front of us as far as the eye could see. We both felt like we wanted to jump and fly into the canyon, maybe one day but not today. The flies were intense, we had to wear flynets. Our t-shirts were covered.

Our guide talked about the history and beliefs of the indigenous people. I learnt more about the country's history than I had in the whole of my time in Australia.

We had four hours left to travel stopping at Erldunda, which was the closest we could get to the centre of Australia. Pressing on to the campsite we enjoyed dinner and slept in swags. So many stars, it was pitch black, just the light from the fire. We could hear howling dingos in the distance as we fell asleep.

9/5/2005

Five a.m. start, strange dreams, must have been listening to the stories yesterday. Breakfast and we were on the bus again, it was still dark. It was only a five-minute drive, we picked a great spot.

All we could see was the silhouette of the rock, the sun's glow started to come from behind us; first the clouds were changing, fire red, pinks and oranges. The rock then started to glow, I watched in amazement. I had never seen anything like it. The colours went through the full ochre spectrum, reds, oranges, yellows even some purples. Just incredible.

The size of the rock was so impressive, the bus dropped us close and we could walk over and touch it, it was very powerful. I understood what people were talking about. We didn't climb as it was forbidden in Aboriginal culture.

Our next stop was Kata Tijuta, where we had the chance to see the massive rocks. We followed the Valley of the Winds walk. There was just no sense as to why these rocks had appeared on this landscape, there was nothing else like it for miles in every direction. The next viewing platform was Karinglana, views were amazing. The scale of everything made us feel like ants scurrying around the world.

As we drove back towards Alice Springs there were a few spots of rain on the bus, we were all amazed. Our final stop was Mount Conner and the Salt Lakes. The vastness of the Salt Lake, it was perfectly flat.

We shared a couple more days exploring Alice Springs, checking out the wildlife and bird sanctuaries.

My credit card was taking a beating. I sorted out plans for the next few weeks and tried to budget. I had to get back to Sydney where I would be flying back to the UK. Only one more experience to book before leaving Alice Springs.

12/5/2005

Four a.m. and we were excited, we were driven out south of Alice Springs, it was cold. An orange glow was just breaking the horizon as we could see the hot air balloon was almost full and ready to go. In the basket, a burst of flames and we rose effortlessly into the air, the world was starting to light up as the sun was coming over the horizon. We floated up to around 1000 feet, the silence was golden. The sun rose higher, colours in the sky changed and we could see Uluru, the Macdonnell Ranges and miles of bush in every direction. It was incredible.

Descending and the ground was going underneath us a lot quicker than before as the wind was blowing. We braced ourselves for landing and came back down to Earth with a bump, what a wonderful experience. Breakfast and a glass of champagne. It was the most amazing end to our time in the red centre of Australia.

We hired a car and drove around to visit Ormiston Gorge, the Ochre Pits, Ellery Creek and Serpentine Gorge. They were amazing to see, completely blew us away how nature can do so much with only a little water and minerals from the rock.

15/5/2004

Our time was up, Gem and I said our sad goodbyes and I was on the bus to the airport, soon after 35,000 feet in the air heading for Brisbane.

Caught up with a load of emails, there had been a lot happening. I wrote a couple of pieces for a travel blog, they came together well, I was inspired. Called to see if Megan was about; her and Colin were on holiday, she had a week's leave.

Sorted through my paintings, I had a few days in Brisbane and wanted to use the time. If I could sell the rest of my work, that would be amazing. Finished, polished and mounted.

Felt like I had caught up with the world again. My last couple of weeks in Australia, I was compelled to go back to Byron. I just wanted to finish with happy memories and relaxing painting. Byron was my escape; my connection to Caroline. Over my travels I had built on her experiences, added plenty of my own, done a full lap of the country, travelled up the east coast twice and visited the red centre. I wanted to appreciate everything we had seen and done.

21/5/2005

Paints out and set up on the beach looking at the lighthouse. I started another picture, I had my stall set out; luckily, I hadn't had to use my credit card again, I still had $50 left from the sales in Brisbane.

I remembered the photo of Caroline and Sarah surfing, they both looked so happy. Every time I had been here it had been perfect, I had shared many special moments. I am coming to the end of my travels now. I hope I have squeezed in enough, I hope I have been able to experience everything she didn't. I miss my little sister. I wish everything could have been different.

I walked on the beach under the stars, sat alone with the sand between my toes looking out to sea. I cried.

I spent a few days alone, aside from brief conversation to passers-by when I was painting. It felt like it was a time for soul-searching, a time to contemplate my travels. I was physically and mentally exhausted and quite enjoyed the overload; Australia had certainly given me so much more than I could have possibly dreamt.

24/5/2004

My final day in Byron Bay, who knows when I will be back again? No painting today. I walked all along the beach and up to the lighthouse, the sun was shining and a slight breeze, it was lovely.

In the afternoon I sat on the beach, looking at the colours and cloud formations. In the blue of the sky there was a giant rainbow, I don't know how this was possible, it wasn't even raining. I laughed and knew Caroline was here. It was a wonderful end to a wonderful time.

I collected my things and boarded the night bus. With a heavy heart I waved goodbye to Byron Bay.

Final time back in Sydney and booked myself a room at The Globe, it been a great place over the last eighteen months, a safe space that I knew would always welcome me. I was a very different man now to the pale-skinned, shorthaired naïve boy who first arrived. My deep tan, long blonde hair and probably a few more wrinkles told the story of the journey though Australia.

I spent my time visiting places and reliving happy memories, painting every day and selling my work, who would have thought it. I felt more confident and noticed the difference walking around the streets of Sydney. My emotions, my psyche and my sense of self had all taken a battering, but I had made it through every experience and felt stronger for it.

2/6/2005

It was my last full day in Sydney, I felt very nostalgic. I enjoyed the routine, morning coffee and chill looking out of the window over Kings Cross. Grabbing my paints and the few pictures and prints I had left, I headed down to the Botanical Gardens.

I was chatting with a few people and before I knew it, I only had a couple of paintings left. How strange, subconsciously I must have been telling people buy these now or never.

Went for food by the fountain and walked over to St. Mary's, lit my final candle for Caroline and our loved ones in the next world.

Sitting in the Botanical Gardens and watched the sun go down, deep breath, my final sunset in Australia looking over to the Sydney Opera House and Harbour Bridge. I took the route past the marina and Woolloomooloo, the big staircase and back to Darlinghurst Road. It was a wonderful day.

3/6/2005

What an adventure it has been. Early in the morning I walked down to the Botanical Gardens. I don't think I had realised how incredible this place was. I had a sudden renewed appreciation for everything around me. My senses seemed heightened, the smells, the sounds and views it was all amazing.

I didn't have long, there weren't many people about. I sat at the window in the Blue Room with a last coffee looking over Darlinghurst Road, I had seen a lot happen here over the last eighteen months. I said my goodbyes last night, it wasn't like before with the old crew. It felt like it had come to its natural end. Cassie who had been working at The Globe since I first arrived waved me off; she had been great to me, we would stay in contact. I jumped on the bus to the airport and finally felt ready to leave Australia.

Sat on the runway ready for take-off I was emotional, I was taking the return journey that Caroline never had. I don't think I will ever go through anything as intense in the rest of my life. When I first arrived one of the questions was, would I fall in love with Australia? The answer was undoubtedly, yes.

I arrived back home after visiting Thailand on the way but that's another story. It was wonderful to see everyone, especially my Grandma.

Chapter 14
A rainbow across the world

Shortly after I returned from travelling in 2005 the DVD, *The Time of Your Life,* was finished. We were really proud. Blair McDonough gave the opening introduction from Ramsey Street. The film then went into different scenarios, they were really hard-hitting and thought provoking. It finished with my piece we filmed in Sydney talking about the charity, Caroline and our story.

Blair and his team visited the UK for the launch. Caroline and I had grown up watching *Neighbours* after school every day, it was one of our favourite TV programmes. She would have loved to have met him. We arranged a press conference at a hotel in York, he was genuinely a lovely guy and connected with Caroline's story. Like many people I had spoken to in Australia, everyone seemed to take her death personally, as if things like this just didn't happen in their country. We got on well and connected over a couple of drinks.

The film was distributed free of charge to educational bodies around the UK. The feedback was fantastic. Teachers were watching it with their students and using the teaching pack. We were pleased, more importantly we knew it was really helping teenagers think more seriously about their safety before travelling.

Later that year, we were presented with an opportunity to have a rainbow mosaic laid in York city centre. I thought it was a lovely gesture, creative and also had great significance with our family's art connection and love of rainbows. Caroline would have definitely approved. Kedadavy Mosaics were commissioned to create the work. The mosaic was laid in the floor in the central area at the Coppergate Centre. We were honoured to be able to put her name to it. We also had a tree planted and engraved stone just around the corner on the riverbank; for me it symbolised the growth of the charity and also matched Caroline's memorial tree which was planted in the

Botanical Gardens in Bundaberg. I have visited the tree many times over the years. Since planting the tree it's been vandalised and destroyed on three different occasions. Who the hell would do something like this? It's a tree planted in memory of a local girl who was murdered in Australia. It made me angry and saddened to realise that some residents of my hometown could do this. Some people have absolutely no respect. Each time it happened, I was lifted by the generosity of people, local garden centres offered to replace the tree free of charge. A beautiful gesture of kindness and in memory of Caroline.

Social media was taking over the world, sites like Facebook were leading the way. Everyone had a website and working online was the future. We redesigned the charity logo and revamped the website. I liked this kind of work; it was creative and I was interested how we could reach more people. We focused our time on rebuilding the website, gathering travel stories and safety tips from experienced travellers. Our primary focus was making sure the information was accurate, we wanted contributions from people who had actually visited the places they were talking about.

This approach worked really well. A lot of travellers were excited to tell their travel stories and offer safety tips. I could feel their passion and excitement through the writing. Reading them certainly made me want to put on my backpack again. They say with travel, it doesn't matter how many places you tick off your list far more are always added. It also reaffirmed that travel was the smart choice, it could change your life, it connected like-minded people from all walks of life and helped people to view the world from a different perspective.

Although my backpacking days were over, I still had a hunger for travel. The romanticised idea of the Grand Tour was back in my mind, holidays and mini breaks in search of culture and higher wisdom.

We were in Rome, what a beautiful city. Around every corner was another beautiful street or picturesque square, wonderful sculptures and art by some of the art world's greatest. Amie and I had first met at The Grange Hotel, she was the General Manager and supported our charity every chance she got. One event I will always remember was a fashion show held at the hotel, it was an amazing success. She had thought of every last detail and even bought a pair of rainbow-coloured heels to finish her outfit.

We walked up to the colosseum arm in arm, imagining the place filled with people, all watching and cheering for the gladiators who were locked in battle. Wide eyed we wandered around the ruins in absolute amazement of what the Roman Empire had built.

We threw coins into the Trevi Fountain, ate some of the finest Italian food and enjoyed many glasses of local wine. Walking towards the Vatican we were watched over by Bernini's sculptures, the architecture was phenomenal. The line was moving slowly forward, we would soon be entering the Great Chapel and be looking up at Michelangelo's masterpiece, the ceiling of the Sistine chapel. Completely breath-taking, nothing I had seen or read about it could ever match the moment. I looked up and saw his inspired work in real life. The experience was all consuming.

Nothing compares to the completely immersive experience of real-life travel when it comes to seeing what some of the worlds true geniuses have created. It is the only way we can truly understanding the great wonders of our world.

Travel is for everyone and as the travel industry was evolving, it was easier than ever for people to visit places on their bucket list.

Each year as the winter drew closer, I was drawn back to the French Alps and Meribel. I found the mountains a perfect place to find space and work, I could hide in the vastness of the piste. It was possible to ride for the day with people, share laughs on the lifts but as soon as I strapped in, I was alone again. I worked for a wonderful family in a private chalet, which meant I had time to paint landscapes of the mountains. I did two exhibitions in Meribel which went really well. I was commissioned to paint the local professional snowboard team and my work was also on display in the lift stations around the resort. I had time to rebuild our charity website, it was extremely time-consuming and I was learning as I went but found the work rewarding. We added new thoughts and pages that we felt would be beneficial for travellers.

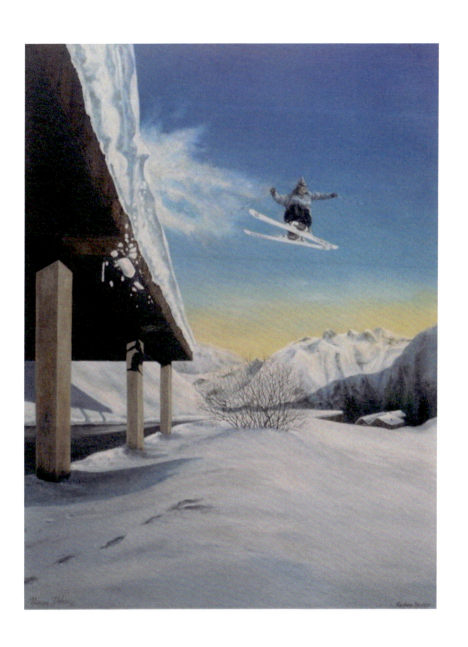

In 2007, Dave Batt who was such a wonderful support while I was in Australia came over to visit in the UK. Megan Hunt and her husband Colin were also visiting. We arranged a dinner at The Grange Hotel. Dave was nervous and spilt red wine on his suit right before dinner, he had nothing to change into. Colin came to the rescue offering an England rugby shirt that he had in his car. This must have pained Dave as it was the Rugby World Cup and Australia had just lost to England 10-12. We all made light of the situation, it broke the ice, and we all had a good laugh.

During dinner Dave stood up and gave a heartfelt speech referencing the shirt, obviously. He went into some detail about Caroline's case and the fact that all members of the Bundaberg Police Force had taken what happened so personally. The team all put in a great deal of personal time to help in any way they could. It had put a strain on many relationships but finding Caroline's killer was of the utmost importance. They all worked tirelessly. I could see his emotion and realised that Caroline's death had made a lasting mark on more lives than I could have imagined. The case had consumed their lives for two years. I will always remember his visit fondly, we had a few drinks strengthening our connections that will always remain.

Five years after the first mosaic was laid in the Coppergate Centre, we had the opportunity to commission an Australian artist to create a mosaic that could be laid in a central park area in the centre of Bundaberg. It was near a few youth hostels, many backpackers would relax around the park. It was the perfect place. For us, the mosaic symbolised a rainbow spanning from York to Bundaberg connecting the UK and Australia, I found it very moving to think that so many people had worked on the idea bringing it into reality. Ideas of sentiment now meant so much.

'September 1 2010 — The Press
Australian tribute to York backpacker Caroline Stuttle

A RAINBOW mosaic in memory of York backpacker Caroline Stuttle has been unveiled in the Australian town where she was killed.

The memorial in Bundaberg, Queensland, was the idea of retired police sergeant, David Batt — the Australian detective who led the investigation into the 19-year-old's murder in 2002.

The mosaic, which is similar to the one carved into the pavement at York's Coppergate Centre in 2005, was funded through donations by residents of Bundaberg.

It has been created by a local artist and lies at the entrance to one of the town's parks, close to three backpacker hostels.

Caroline's brother, Richard Stuttle, said: "It's so nice to have this lasting memorial to Caroline in Australia and it's fantastic that we now have that link between York and Bundaberg.

It also means such a lot to us that it was the people of Australia who did this for us.

Caroline's death really touched the people of Bundaberg because nothing like that had ever happened there. It was quite a sleepy, workers' town and it was a huge shock for them."

Richard, 33, said rainbows were a poignant symbol for his family because Sarah had told them she had seen one in Bundaberg soon after Caroline's death.

As a result, the travel safety charity set up in 2002 by Richard and his mother, Marjorie Marks, in Caroline's memory, was named Caroline's Rainbow Foundation.

Richard said: "There are some days that I really miss her. Birthdays and anniversaries are very difficult and the thought that I'm never going to do certain things, like go to her wedding. It's really hard to swallow."

As positive as the news stories were and how much we needed to promote what we were doing, they always added the heart-wrenching emotional side of things. Rightly so, it was important, but reading it I would always feel a twinge that would sometimes make me shudder. Over time I had gotten used to it and learnt to only focus on the positive.

Over the years we developed close bonds with our local universities and attended many gap year and travel events. They were an excellent opportunity to speak with students about their safety. It was also a great benefit for us to be able to understand what students are thinking about travel and opportunities they found of interest. There had been a significant increase in organisations offering volunteering experiences, students could travel to developing countries and help with building projects or teach

English in local schools. It was a great way for students to see the world without it costing a fortune. We made contact with a few selected companies and put together specific safety tips and advice for these kinds of travelling experiences.

Visiting the mosaic in York again, I noticed the area was busy with families on holiday, shopping and enjoying the city. This led to us think about the risks of travelling with a family. The charity started to look at different avenues of travel. I began to understand how people had to change their mindset when it came to travel and had completely different priorities when choosing destinations.

I was in my thirties and had always viewed travelling from the point of view of the person travelling. When I was younger, I didn't consider the people who were back at home worrying about me, what happened to Caroline obviously completely changed our family's perspective. I talked with Mum as both Caroline and I were off exploring the world at the first opportunity, she was of course now really overprotective. At the time both her and Dad were happy for us to go. Dad said it was a sign that they had done a good job as parents, we were both confident and had enough curiosity to find our own way in life.

We started to include information on the site for parents whose children were travelling. Mum would speak at events for parents discussing the emotional side of losing her daughter, also addressing worries parents could feel when their children went travelling. She said, 'As a parent, it is only natural to feel concerned at the thought of your children heading off into the sunset. The most important thing you can do is to be supportive and help them to figure it out. Talk about their trip, get excited with them and of course listen. Be encouraging, make sure that they are well-informed and understand the potential risks to their personal safety.'

Chapter 15
Life goes on

I felt like we had drawn a line under everything, and I could focus back on my own journey through life. I had a good deal of life experience, but felt I still had a long way to go through bereavement. I read how I was supposed to feel and compared it to what I was actually going through. Everyone is unique and circumstances are always different, but I feel it's important to explain how grief worked for me.

The death of someone you love is one of the greatest sorrows in life. In my mind, there is no greater loss than that of a son or daughter, no parent should ever have to outlive their own child. There are a lot of support groups and organisations set up to help. For a sibling it was different. In my research in the few years after Caroline's death I didn't find as much support available.

Personally, it felt like a part of me was missing, a child is half their mother and half their father. Siblings are parts of their parents but also a part of each other. The loss of Caroline is devastating, but her stolen future hit me harder than anything. My parents will never get to see Caroline get married and have children, if that would have been her wish. I thought further, we will never get to celebrate any future milestones. Significant birthdays, our children hanging out together and our friendship growing long into old age.

Everyone feels grief in their own way, I learnt there are certain stages to the process. I was living in London for the summer and decided to go and see a counsellor, it felt like the right time. A common theory is that there are five stages of grief and dealing with bereavement.

1. Disbelief, denial and feeling numb
In the first few hours and days nothing really made sense. I was in complete disbelief, we all were. I cried uncontrollably, not really comprehending what was happening to us. How could this kind of tragedy happen to our family?

I had of course read stories like this, but it was always at a distance, I never considered for one second that it could be so close. My mind played the different scenarios of what could have happened to Caroline, I was trying the piece together what happened. I felt numb but overloaded with emotion.

None of it really made sense or fitted logically, therefore I couldn't accept it in my mind, it couldn't possibly be true. I had been away for five months, I felt in a daze and didn't want to believe. There was conflict, I still felt hope that it was all some kind of mix up, although deep down in my heart I felt she had gone. It was difficult to come to terms with the fact that Caroline was no longer here. We weren't used to seeing each other every day. It was easy to think she was still travelling, a feeble attempt to trick the mind into thinking she would be back and could walk through the door at any moment. It made it incredibly difficult to comprehend, emotionally knowing the truth and then mentally trying to accept the reality of our situation.

Some days I would wake up completely numb, not really able to feel anything like I had before, even down to my body. It felt I was walking through a Dali painting; a surreal dream my heart knew I could never wake up from.

Looking back now the one thing that convinced me that she was gone was when I saw my Mum's face; I knew she would never get over it. When I saw Dad it was the same, he sobbed like I had never seen him before. Remembering my parents in those moments brought my head and heart together to understand and accept our new reality.

2. Anger, blame

Our situation was slightly different. I was definitely angry, the person who did this to my sister had to pay. For two years I didn't know where to focus that anger; I created a dark figure in my mind and this image was to blame.

I also blamed myself for not protecting Caroline. Why wasn't I there when she needed me? When she came to visit me in the Alps, we talked about meeting in Australia. The decision not to go plagued my mind; if I was there, I could have protected her. Was it my fault that she was gone? I knew it was completely irrational, it didn't matter, I felt like I was fighting an internal war.

During this period, I also felt a huge amount of guilt about the time I wasted, although in reality I had always worked hard and filled my time. It was more the fact Caroline wouldn't have another day in this world to enjoy anything. This contributed towards fuelling my anger. My anger for other aspects of life increased, especially for people's stupidity; I could feel something terrible building up inside me. I always thought when I blow and lose my temper, God help the person on the other end.

It took many years to deal with my anger fully. I was very short-tempered, I noticed that people sometimes danced around me on eggshells. Many not knowing what to say, some wouldn't mention Caroline at all. If anything happened to someone to do with death or murder that I could identify with I would comment. I felt I had the right. I could joke about death as I knew all about it! I could agree with vengeance as I understood it from many action movies. I felt an affinity with the hero whose family had been killed or taken away, I thought I knew what it was like to be able to actually justify killing someone. Although deep down I also knew these thoughts and feeling would never become reality. I wouldn't ever be able to go through with it, I had far too much respect for life.

Sometimes this attitude and behaviour was a mistake, it probably made people feel more uncomfortable. It probably widened the gap and made people feel like they couldn't say anything.

Publicly, however, with the charity I put on the act of a brave and confident person working to stop other families from having to go through a similar situation. Our work was important and that was the person I was most of the time. Other times, I hated the world and what had happened to us.

3. Bargaining

I used Caroline's death to bargain with myself, not initially in a positive way. My behaviour could be erratic. I would let myself off things that I knew were wrong, only hurting myself with the justification that it didn't matter, Caroline was dead. Smoking was the big one for me. Just one more joint or roll up! Caroline will look after me or it's fine after everything we have been through. I realised it was just an excuse, a weakness for things I didn't want to stop doing but knew I should. At times I wanted to bury my head in the sand, a part of me was on self-destruct. I didn't think I was worth it. It stemmed back to confidence, Caroline's death had knocked my confidence and I still feel the ripples today. I was afraid that anything I cared too much about would be taken away; if I didn't care about my life then it didn't matter if it was taken away. It was the same with my career, I didn't feel like I deserved to do well. Caroline was the smart and talented one. I would happily work and help others to reach their goals but when it came to myself, I would make excuses to avoid self-development.

It has taken many years to realise that I had created a loop justifying my behaviour using Caroline's death as my personal bargaining tool. It cascaded and became detrimental: looking back at certain situations, I would make subconscious choices to destroy personal and working relationships, I didn't feel I was worth it. Caroline should still be here, it's not fair, she had far more potential.

4. Depression, sadness and tears

I found a strange addiction to sadness, a sense of comfort in pain. I didn't wallow in it, but I liked to hold it close. My pain defined me. Caroline's death was something that I might never forgive myself for, even though I knew it wasn't my fault. Tears were immediate, I never knew when I could become overwhelmed with emotion. Caroline and I were close, and I still feel a part of her is with me. At times, I could feel her closer or further away and it caused my emotions to fluctuate.

I could also wear what happened to Caroline like a badge, not because I wanted sympathy but because I thought it made me a stronger person. Sadness and pain became as addictive as caffeine and nicotine. Maybe it's just my personality. There was a part of me that liked the darker side of pain, I found it comforting and felt it was mine.

I am not actually sure what depression is, I have been in very dark places but never thought of myself as suffering from depression. This might have been something else I was in denial about. I always thought people are in charge of their own feelings and emotions. Your reaction to situations defines you as an individual. In its simplest form it's personal responsibility. I never wanted help, it was up to me to help myself and only if I wanted to, it had always been my choice. For example, you can only stop smoking when you want to; it doesn't matter how many people tell you it's bad for you or how much support you have, it's down to you.

I learnt to look from different perspectives, it depends on how you view a situation as to how you feel about it. This is where I felt my nature as an optimist helped.

Life is not always sunshine and roses, to me it's like a black and white chequered floor, sometimes you step into the darkness and other times you step into the light. The rationale has always been the darker the bad times the happier the light times; I have always been a person of extremes, monotone represented no life at all.

Emotions are to be experienced, I always want to know everything, my inquisitive mind is built that way. Why would you not want to explore sadness and grief as well as happiness and fun, they are just emotions. Now I try not to look at things as good or bad, it's just experience, and life has always been about experiencing as much as possible.

5. Acceptance

There is a part of my mind that will always fight that Caroline has gone. Acceptance is multi-layered and one of my biggest hurdles in grief. Long term it's the fact that so much time passes we have gotten used to life without her here. Coming to terms she is dead is something completely different, how could I do that? It's not that the pain gets any less, it's just that life raises your threshold and you learn to live with it.

Caroline was a strong-minded young woman and completely unreasonable at times. After her death she was promoted and given angelic status in our minds. Angels we feel should be in heaven, its somehow easier to accept. But she was also a real person and had many different sides, she was loving, caring and a pleasure to be around but she could slam doors just as well as the rest of us. This is what made her human and to accept that this person was gone was hard.

I have spoken with Mum many times about the charity, it was only in one conversation that I realised the commitment we made for Caroline after her death. I hadn't viewed it in this way before but the charity although extremely worthwhile was a large responsibility we had to carry. On the positive side it gave purpose and meaning and we hoped it would go on and help countless people travel more safely. I gave my time willingly, but this also meant that my life was put on hold at times. I would always be

Caroline's brother but it also meant I would always be the brother of the backpacker thrown from the bridge in Australia. It would never change the work for the charity, but acknowledging it as a weight to carry helped greatly in my healing process.

It had now been 19 years since we lost Caroline. As more time passes it's easier to look back and see each milestone from a different perspective. I have spoken with people who have said that they remember Caroline talking to them as clear as if it were yesterday. For some reason, those memories have become cemented in their minds, I believe it's the same with feelings. I have worked through grief, dealing with some aspects more than others. I still have trigger points that can immediately transport me back to the very moment my telephone rang or the moment I saw Mum sobbing as I arrived home. I have coping mechanisms, but sometimes it still feels as if everything is only on pause and at any moment someone could knock the play button.

They say art can be great therapy, it played a large role in helping me to work through the process. We are an artistic family. Caroline was very creative. I still on occasion look through her GCSE artwork. I have always felt that art is a great way to make people look harder and think differently at what you want them to see. For a few years I was painting daily, trying to produce commercial work, but when I had the time, I would also paint for me. I often used very dark colours and some images were completely distorted; I am sure a therapist would have been able to pick apart what I was feeling and thinking. It was the process that I needed, throwing paint on a canvas, hours could go by and I had no sense of where I was or what I was doing. It was impossible to see the journey through the finished work as some paintings ended up almost completely black.

Optimism for me was also a key. I realised my outlook on life helped my grief and this tone was set many years before the loss of Caroline and starting our charity. I always liked to push boundaries and made decisions on instinct but hadn't realised then the consequences of my choices. I chose to take the opportunities in front of me only focusing on the best possible outcome. Training as a chef, working in France, travelling around Europe, changing career and going to Australia.

All these actions and experiences I thought helped build my philosophy on life. I always chose to see the glass half full. I had known other people who had died too soon, we had always poured a drink and toasted their lives. It had been our way of showing respect and reverence. We honoured them by trying to live our lives to the fullest.

I reached a point where I thought that exploring my own mind was the only thing that really mattered. I came to understand that the way I saw the world was already inside me, it was how I was built. I didn't develop my own philosophy I just realised the philosophy of the person I am. I had been chasing rainbows across the world looking for much that was already inside me.

Chapter 16
Art across the pond

I have been very lucky having the opportunity to see many different places and have wonderful experiences. People say, 'I wish I could do that', or 'I wish I could go there'. The truth is that they can if they want to. They just have to make the decision and work towards their goal. I believe one of the ways to find a happy life is finding places in the world you feel at home and most comfortable.

Besides the charity work, I also had to get on with my career; I didn't want to work in kitchens any more although it still paid the bills. Selling my artwork in France and Australia, I was inspired and focused on painting. After a few years painting every day and refining my skills, I was incredibly proud to gain representation by a gallery in New York. I was given the opportunity to exhibit in June of 2011, I was extremely excited and decided to go for it!

It took me around four months, sometimes working well into the night to finish the paintings. I shipped six large- scale oils over ready to exhibit. Using most of my savings I went all in and rented a room in an apartment with another artist in East Village. My plan was to spend two months painting around the city and try to make some contacts. I would sell work in the exhibition which would fund the rest of my stay and allow me the freedom to enjoy New York.

My introduction to the New York art scene said,

'In our annual United in Art Exhibition. Artist Richard Stuttle helped facilitate this adventure with his paintings of pristine slopes in the French Alps, where he spends winters painting and snowboarding, and gritty city streets where he follows skateboarders and parkour practitioners. Stuttle alternates between nearly photographic hyperrealism and a vividly lit and stylized aesthetic evocative of Expressionist woodblock prints…'

I arrived a week before the exhibition hoping to become familiar with my surroundings, meet the gallery team in person and touch up my artwork ready for the exhibition. My first time walking along 5th Avenue was incredible, everything was bigger, brighter and more intense. Caroline would have absolutely loved it; I imagined her raising a glass of wine and looking down from her apartment window over the bustling streets.

8/6/2011

Needed to get out painting, with a small canvas under my arm I walked to Madison Square Gardens. Saw a rainbow in the fountain and smiled. Picked my spot and settled in for the day. Drawing went well, I relaxed and felt back too normal.

Went for dinner with Kristof, who I had previously met at the Arthur Findlay College. A very intelligent, well-educated man, we had connected and were on the same wavelength. After dinner we walked along The High Line, the views across the city were amazing. Mental note; paint from here! We walked past the gallery. I could feel the excitement welling within me. Opening night for the exhibition tomorrow!

Opening night, this was going to be it! I remember getting ready, suited and booted. I was extremely nervous and wondered what the night had to offer.

The gallery had an extensive mailing list, I was told that most work sold would sell on the opening night. My apartment was on the cusp of East Village and Alphabet City. Suit on, I felt out of place for the first five blocks as I walked across town; reaching Fourth Avenue people were dressed more like I was, I stood up proud and tall with a skip in my step. In my head Alicia Keys' *Empire State of Mind* was playing, '…In New York, Concrete jungle where dreams are made of. There's nothin' you can't do. Now you're in New York. These streets will make you feel brand new. Big lights will inspire you. Let's hear it for New York, New York, New York…'

I was early, it was hot, and I sat on The High Line near the gallery. Sent a thought out to Caroline for help, please let everything go well. I hoped she was looking down on me with pride.

I arrived at the gallery; they were filming, I did a short piece to camera. My media experience stood me in good stead. I made nervous conversation with the other artists who were also exhibiting.

An hour or so before the doors opened, the heavens opened and a huge downpour set in for the rest of the night, it definitely stopped people coming out. There was still a reasonable turn out but nothing like there should have been. I made conversation and chatted to people who showed interest in my work, but as the evening went on my heart began to sink. I stayed until the very end; none of my work had a red dot, which meant sold. I was seriously disappointed. Four months' work getting the paintings ready, huge expense in shipping them across the pond and renting a room.

I left the gallery, rain still pouring down and walked back slowly across town. It was 11 p.m., I was drenched to the core. It was like something from the movies, huge buildings towered over me, water flowing down the pavement into the drains. Reflection of the great city lights. It was beautiful. I cried but couldn't tell the difference between tears and rain running down my face. Hours before I had been filled with the excitement, years of work on my art. This to me was the ultimate, I was exhibiting in New York! My heart was through the floor.

At the same time that my exhibition was on, there was a child artist who was also represented by the gallery. I found out her work had sold out, although I can't and don't blame this on my work not selling. Some six-year-old was the talk of the town. I went to see the work. From my experience and years of painting, my opinion at the time cannot be repeated. At this point, I saw the art world in a different light.

I pulled myself together, I had been through worse. I still had hope, my exhibition was on for two weeks. Positive, I went out painting on the streets and handing out flyers for the exhibition.

At the end of the exhibition none of my work had sold. It forced me to rethink how I could earn money to make it through the rest of the trip. I went from going from eating breakfast out and enjoying the city to eating two packets of thirty cent noodles each day.

After some research, I found out places, artists sold work on the streets at weekends. I grabbed a couple of blank canvases and a couple of works from the exhibition and went back to what I had spent my time doing around Australia and the South of France. Painting on location and hopefully selling work along the way.

A few days later and nothing had sold. I had a gold chain which was an eighteenth birthday present, I had no choice but to find a pawnbroker. Only eighty dollars. A few more days and I happily sold one of my paintings. People liked little cityscapes; I painted all day on the streets. I had never been in the position of having to paint for my dinner, I had to be out there to sell. There was no self-pity, no thinking I was hard done by, I asked Caroline for help again.

It took being down to my last few dollars for me to realise that I was the only one who could make it happen. Luck also played a part; I was in the right place at the right time to take advantage of it. It wasn't the sort of luck that catapults you into the spotlight thanks to an acclaimed art critic, but the sort of luck that enabled me to have a real meal, to be able to afford a coffee in New York and have the privilege of watching the world go by.

I became friendly with a guy on the floor below in my apartment block and would pop round for a chill and drink; it was great to have someone in the city that I could talk to about my day. Everyone has a story to tell if you were willing to listen and he was no exception. He had enjoyed an amazing life and I will always remember his generosity and kindness.

One night heading back after a long day painting, I was shattered. Carrying my paintings and all my gear across the city was a long walk. A guy started walking with me and chatting, up until this point I had only met good people and thought nothing different, many people saw my art, heard my English accent and wanted to chat.

We walked together in the direction of East Village. I dropped my bags and paintings, he said there was a party happening on a boat and I was welcome to join. I was tired and felt a bit uneasy but went along with it. He led me around the streets until they were no longer familiar, I had been in the city over a month and knew most areas a little. We ended up walking under a flyover and it felt wrong. A little voice in my head was saying, this is not right. I am sure what I knew about travel safety and our charity made me more aware.

Up ahead I could see silhouettes of a group of people stood around some parked cars, the little voice in my head shouted turn around. I suddenly stopped and turned around; the guy tried to convince me to carry on with him, beckoning me back saying, 'we're nearly there it's just around the corner'. I knew there was something wrong.

Walking quickly into a park, I saw a man with his dog, made my way over and started to make conversation, he must have thought I was crazy. I asked if I could walk with him for a while until I recognised the area. It was a long walk back.

Finally, at the apartment I felt safe again and had time to reflect on the situation, although nothing had actually happened, I knew it was a close call. Something could have easily gone horribly wrong. I was tired and not local, he could see that and must have singled me out as an easy target, but I listened to my intuition and had the conviction to stick with my decision.

As I now say when speaking to students about safer travel, always trust your instincts. If you find yourself in a situation that doesn't feel right, change it. It could seriously alter the outcome. My eyes were fully opened to the dangers of the big city.

Thinking back over the trip, I could have changed my flights and flown home earlier. I could have put the blame on something else, but I was in New York. I pushed myself out of my comfort zone, I was the only person who could do it and make the difference. It was my choice.

I love New York, met amazing people and had some wonderful experiences. I painted in Time Square, on The High Line and many views around Central Park.

One afternoon on The High Line I met a wonderful Argentinian lady called Veronica. We clicked immediately, chatting for hours completely on the same wavelength. Visiting the MET, we admired the art, all beautifully painted and brilliantly done. We went for drinks in a speakeasy, ate pancakes and drank endless coffee while watching the world go by. We both had totally different backgrounds but were able to connect on many different levels. She told me a quote that still resonates. 'Blessed are those who won't trade their dreams for their daily bread' by Facundo Cabral.

During my time in New York, I ate breakfast in the Waldorf Astoria and went to see *Phantom of the Opera* and *How to Succeed in Business without Really Trying* on Broadway. Watched Cirque Du Soleil, Kantara at the Rockefeller Center. Visited some of the city's most famous landmarks, painted nearly every day and chatted with some of the most interesting people. I celebrated my 34th birthday, painting in Central Park during the day and dinner at the Gotham restaurant, wonderful meal and stimulating company.

Even though I didn't have a sell-out exhibition, I didn't feel like I had failed. I sold enough paintings to have money to get me through until my flight home, although a couple of the larger works I had to leave with Kristof. I had highs and lows, but importantly had some incredible experiences. My ego wanted me to sell my work in the exhibition, but that wasn't the reality this time.

On my final few days in the city, I had not seen my roommate, our paths hadn't crossed much over the last month. I noticed the kitchen had not been used. I was out early, coming in late and painting in my room until the early hours, trying to get pictures finished. It was the last day and I needed to get showered and ready, I opened the bathroom door and found him slumped over the toilet. It didn't look like he was breathing, I panicked, what the hell was I going to do?

I rushed to see my friend downstairs and called an ambulance. They asked me whether I was willing to give mouth to mouth. I answered, "No." A few minutes later I heard sirens which were commonplace in the city, when the ambulance and police arrived outside the building it all got very real. Could this trip get any crazier? The paramedics entered and put him on a stretcher, he was still alive thank goodness. They took him to the hospital. My flight was leaving in a few hours and I had to get to the airport. All I could think was now I am going to miss my flight. The police took my statement and luckily said I could go; if they needed anything further, they would let me know.

Sat on the plane, I breathed a sigh of relief and had a chance to think about what had happened. I could have just walked out of the apartment, locked the door and never looked back. I like to think I did the right thing and might have even saved his life.

I arrived back home with dirty clothes, a few pictures and a good story to tell. An incredible two months and I realised that you can give it 100% and it still might not work out the way you think, but I will never think of the trip as not successful. Success, not just about how many paintings you sell it is also about having the confidence to push out of your comfort zone, handling problems as they occur and giving 100%, even its it not in the way you intended.

Chapter 17
A letter to a killer

Over the years I tried not to think of Ian Douglas Previte, he would have one day served his sentence and would be free. I wanted him to understand the world from our perspective and what he was responsible for. I decided to write a letter.

Dear Mr Previte

Do you understand what you have done? Even with your many years in prison and time to contemplate what happened. Do you remember the evening of the April 10th, 2002? I don't believe you fully understand the ramifications of what you have done. I am sure when you woke up on that beautiful morning in Bundaberg, you couldn't have dreamt how the day was going to unfold.

Well, I am sure that my sister, Caroline Ann Stuttle didn't either. Her experiences up until that day in Australia had been nothing but positive, nothing short of amazing. For that, we will always be thankful. I am sure that when she woke it was with a smile, filled with excitement for the places she was yet to see and experiences she was yet to have. Your outlook I believe to be very different.

Australia is one of the most beautiful countries in the world with a reputation of positivity, safety and magical experiences; you destroyed that not only for my sister, but also for everyone who knew her and the thousands of people who identified with her story. Your act of horrific selfishness has not only destroyed our family, but also put a black mark against your beautiful country and struck fear into the hearts of other backpackers.

I want you to understand that by taking Caroline's life, you have not only taken away her bright future, but also destroyed a part of each of us that knew and loved her dearly.

She was a bright, intelligent girl, who did not deserve to cross your path. You had no right to even speak to her, never mind try and take her belongings.

As the years have gone by, I thought more about your life, I am sure you were born like the rest of us with kindness and promise in your heart. I would not presume to know how hard your life has been or what you have had to overcome. That said, no matter what you have been through would it ever justify taking a life or taking anything that doesn't belong to you? You have made your decision. There is only you to blame for this whatever your circumstances. We always have free choice, as adults we all understand right from wrong. No one is perfect, but most of us strive to be the best we can be. Life is precious and the only thing that cannot be replaced. You have taken Caroline's from her without a second thought.

Caroline's death devastated our family and made us shadows of the people we were. Caroline was loved dearly, not only by us, but also by her friends. They send their thoughts to us, her birthday which should have been a happy time is now filled with sadness. We have suffered greatly, not just twice a year on her birthday and anniversary of her death, but every single day.

The lives of Caroline's many friends and their families have also been destroyed, you have made the world a far more unsettling and dangerous place for all of them.

Caroline was only nineteen years old when you took her life. Think of all the amazing experiences you have taken from her. Young adults should be stepping out into the world with confidence and excitement, but sadly for the people who knew Caroline, you have taken this away. You have managed in one thoughtless moment to turn these young people into scared and timid people who might never know the full beauty of what life had in store for them.

You not only took her life and future, but you took away all the times that we could have enjoyed; I will never know who my sister was going to become.

We didn't want other families to feel the same pain and loss. Caroline's light was so strong we set up a charity to try to prevent situations like this happening to others. We created a travel safety charity to warn people of the dangers when travelling, to be aware of people like you. We now help people to travel in a safer environment and be prepared.

So please know that Caroline's outlook and caring nature lives on in helping others. This is what we did with the cards we were dealt. We didn't choose to destroy the lives of others and take things from people that were not ours.

You may consider that your life is ruined spending time in prison, but please know that when you have finished your sentence our sentence will never be over, there is no release from the prison you defined for us and everyone who knew Caroline.

Regards
Richard Stuttle

This letter was never posted.

Death and heartache touch many families, many have gone through the same pain and grief losing loved ones before their time.

Now, when I see stories in the news or read about someone's life who has suffered great loss there is more of a sense of understanding. People find strength and become more resilient. They also gain a whole new perspective on what's important.

Many families have to deal with unfortunate and untimely deaths and deal with loss in their own way. There is no right or wrong, it's down to the individual or family to get through the best way they can.

They say the worst vice is advice but if I can say something to other people who have found themselves in situations where loved ones have departed too soon. There is no right and no wrong way to feel or behave. Do what is best for you and don't try to please others. They will understand. Don't take anything to heart; many people around you won't know how to act, some will offer sympathy or empathy others will avoid the subject all together. Your grief is yours alone and you have to work through it in your own time, no one can help you with that.

Over the years, my friends have become comfortable with me again and now don't mind if Caroline comes up in conversation. They will laugh and joke along with me. Caroline was a loving sister, daughter, granddaughter and a great friend.

It's true when people pass on to the next world they are elevated to angelic status in this world, but I don't feel in Caroline's case this is out of place. One needless act on the April 10th, 2002 and Caroline was robbed. She had her future stolen from her and she was stolen from all of ours.

We shared some of the best times. Many of these have been lost but some are ingrained in my mind and will never be forgotten. If we remember our loved ones a part of them will always be here, although in some ways life can seem a little less bright.

Chapter 18
10-year anniversary

The tenth anniversary of Caroline's death was coming up. We wanted to mark the occasion with something special. York Minster is an historic building and the west front symbolically holds the heart of York. We thought it would be lovely to be able to do something. After speaking with the Archbishop of York we arranged a service for the April 10th, 2012. It was a huge honour for us and we felt would be a fitting tribute to Caroline. We discussed and planned meticulously. There would be readings, hymns and live music.

'On April 10th, 2012 we remembered Caroline at York Minster.

Remembering Caroline (in the North Transept)

Readings by Richard Stuttle and Elly Fiorentini (BBC Radio York). Handel's Aria *Where'er you walk* sung by Julia Riley (mezzo-soprano). Prayers, led by the Dean of York, and an opportunity to light candles.

Ten years after Caroline's death, whilst backpacking in Australia, we are celebrating her life here at York Minster. This service is to remember Caroline. Caroline was a very special person and during her 19 years she lived an outstanding life, fulfilling many personal goals and dazzling all around her with her wonderful personal qualities.

Caroline was kind, confident and intuitive. She will always be remembered for her warmth, intelligence and compassion. Everyone who met Caroline loved her wonderful spirit. In particular, she had a bright, sweet nature and on occasion a daring sense of humour which revealed her independence and self-reliance.

Rainbow Poem
It seems so hard sometimes, to see the sunshine after rain,
To lose one your love, seems a never-ending pain,

You see no joy to life, you feel too low to care,

The weight of all your sorrows feels far too much to bear.

But listen when I tell you, though it is hard not to cry

The love it never leaves you, it never says goodbye.

For it only takes a moment, a simple pause for breath

And when the one you love is near you, never lost to death

For they are all around you in the sky so bright

Glimmering in raindrops, reflections in the light,

You see them in the puddles and even in the shower

And sometimes if you look really closely, they are even in a flower.

So, when you're feeling lonely and you feel all is gone

Take a walk on a rainy day, look closely for the sun,

For you will see a Rainbow, its colours shining bright

and know your love is near you, let your soul take flight.

Because death is not an ending, there is nothing left to fear,

so, keep living and remember your love is always near

For one day you'll be reunited, with no sorrow nor no pain

And you'll be Rainbows together, in sunshine and in rain.

Written by Gail Jones-Martin.

We congregated outside York Minster. It was one of the few times that Dad, Mum and I had been together since the funeral. I felt happy we were here to mark this anniversary. As a family we were nervous, but at the same time extremely proud of what we were about to do.

It was breath-taking to walk into the majestic building which offered grand views in every direction. The Dean of York lead the service saying a few words about Caroline. I sat with sweaty palms waiting for him to introduce me. I had spent weeks perfecting my speech and rehearsed it so many times I knew it word for word.

I had a flashback of Bundaberg speaking at Pastor Errol's service. I took a deep breath and walked to the lectern. I looked out to over 500 people sat in the most wonderful space. I smiled, took a deep breath and spoke. It flowed and I could feel Caroline was with me, she had her hand on my shoulder and helped me through every word.

Next was Elly. She was used to public speaking and did a lovely reading. One of our family friends, Julia, who Caroline and I had spent a lot of time with growing up, sang beautifully. We were finally all led in prayer. It was an amazing experience, everyone felt at peace. We lit candles in memory and the service came to an end.

We couldn't believe it had been ten years since Caroline had gone, time had passed so quickly. The full service was recorded and is available to watch on our charity website.

We walked around to the Minster gardens, the magnificent building which had stood for centuries added to our feeling of pride. Blue skies overhead. As I breathed in the fresh April air, I felt a sense of relief that everything had gone well and that my speech was done. When everyone had made their way into the gardens, we released 500 rainbow balloons.

It was an incredible moment, I felt a genuine release as the balloons floated into the sky, we watched them go and I said a prayer for Caroline. I believed her soul was eternal and she was watching us from another place. I felt like I was freeing a burden that I had carried for the past decade, part of it simply floated away.

The Press:

'The brother of murdered York teenager Caroline Stuttle has spoken in memory of his sister at a moving service to mark the tenth anniversary of her death.

Caroline, 19, died after she was robbed and pushed from a bridge in Bundaberg, Queensland, Australia, on April 10, 2002.

Yesterday, hundreds of people attended choral evensong at the Minster followed by a service to celebrate Caroline's life, after which the whole congregation lit candles in her memory.

Richard Stuttle, Caroline's brother, spoke poignantly of his sister as "a vibrant young girl full of potential and promise". He said: "It has been a very difficult time for us and is still hard to believe she is no longer with us.

"It must be every family's worst nightmare to lose someone who is part of you and who you have shared so much of your life with.

"As a family we miss her every day and it is heart-breaking to think: 'What would she be doing now?' I miss the things we will never get to do or share."

Mr Stuttle said he had travelled the world since his sister's death, visiting places he knew she had seen and others "she would have loved to have seen" and he felt that she had in some way shared in those moments.

He said that after Caroline's death, the family gained hope from Caroline's Rainbow Foundation, set up in her name as a safety guide for young travellers, and added that the way in which Caroline "gave without thought of herself and without thought of reward" should inspire others.

"Today I believe that is her wish for people to not only remember her but to show kindness and love for others," he said.

BBC Radio York presenter Elly Fiorentini also read a poem in Caroline's memory, and mezzo-soprano Julia Riley performed Handel's Aria *Where'er You Walk*.

After the service, rainbow-coloured balloons were released over Dean's Park.

Ahead of the service, David Batt, the Australian police officer who led the investigation which culminated in her killer, Ian Previte, being jailed for life, spoke about the investigation in an interview with the News Mail, in Bundaberg, Queensland.

Mr Batt praised the work of Caroline's mother Marjorie Marks and Caroline's Rainbow Foundation and spoke of how her death had so affected the local community in Bundaberg.'

Chapter 19
Safer Travel app

When we started Caroline's Rainbow Foundation, we never imagined reaching our ten-year milestone. We wanted to do something new, innovative and useful for travellers. As a Board of Directors, we asked the questions:

What are we going to do to mark this milestone?
How can we best help travellers today?

Technology was in the forefront and apps were becoming huge. Our website had pages and pages of safety information about different cities, many travel stories and useful safety tips. Social media platforms were now how people communicated, it made it easy to keep in touch.

I had done a lot of travelling and thought about what would have made my life easier, how could I save time? The concept of a 'Safer Travel' app began to form. Over the next couple of weeks, I jotted and scribbled, pulling together all the information that would have been useful when travelling. We refined ideas and worked together with an app agency to develop our concept. We wanted to see city-specific travel information that included:

Basic city details:
- Currency
- Population
- Map and location
- Dialling codes

Locations and contact details for:
- Embassy
- Tourist office
- Police station
- Hospital

- Airport

Information, website, maps for:

- City highlights
- Places to visit

Important information:

- Annual events
- Customs and traditions
- Local news reports
- Common crimes
- Areas to avoid
- Safety tips

We were excited and had a new a goal to work towards. I started to get prices, the App agency were fantastic and agreed to build the first version at an incredible charity discount. The other side of the project was the content, we needed lots of content! This was going to be an issue. I wanted the content to be provided by people who had actually been travelling and visited the places they were researching.

I contacted a variety of different companies who specialise in sourcing content; I realised that we were never going to be able to afford to buy the content. I was out of options and made the decision and stopped working; this project was too important for the charity. I focused my full attention on the Safer Travel App project. We secured an office space at York St John's University. Utilising their support and opting into various volunteer programs we put out calls to students and experienced travellers.

Looking at the popular travel destinations for backpackers and tourists we came up with a shortlist of countries and cities we wanted to cover. I also contacted people I had met on my travels to help, researching cities, verifying information and entering the information into our custom-built database.

We had a fantastic response and built a team who gave their time generously to help move the project forward. Everyone worked tirelessly and we created a hub in the university, researching, verifying and uploading data. I felt we had momentum. Our Safer Travel app was launched nearly eighteen months later with comprehensive travel and safety information for over 200 popular travel destinations. To everyone who supported the project during this period, I will always be truly grateful and offer my greatest thanks.

'5th September 2013

York Charity Launches Travel Safety App

Travelling attracts many of us for a multitude of reasons. We are attracted to the excitement associated with new experiences. The adventure, growth, culture, fulfilment, new cities, and of course new people. What better way to invest our time than by going on the adventure of a lifetime and embracing the world and all it has to offer? However, it is important to recognise that travelling is not always as safe as we hope. For instance, the streets and the underground subway routes of Tokyo appear perfectly OK until faced with navigating the strange and unknown city alone with only a map in an unfamiliar foreign language as a guide.

The world presents all kinds of beauty, but it also presents dangers that unfortunately we are not guaranteed protection from. Only through raised awareness can we make informed and safe decisions. Therefore, Richard Stuttle founded and directs the charity 'Caroline's Rainbow Foundation'. In addition to raising awareness of travel safety, Caroline's Rainbow Foundation, based at York St John University's Phoenix Centre has now launched a new first of its kind online travel safety app. The app provides global safety advice and city information and is aimed to support travellers whether they are on a gap year, travelling on business, or travelling on holiday.

Richard Stuttle, founder of the York-based charity is the brother of Caroline Stuttle, who tragically died during her gap year travels in 2002. The charity was set up in memory of Caroline and hopes to continue raising awareness of travel safety amongst young travellers and more experienced travellers alike. "The app combines the knowledge and experiences of students and travellers from all over the world, giving valuable first-hand information and insight from people who have visited or come from a destination. I'd like to thank everyone who has kindly donated this information, as it enables the app to provide genuine insights with a personal touch," he says.

An important feature of the new app allows travellers to update live information in order to alert other travellers to news, such as unforeseen hazards and political and social updates. Access to this level of up-to-date knowledge when travelling could be crucial, particularly concerning the safety of the individual. The heart of the charity, as Richard highlights, shall always prioritise the welfare of individuals. The app also acts as a useful tool for travellers to access information such as local news, traditions of the area, places of interest, emergency services, and locations of embassies, police stations, tourist offices, and other useful information points.

September marks a particularly meaningful time for Caroline's Rainbow Foundation as it would have been Caroline's 31st birthday. Undeniably, travelling can be a life- changing experience. Richard highlights that the charity does not aim to discourage people from travelling, but his ongoing work uses his sister's tragic experience in order to promote a positive message of travelling with safety and awareness. "My hope for all travellers is to have amazing experiences and follow their dreams. Our charity will always encourage people to travel as it is one of life's most enriching experiences.'"

The Safer Travel app has become an ongoing project, we are always looking for research and more information about world travel destinations. To date, we have collated comprehensive and accurate information for over 350 cities. It will continue to build until we have covered every traveller destination, even then we will continue checking and reverifying all the information.

The charity was evolving, it was built for travellers, by travellers. We wanted people to put their ideas forward on what sort of information we should start to provide.

With this mindset, two students came to the office with an idea of creating specific pages for hearing-impaired travellers. They wanted to look into the issues faced when travelling. I was immediately interested. They held an event to raise money for the project, we match-funded and supported them. They commissioned a sign language video highlighting the important specific safety information. They also researched hearing-impaired travelling experiences and companies that offered bespoke support. Also, advice for anyone communicating with hearing-impaired travellers they might meet.

All the students were fantastic, they had endless excitement about the possibilities of travel. Working with us helped to improve their knowledge of travel safety and potential risks. Together we were able to produce interesting and useful content covering many different travel experiences.

Chapter 20
Saving lives

When I left for Australia, I was away for nearly two years. It was an incredibly emotional journey. I certainly changed as a person and found out a lot about what I liked and didn't like, as well as understanding life as a backpacker.

It's not an easy decision to make leaving family and friends, but for me it was certainly one I am pleased I made. I would highly recommend it. They say you meet your friends for life at university, I believe the same is true for travelling. I met many like-minded people who shared a similar attitude towards life.

When we started the charity back in 2002, gap year experiences were not as easily accessible and were not considered such a benefit when building a CV. It was normal for students to go from school into further education and from college or university straight into a fulltime job. Today, there is far more merit in taking time out to travel.

Speaking to students and teachers, we discussed at length the positives of a travelling experience before looking for a job or moving on to university. I have known people who have gone travelling or for a winter season and found it completely changed their mind about what they wanted to do for a career. Some friends have carved amazing lives and businesses for themselves in some of the most beautiful environments on Earth, doing what they love every day.

We decided we needed to go one step further from our DVD and develop our education programme. Our idea was to follow up with personalised presentations from people who had completed a gap year or had extensive travelling experience.

I wanted to tell people's stories, highlighting the differences between the travel dream and the reality of donning a backpack and embarking on an adventure.

Making a decision to go travelling should not be taken lightly, it's a hard choice and travelling is not easy. It tests every aspect of self and certainly throws up many challenges. I felt it was important to reiterate what life was like being away from home for a significant period of time. The homesickness, fear of the unknown and constantly living just outside of your comfort zone. Living in youth hostels and shared dormitories definitely takes its toll. There were moments along the way when I just wanted to put my feet up surrounded by the comforts of home.

I was keen to talk about travel. I had completed many winter seasons, spent summers around Europe, travelled to Australia, New Zealand and Thailand, as well as many holidays along the way. After a lot of research and thinking about the simplest way to get the information across in a short space of time I created a basic presentation, including some photos from my travels and a basic outline of important things to consider relating to travel safety.

We contacted schools, colleges and universities, offering presentations on travel safety awareness. They were well-received and a great success; we soon built up a number of venues I would visit each year to talk to students. The feedback was great. The tutors thought the presentations included valuable information for their students. It was also an opportunity for the tutors to reminisce about their own travels before they embarked on their careers.

I did many successful presentations over the years, showing a glimpse of what's out there in the world and talking about the main risks when travelling. One presentation really took me by surprise and not in a good way.

I didn't feel the same energy when I got up on stage, I was speaking to a full assembly. I was more nervous than usual but shook it off, all of a sudden, my mind went completely blank. I had over one hundred students looking at me, I was representing our charity and for some reason I had nothing to say. Pushing through I made the best of it, but I was extremely disappointed. I apologised profusely to the tutors even though they thought the presentation was good, but I knew I hadn't done the best job. I only got one opportunity to speak to future travellers and I knew how important our information was. I was potentially providing information that might help save lives.

My confidence took a knock, sometimes things just don't go as planned. Like anything you do in life, you can never do enough research, preparation and practice. I took the opportunity to think again. On my travels, I asked many people their reasons for leaving everything they knew to travel the world. I also asked what they wished they had known before.

I redesigned the presentation. Still including some travel stories and anecdotes but with more focus on safety techniques and a traveller's mindset, so students could better understand their personal risk management.

Talking about travel safety, the presentation began with a simple statement, 'behaviour that produces damaging or harmful effects, physically or emotionally on people'.

For me the key was 'emotionally', most people think of their safety in the physical and are very good at instinctively avoiding any life-threatening dangers, but emotionally is a different story. Some people don't realise they are emotionally at risk or recognise when they are getting emotionally abused. This could have a huge impact on someone's confidence which can dramatically increase the risk to their safety.

Common sense needs to become common practice. As we grow up, we are taught by our family and peers right from wrong. To look both ways before crossing the road. When in the mountains don't eat yellow snow. These micro-skills take years to learn and eventually become habit, keeping us safe and out of trouble. It follows that we should adhere to the same rules when we travel but sometimes, we choose to break these habits.

I added a couple of simple techniques for travellers to become more aware of their surroundings. My hope was that this would trigger them to find out more about their destinations before they travelled and become more aware in the right moments to reduce risk.

Travel risk assessment — assessing potential hazards:
- Identify the hazard.
- Identify who is at risk.
- Evaluate the risk.
- Take action.

The first thing is to identify the hazard, this could be either from people or your environment.

Identify who is at risk. If you are travelling alone then the primary concern is for yourself, if you are travelling in a group then you will need to consider the level of risk to each person. It's important to remember, each member of the group will have their own thresholds as to what's acceptable, if one person is at risk then the whole group is at risk.

Evaluate the risk, decide if it's acceptable to yourself and other members of the group.

Finally, and most importantly, take action. This could be as simple as pausing before you cross the street or deciding to take a different mode of transport. The earlier travellers are able to spot hazards and take action, the safer they will be when travelling.

The more people practice these types of risk assessment then the more instinctive they will become. Eventually they won't have to consciously think about it unless something triggers in their awareness.

Risk Awareness — understanding people's intentions:
- Reading body language.
- Aggression and mentality.
- People's intentions.

Firstly, reading body language; we already do this subconsciously with people on a daily basis. We know when people are interested in what we are saying, they are making eye contact, arms open and relaxed, and they are facing us. They might also be mirroring our actions.

Be aware, if people are feeling outside their comfort zone, their body language can be more addressing what they are feeling rather than what they think about you. Cultural differences can sometimes confuse matters, some nationalities are more comfortable with physical contact. The Italians, for example, are known for having less personal space, talking with their bodies, arm gestures and more physically animated conversation.

Secondly, aggression and mentality. Again, you need to understand the culture you are potentially stepping into. It can be very insightful talking with local people, you could learn something new and enhance your experience. Some nationalities can be perceived as more forward or aggressive than others; this could quite easily be cultural or traditional and wouldn't impact your safety.

If it's not cultural, it could be because they feel threatened; always check that you have not done something inadvertently to offend people.

Thirdly, I feel this is incredibly important, try to understand people's intentions, ask yourself what do they want? 99% of the time people just want to have a good time; it's the 1% that you need to watch out for. With experience you will know in a few moments if you like a person. Above all, listen to yourself and go with what you think, trusting yourself and your intuition is the most important.

When travelling you meet a lot of people. Some will make a significant impression and others won't. This doesn't mean anyone is better than anyone else but remember your time is priceless and it's your choice who you spend it with. If you feel the need to leave someone's company have the confidence to act.

Putting safety advice into a story format enhances people's understanding, but even if people know the information and find themselves in a high-risk situation, will their head be in the right place to remember what they need?

By understanding the benefits and pitfalls of travel, travellers can learn to minimise risk long before they find themselves in a situation that could become out of their control. It's no good just telling people the information, in presentations I get asked questions like 'where is the UK Embassy in New York?' My reply is always, "Look it up, do your research. If I tell you now, you will only forget; if you understand why and research what you might need to know you will always remember."

The presentations were always to promote travel in a positive light, encouraging people to have the confidence to go out and see parts of the world that interested them. I would always end on a quote, this was one of my favourites attributed to Mark Twain.

"Twenty years from now you will be more disappointed by the things that you didn't do than by the ones you did do. So, throw off the bowlines. Sail away from the safe harbour. Catch the trade winds in your sails. Explore. Dream. Discover."

We approached experienced travellers, developed a training program and standard presentation which laid out travel safety principles and risk assessments. There were spaces where they could add their own stories, anecdotes and points they felt were important.

Our feedback was that the students learnt a great deal from the presentations and the travellers enjoyed sharing their experiences and safety advice.

The majority of travellers return safely and unscathed. Generally, the worst that happens is a bag is stolen or a lost passport. In a minority of cases, something serious could happen and it was those situations we needed to make sure travellers were prepared for.

Through presentations, our DVD and website content, the hope was that some of our advice would stick in people's minds and come to the forefront when they need it most.

One story that made the BBC News was about Heather Burlton and her travels to Nepal. Heather wrote her story in her own words.

'The trip to Nepal was something we'd been planning for nearly a year. Myself and three friends had booked a ten- day trek around the Annapurnas in the Himalayas, followed by five weeks in India.

The trip was exactly what we needed. We'd just finished our exams and felt revived amongst the wonderful scenery and mountain air. Although the air grew a bit thin at the top, we made it over the Thorong La Pass at 5416 meters with only mild mountain sickness, and no sign of the Maoist rebels. The trek ended in Pokhora, Nepal's second city. We spent the first day relaxing, shopping and getting our clothes washed before having a farewell dinner with our guide.

The day our guides left, we set off at 8 a.m. to walk up the 'beautiful forest trail', as described by our guidebook, to the world peace pagoda. With beautiful views of Pokhora, the lake and the Himalayas, it seemed like a necessary visit.

We'd been walking up the wooded trail for about thirty minutes when we discovered we were sharing the path with hundreds of leeches. Walking quicker to get out of the trees and away from the leeches, I failed to notice two Nepalese men on the path above us.

They were in their twenties and wearing bandannas and facemasks. They came down the path towards us and asked for money. This is common in Nepal and India, so we gave our usual reply that we didn't have any. Then one guy pulled out a baton, and we started to feel uneasy, it was made much worse when his companion brandished a knife.

The one guy in our group was at the back, and nearly knocked me over as he pushed past me, I had no idea what he was doing, but at that point two more men came up the path below us, also with knives.

Now we really started to panic. They demanded our bags and ripped them open to go through the contents. They took our cameras, money and wallets. One of my friends begged them to leave our passports, which luckily for us they did. They threw the rest of our stuff on the floor, brandished the knives again and took off down the path.

By this point the other two girls were in tears. We scrambled around on the floor picking up our stuff and headed up the path as quickly as we could. We were terrified and just wanted to get out of there. But we couldn't go down, as that was where the muggers had gone. So, we continued up and fortunately found another path down.

Now we had time for it all to sink in. Whilst I was particularly upset having lost a nearly full memory card in my camera, all I could see in my head was Caroline's Rainbow Foundation's video, where the two lads get stabbed. I kept thinking, that could have been us.

This was when my friend confessed that he had been trying to be the gentleman and protect the three girls by standing in front of them. It hadn't occurred to him that he was a foot taller than the attackers and so would appear aggressive — maybe if he'd seen the video, he would have realised this.

In the end, we were all OK, and still managed to have a wonderful time on the rest of the trip. It wouldn't stop me travelling again, but it has made me much more aware of safety.'

Chapter 21
Another life

I was proud of what the charity had achieved. We were in a good place, the Safer Travel app was doing well, our presentations and education program had a stable list of places we visited each year.

Caroline's death had defined many years and the charity had taken a great deal of time. I had always worked because I wanted to learn something new or the job could take me to places I wanted to visit. I had once taken a cooking job in a fine dining hotel restaurant in Scotland for a lesser position and less money because I hugely respected the head chef, what I learnt took my cooking abilities to another level. It was a far greater benefit to my life and CV than just working for the financial reward.

My career was varied to say the least, I didn't really want to be in the kitchens any more and was looking for something new and inspiring. My artwork was not selling, and I had finished with the winter seasons. I was getting by as a freelance chef and consultant. I wasn't feeling inspired and could feel a change coming. I have always been a creative person, whether it be food, art or design. I enjoyed the charity work, learning about apps, marketing and web design. The presentations had built confidence and I had completed many courses at the Arthur Findlay College and had been mentored by some fantastic world class tutors. I will always be indebted to Janette Marshall and love her dearly.

In my personal life, I had met some very special people and shared some wonderful moments, but it has never worked out quite right. Looking back, I felt my grief played a major role. I watched most of my friends get married and have children. I became good in small doses, seeing people for the occasional coffee, beer or smoke. I liked just popping in, having a laugh and leaving before any further responsibility was placed on my shoulders. It was a cycle that I feel was compounded by living a seasonal lifestyle.

I was incredibly lucky to meet an inspiring gentleman who I will always be indebted too. He had seen my art and our charity work. He was building a new law firm with a completely different methodology, looking to change the legal profession and create an entirely new way of helping customers. I had the privilege of meeting Gary Gallen and found we had the exact same outlook on life. He offered me a role leading his design department; excitedly I took up the challenge.

Sometimes life can be stranger and more aligned than I ever thought possible. A few significant moments can set the next chapter of your life. I recognised certain points over the years, and they act as a reminder as to how magical our world can be.

We met in a pub; Sarah was working for the company and I was setting up the kitchen for a friend who had taken on the business. We immediately felt sparks between us and both knew in that moment that our lives had changed completely. Over the following weeks and months things moved quickly.

One weekend, less than a year after Sarah and I had met, I planned a surprise trip. We had already been looking at houses and talking about our future, an alert came through on my phone, it looked like the perfect house. We booked a viewing for Friday afternoon. Arriving at the property it looked perfect, stepping through the front door we knew immediately that it was our new home.

The next morning, we flew to Venice, neither of us had visited the city before. We stayed in the amazing Bauer Hotel and wandered happily around the floating city. Sunday evening, after a wonderful dinner, we went up to the balcony of the penthouse suite, the sun was setting behind the Basilica di Santa Maria della Salute. I had arranged for a bottle of champagne and a dozen red roses to be on the table. It was a beautiful evening, I got down on one knee and asked her to be my wife. She said, 'Yes.' Completely in love and happier than either of us had ever been, we enjoyed Venice.

Monday morning, we flew back to the UK. As we landed, I had a voicemail saying that multiple offers had been put in on the house. We immediately called. The couple accepted our offer partly because we reminded them of where they were five years ago when they bought the property.

In the space of one weekend, we got engaged in the most wonderful of way and bought our new home. Our lives changed forever. Less than a year after moving in, we were married.

In 2017, I turned forty years old, Caroline would have been thirty-five. I was married, Sarah and I had been on many amazing holidays and we lived in a lovely home together. I had joined the Freemasons, Dad put me through my degrees and I was now a Master Mason. I didn't get much time to see family but on the whole life was good.

I had made the decision with a heavy heart to leave the law firm. It had been an amazing experience with inspiring people. I just felt it was time to do something different and my wife needed me, I would be back in the hospitality industry, working with Sarah building a restaurant brand. We were consumed by work; it was an exciting new challenge. The time I had free, I continued with the charity work, delivering presentations, managing student internships and updating our online presence.

The world was changing extremely quickly and I had watched with interest the rise of social media and influencers. There were amazing people I admired who had a voice and were able to publish wonderful content to a wider audience. Others were becoming famous for what I considered the wrong reasons. I came to believe that technology, especially social media could be extremely detrimental. We could be easily distracted and were quickly becoming addicted. In relation to travel I would see pictures of beautiful people in beautiful locations, the images and captions were positive and portrayed an idealised view of the world. They weren't necessarily depicting an accurate view of what it was like to really travel and the risks involved. I felt concerned, younger people had shorter attention spans and were been fed an unrealistic view of the world. It could have a detrimental effect on the safety of inexperienced travellers.

I was inspired to write, revisiting my travels to Australia and looking back through my diaries. I had some wonderful memories. All I travelled with was a basic mobile, camera, sketchbook and paints, we had no knowledge of social media and what it meant to have an online presence. We visited places, sat and chatted soaking up the atmosphere. We shared our experience with the people who were there with no distraction. I'm not saying that doesn't happen today, but I have seen countless times where people have stood looking out over a wonderful view, taken a quick photo or selfie, turned and left or sat down on a bench and started scrolling. Visiting wonderful galleries or museums, many people are more interested in the café their phones. I am aware it's a bit of an old man's view of our next generation but there was genuine concern and it saddened me to think these people weren't getting the most out of their experiences.

Chapter 22
Competing with angels

The natural world played a large role in my life growing up. Like many people of my generation Sir David Attenborough was one of my heroes. He always spoke with such passion and sensitivity about the natural world and the animal kingdom. I was glued to the TV whenever any of his programmes were on. He taught me that life for everyone on this planet was a battle, survival of the fittest. Every living thing completes a life cycle; birth, growth, reproduction, death and feeds back into the food chain. It's a balancing act that's taken hundreds of thousands of years to perfect. Our world is dependent on every living thing to thrive, no matter how large or small. I understood that life on this planet is hard, so why should it be any different for us? We just have different struggles, thankfully most are not life-threatening but that doesn't necessarily make them any easier.

As humans, we are blessed with consciousness. There is something very powerful within us and our conscious mind; belief and our understanding of death sets us apart from all other species. Some people are willing to sacrifice everything for what they believe. It can even override our instinct for survival and self-preservation.

After Caroline was gone, I didn't know what to believe. Was she now an angel? How could my life live up to what hers could have been?

I wondered if her soul was still around in some form or another. When I was around eight years old, another of my heroes was my Grandad. We had so many amazing times which I will always remember fondly. After he died, I was upset, but eventually asked the question.

"Mum, Dad, what happens when we die?"

I can't remember word for word. We talked about life. Dad told me that minutes after I was born, he held me in his arms, to him I was an amazing new life. He thought, who is this little person? We all talked about growing up, becoming a teenager, an adult, eventually a parent and grandparent just like Grandma and Grandad. They explained when you die you go to another place, but you are still around looking over your family and friends. The conversation must have planted a seed in my mind.

Since Caroline's death our family have talked a lot about life after death. I have had many experiences that I feel are far more than just coincidence. Dad told me a story from when Caroline was little.

'Dad,' she said.

'Yes Caroline?' he replied.

'When I go to bed a man comes to visit me at night,' she said, very relaxed.

'OK, what does he want?' Dad replied, surprised but calm. He knew the house was secure and no one could have gotten in. She could have been dreaming.

'He just wants to chat, but the thing is Dad, I can see straight through him.'

'Right. No problem, next time he comes to see you tell him to come and see me,' said Dad.

The next morning, 'Dad, the man came again last night, and I told him to go and see you.'

'OK, then what happened?' Dad asked.

'He came back and said you were asleep,' Caroline replied.

'Next time he comes to see you, ask him to go away so you can get some sleep,' Dad said.

'OK,' Caroline said.

After that, she never mentioned the man again and slept well.

I became interested in life after death, what had happened to my sister? Where was she now? I believed that there was more than just our physical world, but didn't know what. Over the years I have been able to study at The Arthur Findlay College. The college was left by Arthur Findlay following his death to further advance Spiritualism and the psychic sciences. It delves into the subject of life after death and the continuation of the human spirit.

I have always kept an open mind and over my life tried to listen very much to my intuition, the little voice inside me that knows what's best for my well-being. I always tried to listen carefully and develop my sensitivity to the world around me.

My thoughts would go back to hearing the organ playing in the weeks after Caroline's death and the significance we had placed in rainbows. I have been lucky enough to be around many world-class mediums and the information they have given has been incredibly accurate. It always made me wonder where the information came from?

Our belief in another existence has given us as a family a common bond to hold close. We like to think Caroline and our other loved ones are looking down on us, watching and guiding us in this world.

I believe as humans we are blessed with a soul. Our lifeforce is so strong, complex and well developed that I find it hard to believe that it only popped into existence when we were born and on death it just ends. It's the essence of what makes us individual. I know there is something which allows us to connect with people on multiple levels, this is evident with all the people I have met throughout the years. We are able to connect through mind, body and soul.

I found comfort in the thought that Caroline is continuing her work in the next world and her energy still exists in some shape or form.

The way I understand our different worlds is through levels of vibration. Everything is vibrating at a different frequency from trees in the forest to the table we place our coffee cup on. I imagine an infinite number of guitar strings all tuned to a different note; to listen it's a case of simply plucking the string and attuning to harmonise with that vibration. After death, our energy or soul departs our physical body returning to another frequency.

I believe Caroline's soul has returned to become part of the vibrational energy of the universe (as we all are). I can attune into her frequency, feel her energy and know that she is still around.

Attending courses at the Arthur Findlay College, I have learnt about energy, healing, spirit art and mediumship. It opened up a whole new level of potential, looking deeper into ourselves as well as beyond our physical and materialistic worlds.

When I was working in the Alps, I had time and the opportunity to paint as well as complete various spiritual courses. Painting put me in an altered state and allowed me to look further into myself and areas of life that interested me. Expanding my mind was important, it's a way I could explore and feel out of control that didn't rely on anyone else.

One occasion shortly after Caroline's death, I found myself in a situation with a group of people I had not met before and they didn't know our story. They asked if I had any siblings, and for ease, I said 'No'. Immediately I felt a pain inside and pull on my heart, it was as if she was shouting, I'm still here! I had just denied Caroline's entire existence. I still think back now and cringe, I felt absolutely terrible. I have never done it again. I tried to understand why I said that; a part of me wanted to save them experiencing the pain of our story, another part didn't want them to feel sorry for me. I have never wanted sympathy but that was no excuse in denying my sister's life.

Seeing Caroline in the chapel of rest made me aware that it was Caroline's essence or soul which made her who she was. That was the spark of life and it was no longer in her body.

I feel it's important for us to consider our own evolution in order to understand our own spark of life. Appreciating the simple pleasures. Watching a beautiful sunset, taking an evening stroll along the beach or catching up with friends for dinner. These experiences can evoke feelings and emotions within us, I have always been curious why people like certain things more than others, why people fall in love.

A quote by one of Spiritualism's great pioneers, Gordon Higginson, resonated strongly, 'Before you can touch the Spirit, you must find it within yourself. For all truth, for all knowledge and all love, must be found first within oneself.'

Through better understanding our feelings and emotions we can enhance our awareness. We can experience more from the sunset or the stroll on the beach, we are able to forge deeper connections with the people around us.

I can liken this development to painting, for portraits and life drawing there are techniques to learn, ways to look at a subject that make the work more accurate and captures the feeling and essence of the person. Firstly, it's about the physical form, facial features, tone and shadow. Next is to look under the skin, understanding bone structure, weight distribution and muscle definition. Once an artist has gained this knowledge, they can produce an accurate resemblance of the sitter, but there is more to it. An artist then needs to look not with their eyes but with their feelings and emotions, they need to capture the essence of the person. This is far more difficult and not a skill to master; it's a knowing that needs to be understood in every brushstroke. Some painters just have the touch, they have that ability to capture the sitter's true self on canvas. Looking at the works of the greatest portrait painters, they have captured far more than just the resemblance. Their paintings can evoke the same feelings as if you were actually interacting with the person they painted.

I have been asked many times, do I consider myself a religious man? My belief played a role in dealing with what we had been through. I have been interested different aspects of Spiritualism and other religions for many years and feel that the belief in more than just myself has given me a greater sense of peace. Socrates heard a voice in his head, a divine or guiding spirit who advised him throughout his life. Had he achieved some deeper understanding of life, or had he tapped into his intuition? Was it another part of himself in the spirit world communicating with him or was it God? We will never know the answer, but I believe that you have to be true to yourself, listen to the voice inside yourself which understands your divine path.

I am sure my ideas and beliefs will continue to change over time as they have done up until this point. I think that any person who holds the same philosophy all their lives is either a born genius or unable to consider new ideas and evolve. It's incredibly important to try to incorporate what we learn into our daily lives, be willing to change our way of thinking as we meet different people and have new experiences.

Life is a pendulum, as much as it swings in one direction it swings just as far in the other. I now try not to view what happens as good and bad or black and white, everything is just part of life's experience. I feel safer in the knowledge that nothing will ever be as bad as the devastation we have already been through. If it turns out I am wrong and something far worse happens, I feel safe in the knowledge that I have already gotten through experiences in life that I never thought I would be able to.

Sadly, we will never know what Caroline's life could have been in this world. I believe we have our own lives to live, we both have a great deal to do and will be working together for many years to come, just from different worlds.

Chapter 23
Travelling today

Since 2002, there have been huge changes in the way we travel. Not only in opportunities open to travellers but also the mindset of how people want to explore the world. The internet had made the world a far smaller place, when it comes to researching destinations all the information you need is at your fingertips. This could be overwhelming, for some there we too many options, for others it opened a Pandora's Box that could define the rest of their lives. Travel is a blessing but can become incredibly addictive.

One of the biggest considerations for young travellers today is responsible travel, people are hugely concerned about how we have treated our planet. Sir David Attenborough said, "The moment of crisis has come," when talking about climate change. He has been a huge influence and I have always great respect for his knowledge, enthusiasm and insight into the natural world. He has always spoken passionately about climate change and it seems in today's world we are definitely at a crisis point. Our presence on the planet has dramatically sped up natural evolution and is responsible for the destruction of many idyllic natural sanctuaries and eco systems.

Over recent years, places are experiencing record temperatures, the fires in Australia and severe lack of rain destroying habitat and homes. I have such an affinity for the country, it's heart-breaking to think how some of the beautiful landscapes I enjoyed back in 2003-2005 will look completely different today. It saddens me that future generations won't be able to travel so freely as I did.

The rise of technology over the last decade has enhanced our travelling experiences in so many ways but has also had a dramatic effect on our planet. Airlines for example have responded to customer needs by scheduling flights to almost anywhere in the world. Customer need and the pursuit of financial profit should not be encouraged if it is detrimental to our planet's wellbeing. Places like Maya Bay suffered significantly, the area was made popular by Alex Garland's book *The Beach* and Danny Boyle's film adaptation starring Leonardo DiCaprio in 2000. The book did the rounds in our backpacker circles. Tourists flocked to the small beach, at its peak around 5000 tourists visited per day. This soon destroyed what was a natural paradise. The beach closed in 2019 and won't reopen for the foreseeable future. The irony is that our lust to see and experience untouched paradises has played a huge role in helping to destroy them. I believe we have drained and destroyed our beautiful planet and if we don't act now it will be too late, but I am optimistic, and this is where I hope our genius of consciousness might be able to help.

I applaud our next generation of backpackers; they are incredibly mindful of how they travel. Sustainable travel now features highly as a factor in people's considerations when choosing destinations. It goes beyond looking at transportation, eco-friendly accommodation and supporting local and tourist businesses. Travellers are aware of their own carbon footprint and work to offset it. Sustainable travel matters if people want to continue to enjoy travelling our world.

There are of course things that are out of our control when travelling, natural disasters such as the earthquake and tsunami in the Indian Ocean in 2004, the volcanic ash cloud in 2010 from Iceland's most active volcano. These have all disrupted our world. I feel with these your safety is partly down to luck, whether you are in the right place or the wrong place at the time these things happen. Though in all of these events I am humbled by the support people offer and our willingness to selflessly help others. As a charity we can't help when it comes to natural disasters, there are other organisations in place but where we can make a big difference is with personal safety in day-to-day travel.

A common question I have been asked by students throughout the years is, 'what are the most important things I need to understand to improve my safety when travelling?'

I have given this great thought and have developed a simple safety awareness system called K.A.R. Three key areas that if understood on multiple levels can dramatically improve safety and reduce risk. During public speaking engagements, I usually only get time to answer in brief, but I will take this opportunity to expand further.

K.A.R is in its simplest form a mindset. It incorporates everything we have already learnt over many years; safety tools, risk assessments and awareness strategies that we have been taught in order to live in our world. K.A.R offers three principles that if understood can be applied at the right time when travelling to significantly reduce risk.

K.A.R stands for:
1. Knowledge
2. Awareness
3. Response

Knowledge — Let's start with knowledge; simply put, nobody likes to look stupid in any situation. Why wouldn't you find out as much as you can about the places you are visiting?

Research is always number one. Consider any place you have a desire to visit, there's an interest that makes us want to find out more, ultimately the more you know the better your experience. This is certainly true when visiting attractions and historical landmarks. Sarah and I were travelling in Bali and staying in a beautiful hotel in Ubud. On a day's excursion we went to visit the Monkey Temple, which was located in Mandala Suci Wenara Wana or more commonly known as the Monkey Forest. We discovered that the forest is around 12.5 hectares with a staggering 186 different species of tree and is occupied by around 700 Balinese long-tailed macaques. The three Hindu temples were constructed around 1350 AD: the Pura Dalem Agung Padangtegal or 'Great Temple of Death' was used for worshipping the god Hyang Widhi, the second is the Pura Beji and is known as the bathing temple, the third is called the Pura Prajapati and receives the bodies of the dead. All three play a large role in Balinese culture and tradition. The more we learnt about the temples, the more appreciation we had during our visit. If we hadn't done any research, it would just have been a bunch of old ruins with lots of monkeys running around.

Regarding our safety, we knew what to expect and understood the risks were low; we had read the reviews and we felt safe enough not to worry too much about anything happening. This meant we could relax a little more and enjoy our visit.

To me research is part and parcel of your travelling experience, it means you can start getting excited long before your departure date. Once you step foot off the bus, train or plane at your chosen destination every second counts, don't waste time researching where to go and what to do. Be prepared. Find out about the culture, history and importantly common crimes, local events and even the political situation. All of this knowledge can help you understand the environment you are in, reduce risk and improve your safety.

Many countries have unique laws that you might not agree with but must be followed. Leaving Bali and stopped in Singapore. It is one of the most inspiring and cleanest places I have ever been. They have strict rules about drinking alcohol. Drunk and disorderly conduct is treated seriously. Penalties for convicted offenders include fines, imprisonment and possibly corporal punishment. It is also illegal to drink alcohol in public places from 10:30 p.m. to 7:00 a.m. during the week. These restrictions are imposed for 24 hours over weekends in specific areas and designated Liquor Control Zones. If travellers are not aware of the laws, they could easily find themselves breaking them without even knowing.

Another essential part in a traveller's research is anticipating what you might need before you need it. Inoculations can sometimes take up to three months before you are fully protected. Taking out the correct insurance, always read the small print and make sure you are covered for any extreme sports or unusual activities.

When talking to students, I stress the importance of knowledge preparation. Using exams as an example, most people wouldn't dream of going into an exam without first revising. Through the education system we have already learnt the tools for effective research.

A beneficial thing to do in relating knowledge to safety is to act out potential scenarios, what to do if something goes wrong. For example, if you lose your passport can you answer the following questions?

- Where do I go?
- Who do I ask?
- What do I do?

As I mentioned knowledge is about understanding the mindset, think of what might happen and develop the ability to solve the problem in your mind. I am locked out of my room. I've lost my friends in a city I don't know. I have had my bag stolen or my luggage didn't arrive at my final destination. If travellers can understand this knowledge mindset then if something does arise, they will be better equipped to effectively deal with it.

Increased knowledge will help to control stress if something does occur. Your problem-solving skills will remain efficient, and any potential negative impact will be minimised. Travelling automatically puts you outside your comfort zone; another key area of knowledge is knowing how you will react. It's natural to feel uncomfortable if we don't feel in control:

- Our stress levels rise.
- We become anxious.
- Start to feel uncomfortable.
- Become unsure of what to do.
- Start to feel nervous and nauseous.

All of these points can send our emotions into overdrive, detract from what's happening around us and have a dramatic impact on personal safety. Opportunists are looking for people who look out of their comfort zone as they are easier to take advantage of.

Also be aware that opportunists might also come in disguise, they might offer to help or offer to solve your problems. If you are not in your right frame of mind you might not be able to tell the difference between someone who is genuine or someone who wants to take advantage of your situation.

Research doesn't just stop when you start travelling, chatting to other travellers in hotels or youth hostels can offer great insight. Knowledge is very much passed around the travel community; the best companies to take the trips with or the best times to visit attractions. Talk to people who have actually been and done it, they can say whether it was worthwhile and what they gained from the experience.

Many people who take a backpacking adventure travel a similar route. When I was in Australia, I bumped into people time and again. The worst things to say are, 'We didn't see that I wish we'd known.' or 'Yeah, we went but it was closed.'

Awareness — Armed with knowledge of possible risks, relevant safety tips and all the exciting things you are going to do, the next aspect to consider is your awareness. Raising your awareness at the right time enables you to spot possible hazardous situations before they start to unfold and if action is taken early enough you can prevent your level of risk from increasing.

There are a few simple techniques, firstly risk assessments which we touched on in the earlier student presentations. The simple process which if done regularly will become automatic. What is the hazard and who is at risk? Is the risk acceptable to myself and the people I am with? Take action if required.

Another important part of being aware is understanding people; this is what Caroline was very good at. She could read people and see past their words to their true intentions. Some people are better at this than others, but it's a skill which can be honed over time. We automatically read body language, it's a case of being conscious of what we are reading. We know if people are open to a conversation before either party even says a word.

Another method of understanding when to raise awareness is to use our imagination. If we are able to imagine a situation before it arises, we can create a plan of action. One example I use is to imagine visiting an airport, it's a busy place, screens are updating flight times and departure gates every few minutes. People busying about, their main concern is getting to their destination but there is always a lot of time to wait. We know opportunists are looking to take belongings from people when they are not aware. In your mind, take a look around the airport, how many people are on their mobile phones? Can you see their hand luggage? Could someone take it without them knowing?

A simple way to reduce this risk is to make a conscious decision, when waiting at an airport (or any busy location) leave your phone in your pocket and keep an eye on your bags.

Now imagine you have arrived at your destination. How many people are on their phones Googling what to do, searching for the easiest way to get to their accommodation. Where are their bags? Can you see any opportunists? Knowing your route and pre-booking transport can reduce the danger of been taken advantage of.

Having risk assessments, awareness strategies and the foresight to anticipate potential problems and find solutions as part of your skillset is incredibly important. Its then simply a case of raising your awareness, becoming present at the right time to keep you safe and your stress levels low. Most people wouldn't dream of crossing the road without raising their awareness and looking both ways before stepping out.

Listen to your own intuition. The more you listen to yourself the more you will believe what your intuition tells you. It will automatically alert you when you need to be fully aware. If something doesn't feel right, change your situation. You are in control and your safety is your responsibility.

Nobody can be fully aware all of the time, it's impossible. Your senses and knowledge will let you know when you need to raise your awareness. Your responsibility is to not be distracted when these moments occur.

Response — Comprehensive knowledge and raised awareness in the right moments means your risk level should remain low. Sometimes however you may be unable to avoid a potentially hazardous situation, in these moments your actions become incredibly important, how you react could dramatically change the outcome.

If you have recognised a potential danger early, it will give you time to process and decide on the best course of action. If there is no choice but to participate in a confrontation, there are a variety of diffusion techniques. The simplest I found consists of three main actions.

- Stop.
- Observe.
- Respond.

If a situation is becoming out of hand the first thing to do is to stop, breathe and gather your thoughts. Give yourself time to process what's happening with the people involved and the surrounding area. Recognise that you might not be the cause of the person's anger or aggression. Step back both physically and mentally, this in itself can defuse a situation if you were perceived as a threat. It will help you gain a better perspective of the situation. Be aware that if you are travelling in a group then it could be the group that is causing a situation to escalate.

Observe what's happening, clarify and rationalise what is actually happening. Try to understand what the person or people want. In many aggressive confrontations the person simply wants respect or is in fear of losing respect. Try to control your emotions, these can quickly and easily cloud judgement.

Consider your reply carefully before you respond. Speaking calmly, slowly and in a softer tone can also help defuse the situation.

If you are confronted by an opportunist that clearly wants to take your belongings, the most important thing at all times relates back to what happened to Caroline. If someone forcefully tries to take your belongings, just let them go. Nothing is worth more than your life.

Understanding the K.A.R principles can give travellers a greater sense of security in their own abilities, this helps to increase confidence which in itself can reduce risk. Confident people who know where they are going are less likely to be considered a target by opportunists.

This mindset combined with extensive knowledge, the ability to raise your awareness when required and to respond appropriately in challenging situations means risk to your safety will be reduced when it matters most. As a result, you can focus back to what you should be doing: enjoying the places you are visiting and ultimately following your travelling dreams.

Chapter 24
A new decade

A year that I don't think anyone could have predicted. No one expected 2020 to unfold in the way it did. COVID-19 has become the unseen killer. Our times are unprecedented due to the freedom of travel and how over the last half a century we have made the world a far more accessible place. Unfortunately, we don't live in harmony with our environment and we consume far more than we need. I think this is partly nature's way of telling us to cease our reckless and thoughtless actions in pursuit of the wrong goals and to stop destroying our beautiful world.

There were huge changes in the travel industry, lockdown stopped all non-essential travel, will it ever go back to the world we knew before? I sincerely hope our future generations will be able to have the freedom of travel that I had the privilege of enjoying. I hope there are places that remain unspoilt, where travellers can appreciate the beauty of our world, meet like-minded people and learn skills that will help their future lives and careers.

For our family, 2020 held something else that we didn't know how to deal with.

Diary Entry — May 2020
The 75th VE Day was very different to that of previous years. I still felt a huge sense of pride to be British and part of the United Kingdom. I have the utmost respect for all those souls who died for us, died for a worthy cause. We are here now only because they fought so hard for our freedom. Soldiers killed for a reason, Ian Douglas Previte killed for nothing. My body went weak and was physically deflated, today the man who murdered my sister is going to be released. Thoughts of the telephone call in the Alps all those years ago and sitting in the courtroom in Bundaberg came flooding back into my mind.

Press release had gone out, the Australian media had picked it up. Calls and emails requesting interviews and statements. Another piece went out on the local news which I recorded yesterday.

Working from home, sat in the garden with my laptop. The thought came into my head, Australia is currently nine hours ahead. Could he be a free man now? He might be looking up at blue skies, breathing fresh air. No bars, he is no longer in a cell and has been granted the same rights and freedoms as me. It hit me harder than I thought, but in a different way. I no longer wanted to go over to Australia, visions of waiting at the prison gates for him to be released and the pain I would inflict had long since gone. He has served his life sentence, and what I now realised is so have we.

I always thought that his payment of fifteen years of life was not enough; when he was released, he would be free, but our sentence was always forever. I now thought that he will never experience freedom, he will be forever tormented by what he's done, he will never be able to get the sound of her final scream out of his head. I know Caroline, she will haunt him for the rest of his days.

We will always miss Caroline. She was taken far too soon from our lives, but it was not our fault. There was nothing we could do to change what happened. Life is hard, bad things happen and some things are just out of our control. It was time for us to be free, we have also served our sentence even though we committed no crime. It was time for us to release ourselves from our mental prison and undo the shackles of pain and grief we placed around our hands and feet.

Many lovely thoughts and messages on social media, incredibly touching. Stories featured on TV and in the papers in the UK and Australia. Reading some of the comments, there was anger, strong feelings as to why he was getting released, he should spend his whole life behind bars.

'Bundaberg Now
The family of murdered English backpacker Caroline Stuttle have spoken about their grief and her legacy after learning convicted killer Ian Previte was due to be released on parole today.

In 2002, Caroline Ann Stuttle from York was travelling with a friend on her gap year around Australia and Bundaberg was her final destination. On 10 April 2002 she was thrown from the Burnett Bridge and lost her life. Her murderer served 15 years of a life sentence after being convicted in 2004.

Caroline's Rainbow Foundation was set up by Caroline's mother Marjorie Marks-Stuttle and her brother Richard Stuttle, after Caroline's death. The charity promotes travel safety awareness for anyone going abroad.

"The release of the man who stole my sister's life has hit our family harder than we thought; it's been 18 years since we lost Caroline and life without her still hurts every day," Richard Stuttle said.

"We strive to stay positive, reminding ourselves of Caroline's Rainbow Foundation and all the work we have done to support backpackers and young travellers, helping to keep them safe when travelling."

"This is Caroline's legacy and how she will always be with us."

Bundaberg Region Mayor, Jack Dempsey said he has great empathy for Caroline's family.

"Caroline's murder was a tragedy that took the life of an innocent, caring and energetic young woman," Mayor Dempsey said.

"Caroline was kind, confident and intuitive. She will always be remembered for her warmth, intelligence and compassion. Bundaberg is a welcoming community and we regret this terrible crime occurred in our city. Caroline's rainbow continues to brighten Buss Park and her legacy lives on, providing travel advice for young people and encouraging them to follow their dreams."

Mayor Dempsey said former Bundaberg City Mayor Kay McDuff played a key role in leading the community's condolences after the murder and supporting Caroline Stuttle's family in their grief, also visiting England in 2007.

The Caroline's Rainbow Foundation and Safer Travel website has comprehensive safer travel information, safety tips and travel stories to highlight the benefits and pitfalls of world travel.

In 2012, for the charity's 10-year anniversary, they launched the Safer Travel app on Android and Apple. It's a comprehensive city-specific safety guide covering more than 350 world destinations.

Richard visits schools, colleges and universities around the UK talking to students about his travelling experiences, offering safety advice and awareness strategies to help them stay safe when entering potentially high-risk situations.

Richard has recently finished writing a book about Caroline Stuttle, which includes stories from his travels, founding the charity and attending the trial for his sister's death. He also goes into detail about dealing with grief and coming to terms with life without his sister. There are contributions from Caroline's mother and father as well as some of her close friends and people who worked on Caroline's murder investigation. He is now working with Pegasus Publishers, and although no release date has been set, Richard is hoping the book will be released towards the end of this year.

Richard hopes to return to Australia in the future and visit Bundaberg again. "I have visited Bundaberg a number of times, some visits have been incredibly difficult," he said.
"I have always felt moved by the place and people in a positive way. Everyone has always been so kind and generous. A lovely memory I have is visiting the Botanic Gardens with my father and seeing the tree planted for Caroline. I have seen photographs of the rainbow mosaic that was created in 2010 and would like one day to see it in person.".'

In the days after the release, the UK was still in lockdown. Rainbows had become a symbol of support and love for the NHS; obviously to our family rainbows had another meaning, I thought it was strange. It almost felt like an outpouring of love from Caroline, she was flooding the world with rainbows. We stood on our front step and clapped with pride for our country pulling together and the heroic work of our emergency services and key workers.

Previte had served the sentence for his crime. This by no way meant I thought the sentence was fair. Taking a life to me should mean life. I was not prepared for his release but how could I have been? It hit me in a different way to which I thought. I was struck by a huge sadness for Caroline, her missing out on life was the only thing that hurt. I was also feeling a strange sense of relief, our sentence was also over too. As the realisation processed, I felt it cascading though my mind, body and soul. I was forgiving a part of myself that I didn't know needed forgiving. I felt it was happening naturally. A friend shared a powerful story with me about loss and mourning; the part that resonated was a lady saying, 'forgiveness is for the person who forgives not the person who has been forgiven.' She was right, we forgive for our own well-being and not the well-being of others. This was also true for forgiving myself, forgiveness for living life on my own terms, forgiveness for still being here.

In June, there was another unexpected event. My marriage sadly came to an end; five wonderful years together and so many amazing experiences. We were both absolutely devastated. It had been perfect in so many ways, fantastic adventures, wonderful holidays and building businesses together. We had sadly reached a point where we were both heading in different directions, we wanted different things from the next chapter of our lives. It was an incredibly difficult decision but we both knew deep down it was the right one. We will always love each other and will be there if either of us need anything.

I had been working on my manuscript most days over the last year, although many pieces were written years before. Something compelled me to bring it all together, it was a leap of faith. I had no idea how it was going to turn out or whether it was even worthy of publication. It had become an opportunity to go on another journey reliving my travels again. The experience had been an emotional rollercoaster, definitely cathartic and maybe contributed somewhat to the release and forgiveness I was feeling. I had been on some crazy adventures over the last couple of decades. There were many fearful days, wonderful memories as well as a great longing to be living it all again. I felt like I have lived many lives, some sadly now a distant memory and others I'm happy to have survived.

The world keeps turning and people keep moving, all these interactions and people bumping into each other sharing precious moments in time. Life is incredible.

A friend of mine asked me recently, 'How is your self-responsibility?' I felt at times I had not treated myself as a person or an individual who deserved respect. Now in my early forties, I have to make time for myself, increasing my knowledge and understanding, openness for my soul and respect for my body. A quote by Carl Jung which I became aware of through the incredible insights of Dr Jordan B Peterson, "The fool is the precursor to the saviour." He explains it so perfectly; my basic understanding was, unless we are willing to become the fool again, we would never develop. Without becoming a beginner with no knowledge or insight of a subject, it's impossible to learn anything new or evolve to the next level of our own existence. The willingness to start at the bottom had featured many times during my life, through my travels, changing careers, joining the Freemasons and taking on the challenge of building a charity. I could trace the mindset back to my years of skateboarding. Which strangely also features in Dr Peterson's book, *12 Rules for Life* as Rule 11: Do not bother children when they are skateboarding. It's an incredibly difficult sport and one after all these years I am still in love with. It takes its toll mentally and physically. Learning new tricks is hard, all skateboarders have spent many years picking themselves up off the floor. Trying tricks hundreds or even thousands of times before finally landing them. They have spent hours nursing injuries and thinking about how they can become better. None of this stops them from getting back on their board and trying again; the rewards are great, and the pleasure is immense. Simply put, skateboarding teaches you that when learning a new trick, you are always a beginner, you must analyse problems, push your limits, get up and keep trying until you make it.

So, I look to the future with the knowledge I have today. Will I make more mistakes? Yes, of course. Am I willing to start again at the bottom and try something new? Yes, of course. Is life going to be hard? Of course. Am I looking forward to the rest of my journey? Definitely, yes!

Chapter 25
Caroline's legacy

Every milestone that Caroline misses brings sadness. The love and positivity of family and friends enables us to get through it together.

The charity has given us strength and something to work towards, it pushed us out of our comfort zone. We have no way of really knowing whether Caroline would have approved, none of us asked her permission. All we can hope is that she would have been proud, her passion for travel and different cultures has now been combined with safer travel. For a family with no prior experience in the travel or safety industries we have done our best to build something that will help others.

Caroline will always be my little sister. She loved life, was meticulous in her work and very creative in the way she thought. She was feisty and hot-tempered, if she wanted something she would go out and get it. I will always remember her with compassion and love. She will never be forgotten by everyone who knew her. Caroline had nineteen years with us, and when writing this we have nearly had nineteen years without her. It has gone in the blink of an eye. Now she lives with the angels. She will be doing good work in the next world, keeping busy and helping others less fortunate than herself.

Caroline's Rainbow Foundation has been going strong since 2002. I will always give my time freely and willingly to help and support anyone going travelling and wanting to broaden their horizons. I know the benefits and what seeing different places around the world has done for me. The support from our local community has always been above and beyond, completely humbling us with everyone's generosity. We have spoken to thousands of students about the amazing experiences that are out in the world and how they can travel in a safer environment. Our website and social media offer inspiring stories, up to date travel information, safety tips and insights to help prepare travellers to have the best times possible. Building our Safer Travel app brought people together, uniting experienced travellers, researchers, editors and data entry volunteers. It is now a solid, comprehensive resource for anyone travelling.

Where is the charity going in the future?

We filmed our presentations so students can access our important information online. Recently we launched our 'Safer Travel Talk' podcast series, talking to experienced travellers from around the world who all have fantastic stories and safety advice to share.

We are expanding our travel guides, building our new website www.safertravel.org and have started reverifying and transferring all content from our app database to the website. Visitors can now access city specific information directly online as and when they needed it.

We are also developing fully immersive experiences using virtual reality so young travellers can better understand the risks and prepare before they embark on their travels.

We will continue to be inspired, our aim has always been to encourage and inform young travellers who have all the excitement of first-time travel, but need more insight in order to make the best of their adventures.

One strong message that has rung true throughout the years is the message of positivity and encouragement to travel, I certainly have never been put off travel with what happened. We always focus on the benefits of travel and how it opens doors to new possibilities. Our motto of 'follow your dreams' has been with us since the beginning.

The travel industry will always be evolving, I believe the fundamental drive that people have to explore will always be there. For some it's in their DNA and for others it's just meant to be. Our hope is that Caroline's story will encourage people to travel, consider personal safety carefully and hold their life in the highest regard. If we have helped to save just one life, then it has all been worthwhile.

Caroline will always be in our hearts. Today we laugh about the funny things she said. I would like to finish this book by sharing a story that always makes us smile.

On the plane we had our usual fight for the window seat, the sweeties handed out by the cabin crew stopped our ears popping. Once airborne and the seatbelt signs were switched off, Dad asked one of the crew if Caroline and I could go up to the flight deck to see the captain. He said it was for us, but really, we knew he wanted to see the cockpit just as much as we did. Imagine a request like this on today's flight, it would be seen as ridiculous. Once the flight was well underway, one of the cabin crew came over and escorted us to the front of the plane. Opening the door to the flight deck, the captain and first officer were sat at the controls, we nervously went in. I was amazed by all the instruments and dials, it all looked so complicated, I was in awe. Out of the front windscreen I could see we were flying way above the clouds and could see for miles to an endless horizon. The captain asked our names.

'My name is Caroline,' she said.

'Hi Caroline, do you have any questions?' the captain replied with a smile.

Caroline looked out of the front windscreen, thought for a moment and asked, 'Are we going to see God up here?'

'I hope not today!' the Captain replied quick as a flash.

Thank you from the bottom of my heart for reading this book. My hope is that it's been an inspiring and positive read, sometimes ordinary people find themselves in extraordinary circumstances.

Everyone is searching for their pot of gold and it's a very worthy pursuit, but until we realise part of it can only come from travelling around our planet and finding out more about who we are, we will always just be chasing rainbows.

'You only have one life and it's the most precious thing you own, live every day to the fullest, travel safety and always remember to follow your dreams.'

Everything between my sister and I, has always been equal. 50% of the proceeds of this book will go directly to Caroline's Rainbow Foundation.

Thank you for your time and supporting Caroline's Rainbow Foundation.

Appendix

Our parents

Mum and Dad helped shape us into the people we became. The expression 'no one should outlive their own child' is true. The loss of a child I can only imagine must be the hardest thing in the world.

A mother's journey — Strength out of tragedy

After nearly 20 years, we look back on how we coped with our loss and I am a very proud a mother.

Today, as I sit on the swing in our beautiful garden, I have tears rolling down my face. The emptiness still hits the pain in my heart. I watch the butterflies and remember the days, my beautiful daughter loved nature. It is now so many years since Caroline was taken. This week I should be happy, as it's my birthday.

Sweet Caroline how I miss you so. I know you are only a breath away; I hear songs to remind me, I see places to bring back special moments. My heart breaks for all the memories that you would have made in your future. Your life taken by someone who didn't care.

Missing out on a lifetime of what should have been. Her graduation, her wedding, her family and all the things we talked about. I miss your friendship, but over the rainbow you wait, sending me signs to give me strength to continue.

When Caroline's Dad chose to end our twenty-five-year marriage, I thought my future and all our plans were over. Caroline was in the middle of her GCSEs planning to go to university and Richard was working as a chef in the French Alps. Plans can change in an instant. The break-up of a marriage seemed nothing compared with the heart-wrenching thought that someone had destroyed my daughter's life for their own gratification for drugs. Tomorrow is never promised, and you have to enjoy each day.

My parents taught me to be kind and caring and I have always tried to help others. When something so awful happens, through the tears and pain it feels as if there is no way forward. I remember my thoughts were 'I just want to die'. I believe in God and I knew Caroline was in God's arms and was an angel in heaven, but I just wanted to be with there with her.

I wake in the night, my dreams taking over so I couldn't close my eyes again. Shall I write my thoughts down? No, I will tomorrow. It's always tomorrow, but tomorrow I will have forgotten again, as the pain is too much and I go on distracting myself with anything. I look at the clock - as usual 3.00 a.m., a time when many lay awake.

Our stresses come out in our dreams, nightmares or thoughts as we lay awake looking at the ceiling or cuddling Caroline's teddy bear. My nightmare years ago was a stick man running across a bridge, a recurring dream. Now I know why and how we relate our dreams to reality, and knowing it was my daughter running for her life.

As a mother, you want to protect your children, but we are here to encourage and give our children the tools to develop and be independent. When your life is turned upside down you question, why us? But why not? Your inner strength kicks in through your pain and broken heart. As so many parents say, we have to help. No, you can't save the world, but you can make a difference and hopefully through your experiences other families won't have to go through the pain you have.

I will go back to the beginning. 3.00 a.m. there was the banging on the front door. I was already awake. Living on my own I had to go to answer the door, two young police officers, a man and a lady faced me with very sad faces. "Oh no, is it my mother?" I asked. Grandma was ninety-one and lived around the corner. I felt cold but had no idea the next few words would destroy my life. "Caroline has been found dead…"

I screamed. "Are you sure?" Hysteria took over and they tried to comfort me.

Who are these strangers telling me my daughter has gone? When we spoke two days before and she was having the 'time of her life'.

The next few hours were blank. I try to recall, but I don't want to as you don't want to believe you will never see your daughter again, except in a coffin with no resemblance to the precious soul who had so much to offer the world. I ask myself daily what she would have been doing now, her future destroyed and our endless pain lives on.

In the days that followed, we sat around talking: what can we do?

Cuddling Caroline's teddy, I wandered around surrounded by so many friends, flowers, cards and lots of tears. So many parents have suffered loss, what could we do to help? My family were nurses and I was a nanny, training as a nursery nurse it was in my nature to want to support others.

I never had a chance to say goodbye to Caroline. How could this be happening on the other side of the world without her mother to protect her? It felt unreal, as Caroline was in Australia. It felt like she could still be coming home. I had a wonderful, kind, caring, strong-minded daughter for nineteen years, who left a lasting legacy on all she knew and touched but that ache inside as her friends move on will never go away.

I don't want to go to that black hole again, maybe reading this might help people to know that there are lights in life we can enjoy still. For everyone facing grief, there is no time limit, and the loss of every loved one is dealt with in its own unique way. Losing Caroline's godmother, Janet, who I had known all my life and the loss of my half-sister, Jean, were different forms of utter devastation and grief. No-one can say move on, no-one will judge you. Each day, you take a deep breath and put one step forward. You realise the kindness of friends and that it's okay to cry, to scream, to keep running; but take one day at a time.

I had been on my own for five years running the gallery while Alan had been working away, the business was up for sale. Wendy, a close friend, knew David who was a Manager at Tesco's and they had worked together for thirty years. She thought David and I would be perfect together, although opposites we complimented each other. David came into the gallery and asked me out for lunch to discuss business.

That morning I got a text from Caroline saying have a lovely time she was very excited for me, did he like shopping? Oh yes! Always punctual, he arrived at 12.30 p.m. Australia is nine hours ahead and Caroline died at exactly the same time David was collecting me, but of course we didn't find out until the following morning.

David and I had lunch at a local Italian restaurant, we knew immediately we were soulmates and perfect for each other. Italy became important to us, as Caroline loved Venice. I had taken her there after our trip to Florence, where I had worked as a nanny for a lovely family. She said she would visit with her boyfriend, as it was not romantic visiting with your mother. It was still a wonderful and special trip to treasure. David and I went to Italy for our honeymoon two years later and returned to Venice to light a candle for Caroline.

The morning after our first lunch date, I had an early phone call from David to say he would come over but needed to know my address. Already close friends had arrived, having just met him he came into my life and gave me so much support and care. My initial thought that he was my soulmate proved to be right.

Countless times I have driven from where we live to where Caroline rests. I cried all the way home and just wanted to hug her. Following a car, there's a sign, a number plate 'CAZ' which was her nickname. "I'm around Mum," she is saying.

On my sad days I cannot remember her voice, but on happier days I remember her smile and laugh and her sense of fun. Richard taught her to cook as she was not the practical one, but she thought it would be useful when she went to university. When I came in from work, she was the one who cooked a meal for me. She used to love going to Grandma's to have chicken dinners and luckily Grandma lived around the corner. My mother was like my best friend and was always there to support us.

I have to have a belief in trying to help other people, it's what Caroline would have wanted. God gave us the strength to start the charity as we felt we must do something positive. We don't want others to go through the same pain and we wanted to do something for Caroline. We tell ourselves that we want our children to grow up and be independent, to challenge the world and make a difference, not expecting the difference Caroline made from the day she came into our world.

Caroline's Rainbow Foundation emerged and will continue to remember a special young lady and push us forward to help other young travellers to be aware, to follow their dreams but to do it safely.

Here we are with so much support from family, friends and people who believe in what we do. A lasting legacy as our next generation face a difficult world, but there is still beauty all around us. Take the time to stop and smell the roses.

Our pyramid started. I always felt it was important to build on a good foundation. I did many talks, TV and radio interviews and magazine articles. BBC Radio York took us on as charity of the year. I remember sitting at the Heart of Yorkshire Awards 2003 as a runner up with David and Richard.

We were at the same table as the Calendar Girls and Jane Tomlinson, who had all overcome adversity. We are all driven people.

I had the honour to meet Diana Lamplugh from the Suzy Lamplugh Trust, who had been running her charity for some years. Having someone so experienced was a great help. Her words of advice were to take time to grieve and in the early days she always supported us. We did a few events together with an overall message to stay safe.

A few years later, a great honour for the charity was to have an invite to a garden party at Buckingham Palace as recognition for everyone involved in our charity. It was a wonderful day David and I will always remember. I know Caroline would have been very proud.

You feel like you're on a hamster's wheel pushing and pushing, round and round. Only years later did I look back and think we have achieved something positive.

The memories in your heart remain. Caroline was such an animal lover, stopping to look in the pet shop on our way to school. She persuaded us to bring home goldfish, hamsters, mice, gerbils, guinea pigs and rabbits. This led us to taking Jude, our black labrador, from the RSPCA. At fifteen, Caroline went for long walks after school with Jude and her close friends. As she was a rescue dog and was already an old dog, she passed the day Caroline finished college, she was there for us when we really needed her. Throughout her life, Caroline gave to others. We have had letters of thanks from friends who, unknowingly, she had helped in different ways.

Caroline was excited after studying psychology at college and getting top marks. The day her results came through she got a place at Manchester University to study psychology. Her dream was to be a criminal psychologist in New York. Those words haunt me, she wanted to go on her gap year to New York, but we felt New York was too violent and her friends were going to Australia. I remember waving her off at York station with her friend Sarah's mum. Caroline did not want me to go to the airport, her boyfriend Ian accompanied her, she said how brave I was not to cry. The loneliness without her meant many tears flowed.

Richard has been my strength and support, he stayed strong for me. We shared our pain, but he kept so much of his pain to himself. As a mother I feel guilty, but I know we all had to deal with it in our own way.

I look back over the years and realise with all the talk of mental health how I have coped with depression. The questions of why me, why us? We want life to be perfect, unfortunately it rarely is but these things make us stronger. I am lucky to have a strong circle of friends who have supported us every step of the way, all I can say is a heartfelt thank you.

As so many parents who cope with loss say, we do not want anyone else to go through the pain we have gone through.

Richard and his father went out for the trial of the man who took our precious daughter away from us. I couldn't face it. You try to be brave, but to go to the other side of the world is another thing entirely. I wanted to stay in my comfort zone. Richard had his father for support and I kept in touch. Eventually, I felt well enough to make the long journey to Australia.

We arrived in Melbourne on April 10th — the day Caroline died. We went and lit a candle. Everywhere we go around the world we always light a candle for her and David's late wife, Barbara. We went on to Brisbane and were kindly met by Megan and Colin, who had worked so hard through the Foreign Office on our behalf. They invited us to stay. So much kindness. They drove us up to Bundaberg. We called in at Childers and the Palace Backpackers, where so many had lost their lives in a fire and saw a memorial for them, and I remember thinking it is not only me suffering a loss.

We went to Bundaberg and met the detectives who worked so hard for two years to find the murderer. It had obviously affected them so much too as Bundaberg is such a quiet place. The mayor and other wonderful people were there to greet us. We were donated flowers to lay under the bridge, which was so painful. As I stood there, the place Caroline's life ended, I wondered was she in pain? Was it instant? Even those seconds when she fell, what were her thoughts? All of her future gone in a flash. It was a long drop; how many seconds were her frightening thoughts? I couldn't comfort her as I stood there looking up at the high bridge. Everyone was so kind, but the pain was so unbearable to see how Caroline had no chance with such a brutal act.

After a few days, Megan and Colin drove us up to the rainforest, a beautiful day and all the way I said Caroline will send us a rainbow and she did as we arrived and said goodbye to our wonderful hosts and friends. My caring husband had arranged for us to go on a cruise and as I learnt to snorkel, I ran out of the sea crying as I had seen a rainbow fish.

We had six weeks in Australia and finished up in Sydney. As I saw the famous bridge, I burst into tears, as we have a photo of Caroline there, smiling and so happy. So many memories we will always treasure, the kindness of people will stay in our hearts. So much pain in the world. I wanted to change the suffering, a smile, a small word of kindness or support helps someone, we can only do our best.

We continue to develop our charity with safer travel in mind. Her legacy is changing, inspiring people as well as informing people, whatever age they choose to travel. It is such a wonderful opportunity to learn about different cultures, meet wonderful people and see amazing sights. We talk to young people; they are excited about their future. No one wants to stop them following their dreams, just to prioritise their safety.

We hope this story about Caroline will help others to see light at the end of the tunnel as helping other people has given us the strength to continue. She was so special and gave everything to so many people. I am, and always will be, a very proud mother. She has now been cruelly taken from us but the years in between gave us joy, heartache, pride and sometimes exasperation but her character shone as she worked so hard to achieve her goals. She didn't let time slip by as she had to fill so much into her short life.

Her energy drove us and still does to provide a lasting legacy so she will not be forgotten, giving us a purpose through the happy and difficult years. She brought so much joy to us and her friends. She left a big hole in our lives and each day that hole stays empty as she is not here.

Until we meet again, my darling daughter.

David's story
Such a difficult time, I had just met this wonderful, kind caring lady. She was then utterly destroyed by the worst news anyone could ever have, to lose a child in such violent circumstances was devastating.

The early morning phone call came from our friend Wendy. I heard the horrendous news and immediately wanted to be there for Marjorie. 6:00 a.m. news travels fast, I realised how many press and media were outside wanting information. I met the Police Liaison Officer Richard Crinnion, the first hurdle was to speak on Marjorie's behalf, as she was inconsolable. I gave a statement and they gave their word they would leave the family in peace.

Marjorie was a warm beautiful lady, who took my heart instantly, why should this happen as we had only just found hope in our lives. I could understand a little of her pain, my late wife and I couldn't have family but we both went through great suffering as I watched her die of cancer.

The next thought was to support the family, I could do the practical things. Speaking to the dentist regarding dental records to confirm it was Caroline. After a difficult conversation, I was then able to send the required details through a secure line to the Foreign Office. I was in regular contact with Megan Hunt regarding Caroline. After the awful phone call from the police in France, Richard spoke to us and said he would drive home. I offered to collect him from Liverpool Airport. It was the first time I met Richard as we faced the awful journey back to York. It was not how I expected to meet Marjorie's son, during the journey I did feel we had a connection.

I was able to devote time to helping and meeting all of Marjorie's friends. I felt that I couldn't leave everyone, although it was hard to be involved as an outsider who had never met Caroline. Did the family want me there? I wasn't sure but I felt compelled to help. I felt Marjorie needed my support. Between myself, her mother and Marjorie's friends we made sure they had everything they needed. Marjorie's mother Nora and I understood each other. As an ex-smoker she asked me for a puff on my cigarette without telling Marjorie.

The funeral of course I left to the family and was only there for support — I pushed Nora around in the wheelchair.

Over the following weeks as we talked about Caroline, I felt I was beginning to know what a sparkling character she was, she was spoken of so well by all her friends. The number of sympathy cards and flowers arriving, I knew I was around wonderful people.

Marjorie and Richard were talking about how they could honour Caroline and had the idea for founding Caroline's Rainbow Foundation. I thought I would be able to help. After years working in Tesco as a manager I had retired early, missing work and my colleagues, I could use my expertise in a new way to make a difference. I had been involved with so many charities and fundraised incentives throughout my working life I had many transferrable skills. Marjorie and I travelled to many TV studios and interviews, where I was able to offer my support. We also hosted many fundraising events for the charity.

As I fell in love with Marjorie over the following weeks and months, I asked her to marry me; we were married two years later. I am very proud of both my wife and stepson and everything we have achieved.

A father's story — Memories live in your heart forever

I am proud of my children, as a parent, I always will be. Memories of a time that has past will always be ingrained in my heart, good and bad times. For Marjorie and me, our children were the biggest part of our lives together.

My son Richard and I have written extraordinary amounts about what happened in the year of 2002. We have discussed at length the therapeutic value of writing; in the subsequent years, writing has helped us understand more about our grief and the devastating loss of Caroline.

I have an old mobile phone I had back in 2002. The phone is old and battered, worthless in monetary value, but priceless to me. It still holds texts messages from Caroline when she texted me from Oz (as she called it) Her last message, 'I will be in touch, love you Dad'. Simple words but meant so much.

Richard and I said goodbye to Caroline in a tragic yet loving way, holding her hand in the chapel of rest. I placed a wooden cross in Caroline's hand and a gold one in Richard's to mark a connection with past and future. Life always goes on, but from that moment in a very different way.

I have been an artist all my life. When Caroline was young, we used to paint in my studio in York, she also had a gift for art and was very creative. She took Art GCSE, which made me very proud. Her work was great, done with feeling and emotion. When I was fifteen years old, I won a painting competition, the prize was an easel, which I still use today. I thought a fitting tribute to Caroline would be to help art students at her old school to develop their talent. Both Richard and Caroline attended Huntington School which was only a short distance from our home. We had the idea for and created the Stuttle Painting Bursary. A monetary prize was to be given to the top art students of the year, so they could continue their artistic endeavours. My hope was to inspire them to enter into the arts as a career and give them a boost to start their journey.

The special remembered times always in my heart and mind were trips Caroline and I took in our motor caravan to the Yorkshire Dales, the Yorkshire Moors and Highlands of Scotland. Caroline and I would pack up supplies for a few days and go and paint. On a couple of occasions our dog Jude also came with us. One place I remember in particular was Loch Lomond, Caroline and I stopped at a lovely campsite by the side of the loch and painted together. I still have those paintings in our studio. It was a wonderful time which I try to remember often.

One of our Yorkshire Dales trips was extra special, we stayed in Mucker and painted rainbows. Just beautiful at the time, but even more special with the charity Richard and Marjorie created and the significance rainbows hold. I painted and Caroline sat beside me, she had to do her homework for school. She was one of the top students and I always admired her work ethic.

The last painting I made in the Yorkshire Dales, was of New House, Caroline was in Australia at the time. Driving home along the beautiful country roads I saw three rainbows. I wrote about it in my book *One Hundred Days of a Father's Mourning*.

I now can't do anything more for my daughter but remember the good times we all had as a family before it was savagely destroyed by a mindless act. I would not wish any parent or sibling to go through what we have been through and will continue to go through for the rest of our lives. Our pain will never end or be forgotten.

At the age of eighty, which I am now, I have had a full and rich life in so many ways. One act of evil had tainted my years, but this is a cup from which I do not want to drink from. I try to stay positive, some days this is harder than others, Caroline's death can sometimes seem only a moment ago.

Remembering the blossom in the springtime of life. This was all Caroline had, she was young, full of energy and life. It brings me some comfort to know she was having the best of times. I am now nearing the end of my lifetime on this beautiful planet. There is only one thing I would ask from the almighty spirit; pray take away the pain of a parent whose child was murdered.

A big thank you to Richard, the author of this book. I am so proud to call him my son.

Caroline's friends

Caroline in life and death inspired people. Their positive memory of Caroline prevailed. When writing this book, I approached some of Caroline's friends them asking if they would like to write something in memory of her.

Sarah Taylor (Holiday)

'Caroline and I had been friends throughout high school, but our friendship really blossomed when we both decided to go to Sixth Form College instead of staying on at school, as most in our year group did. From that time on, we became joined at the hip. What I remember most from those precious years was laughter. We would get up really early to get two buses across town to get to college until Caroline learned to drive, but despite being bleary eyed we would chat incessantly and laugh the whole way there. This earned us our nickname of Duracell Bunnies by one of our fellow bus passengers, as our energy seemed boundless. We both kept diaries during this time but because so many little things made us laugh each day, we bought our own special notebook (our Funny Book) just to capture them all. We were exploring early adulthood and our new freedoms together. Going clubbing for the first time and realising that the most fun part was actually getting ready together beforehand in one of our houses, and the Chinese we would inevitably end up getting at the end of the night.

After having dreamt of our gap year for so long, I remember the surreal feeling when we finally arrived in Sydney. I suddenly felt so small (Caroline and I were both not much over 5ft — our backpacks were almost as big as we were!) and far from home. But we soon found our 'new normal' together and got into the travelling groove.

We remained inseparable from the second we woke up in whatever hostel we were staying in, throughout the day's adventures until going to sleep again. We packed so many experiences into our months in Australia. One of our favourite places had been the chilled-out town of Byron Bay, where we got up to see the sunrise at its most easterly point, spent hours relaxing on the beach, learned to surf and took slow walks just chatting and soaking in the atmosphere. It was on one of those walks that I remember us wistfully reflecting on our travels so far as well as sharing our hopes and dreams for our futures. The sun was just beginning to set, and a street performer was singing The Beatles' *Let it Be*, the song that would be played at Caroline's funeral just weeks later.

To this day, it still overwhelms me to realise how suddenly and violently life can shift. How a day can begin like any other but end in tragedy. On the evening of Caroline's murder, I remember we had written a grocery list for the next day. Planning meals and doing our own food shopping was still a bit of a novelty for us so we had given it a title — "Caz and Rah's Shopping List". Caroline called me Rah since everyone else abbreviated my name to Sar. The more unusual "Rah" was a tribute to the special status of our friendship! But soon that innocent list of pasta, bread and milk was to become gathered up by police in the aftermath of Caroline's death. The days that followed are still a blur. Hours spent being interviewed by the police. Identifying Caroline's body. Being taken somewhere peaceful for an hour or so by a member of the embassy. I remember on the plane journey home they were showing Legally Blonde 2. Having loved watching the first one together, Caroline and I had looked forward to the sequel. Since we would never now get to see it together, I watched the film for us both. To others on the plane who knew who I was, it must have seemed an odd thing to be watching in the circumstances without knowing why I was doing it.

What I would want another young person to know who is going through loss or trauma is that there is no single right way to feel or be. Grief doesn't follow a neat line. And I would want them to have self-compassion for their own pain — in whatever way it manifests. That's been a big lesson for me as for years I would feel guilty whenever I reached a certain milestone that Caroline never would — like graduating from university or getting married. But Caroline had such a big and kind heart that it feels more meaningful to honour that by living fully and joyfully rather than dwell on "what ifs".'

Laura Lister (Roberts)

'I will always remember Caroline so fondly. I actually met Caroline when we were about fifteen years old, although we went to different schools, we had mutual friends so our paths crossed regularly at Fibbers, a local music venue, where we would both go to see bands such as Vacant Goldfish and Baggy Blue Sky.

We first became good friends on our enrolment day at York Sixth Form College. We ended up sitting next to each other in the queue. Caroline had come with her mum, Marjorie, and the three of us sat and chatted and were surprised to find out we had chosen the same three A-levels! It was from then that we realised how similar we were, and it became an on-going joke between us. We made arrangements to meet on the first day of college as Caroline was moving over from Huntington and didn't know many people. I met her and Sarah on Tadcaster Road and the three of us walked into college together.

Caroline was nervous going in on the first day, but she soon made lots of friends with her bubbly, positive and friendly nature. I remember Caroline being so kind, gentle and humble. It's funny as I can still hear her saying, 'Hiya Laur' each day as I walked into the room where we had English Literature together.

We always made sure we sat together in these lessons so that we could read the books together, as well as have a gossip. We both really enjoyed English, especially those lessons with our tutor Huw, who we both thought so highly of. He sent me a card when Caroline died and had such kind words to say about her. He made a comment even then about our friendship (and chatting in lessons when we should have been reading *Catch-22*) and how similar he thought we were, right down to our handwriting as he said he could never tell our essays apart to look at them.

We spent two years at college becoming close friends, spending lots of time together in lessons and in the college canteen. Caz would sometimes come to my house after college and meet her mum there, so Marjorie could walk their dog Jude on the Knavesmire near my house, giving us more time to chat! We also enjoyed shopping together, I remember Caroline liked Warehouse, so we often went in there to try on clothes for the latest planned night out. There were of course lots of fun evenings in town too, usually ending up at The Gallery nightclub. I remember being on a night out with Caroline and Sarah, we were laughing about the height difference between us. I would tower over them both and always called them the munchkins.

When I went straight to university in Chester, the following September, Caz kept in touch and I often heard from her via emails and MSN messenger — that was all we had back then. It was great to hear from her in Australia, learning all about her travels and how much she was enjoying herself with Sarah, even meeting up with our friends Ben and Jimmy. I took comfort in the fact that she was having the time of her life and she was so content, happy and relaxed in those last few months. We made plans to meet once she got home and I looked forward to her being close as she had chosen Manchester to go to university the following September.

I will always remember the day I found out. I was in York with my friend and my mum called me, as I was home for the Easter holidays. She knew I had been on messenger to Caroline only a few days before. I remember just feeling like I was in a bubble, I couldn't take it in. I walked down the high street and there she was on the front page of every newspaper. I went home and the first thing I did was to check my emails and there was one from Caroline. It was so difficult to read knowing what had happened. I still find it hard to grasp that just a few hours after her writing those last words to me, the unthinkable had happened. It took me a long time to process it, as it did all of us, and even though we were only close friends for just a few years she has left a lasting impression on me and I am lucky to have the memories I do.

When Caroline died, Ben and I went to see her mum, Marjorie. I remember feeling so nervous as I didn't know what to say to her or Richard, but I am so glad I did as Marjorie has been in my life ever since and I think Caroline would have liked that. When the time came, I helped Marjorie sort through Caroline's room. I remember finding her copy of Catch-22 and opening it to see her familiar handwriting and all the notes that we had written to each other in the back when we couldn't get away with talking in class. Marjorie kindly let me keep it and I still have it today, a very treasured memories of our time together.

I will always remember Caroline and the fun college years that we shared. I was envious of her taking a gap year and pursuing her dream, often wishing I had made the same choice. It is so heart-breaking to comprehend that her dream was cut short and her future taken away. Marjorie and Richard set up Caroline's Rainbow Foundation to try and ensure that this didn't happen again. They wanted to encourage young travellers to go and see the world while providing them with the information they need to stay safe and I know Caroline would be very proud of them both and the legacy that she has left behind.'

Sophie Bloom

'I remember in Caroline's room she had a poster of sunflowers, and if I had to choose a flower that best represented her, it would certainly be that. Caroline's positivity and warmth shone through; so much of our time at school was spent laughing and smiling. She was one of the kindest, most generous and thoughtful people I have ever had the privilege to know.

Particular memories that stand out for me are when she gave me one of her rabbits (she was a natural with animals and took such good care of them) and when we made up a song about food in German, it wasn't homework, but we performed it in front of the class in hysterics. Despite my terrible memory, I can still recall all of the lyrics and actions to our awful song!

Losing Caroline has made me so much more grateful for life and the people around me. I went travelling after university, much of it alone, and I often reminded myself to be adventurous, brave and enjoy every moment.

At each major milestone, I wonder if she would have been doing something similar. In 2017, my husband (who also went to school and worked with Caroline) and I were blessed with a baby girl. We named her Francesca Caroline, in memory of our incredible friend. We have since had a second daughter and if our girls are half as caring and passionate as Caroline was, then I will be a very proud mother indeed.'

Sarah

'I feel very lucky to have had such an amazing childhood friend. Caz was probably more of the leader between the two of us and even as a child she encouraged me to step out of my comfort zone. I was always a bit in awe of her; she was always cooler, prettier, funnier. I always thought the world of her and was proud to call her my friend. We lived very close to each other, but it wasn't a forced friendship — we naturally came together and had a lot of shared interests.

One of the things that I miss the most is talking about the memories that only the two of us shared. Shortly after what happened, I realised there were so many things that I would never get to laugh about with Caz again, or simply say "remember that time when..." These are the things that no one else experienced and will forever stay hidden.

I would always say that I had a happy childhood and the predominant part of this was Caz. She took us on adventures, we made up lots of terrible dances and we explored our local area; things always felt very carefree. She was curious and creative. She is one of those rare people that you never heard anything negative about.

Caz, like many teenage girls, had her insecurities but she was always truly beautiful. I still miss her and also miss the future she would have had. It still doesn't feel real that she is no longer here and that will remain infinitely and incredibly sad. However, how lucky we all were to have had her in our lives… and in so many ways she still is; in our memories, in our present lives and in every rainbow.'

Ben Fogarty

'Caroline was a marvel. She had the most incredible smile. It is often said that someone's smile can light up a room. Caroline's smile could light up your soul. I only met Caroline in September 2000. Disgruntled with our respective A-Level choices, we had both made the bold choice to drop one of our current subjects at the start of Year 13 and opted to take up history as a night class at the local college instead.

It was hard work, three hours a week sat in a room of fully-fledged adults (we, or at least I, certainly did not consider ourselves so) listening to long lectures about Soviet Russia and Nazi Germany. We sat next to each other, and I would furiously copy Caroline's notes in the hope it would help me to absorb what was being said. Every week we would have a fifteen-minute break, and this for me was a haven. So wrought was I with all the insecurities of adolescence, and so kind, honest and mature were Caroline's ears and words that we developed a wonderful friendship. We would talk about all of our hopes, dreams, our fears.

We discussed our plans for university, agreeing not only to attend the same university in Manchester, but also the same halls of residence. We also spoke of our plans for travelling the following year, whilst my friend and I were going to be in Australia, Caroline and Sarah would be there too.

In a short space of time, Caroline had become my best friend, and I fully expected that it would be a friendship that would last forever.

In 2002, after my friend and I had been to South Africa and New Zealand, we finally arrived in Australia, where we quickly got in contact with Caroline and Sarah. We spent an incredible, few days in Byron Bay, and later in Surfer's Paradise. We felt free, and so full of the optimism of youth — we were discovering that life was a wonderful thing, and we were truly excited about all that the future held.

When I found out about Caroline's death, I was devastated. We were due to meet her in Bundaberg just a couple of days after that fateful night of April 10. We literally could not believe that she had been killed — all of that joy we shared had been ripped away, and a life full of promise was gone.

I embarked upon the long journey home, and over the next seventy-two hours, I made a number of promises to myself, all of which were taken in Caroline's honour: I had often confided in Caroline that I wished to be an actor, but I never would because I was too scared. When I left university, I went to drama school and became an actor, a career which lasted a number of years and met with some success — all of which I owe to her. I vowed to always continue travelling, no matter what, as I knew that is what she would have wanted — for us to continue to seek and experience new cultures and adventure, and I have since been fortunate enough to visit India, the Far East, the Middle East, East Africa and most of Europe. And I also promised that I would always say 'yes'… to everything.

Caroline was so very openminded, optimistic and enthusiastic — saying yes epitomises those attributes, and whilst it may have got me into a few scrapes… it has also enabled me to see the world through a lens which is so much more positive than I would have otherwise managed. Finally, Caroline's life taught me so very much about the world. Her passing was a tragedy, but her memory is a joy, and I live with that joy today, tomorrow and always, by striving to do what is right and good. I miss her dearly.'

Dedications and insight

Megan Hunt
Vice Consul & Head of Consular Services

The Foreign and Commonwealth Office supports British families across the world when tragedies happen. In April 2002, I was the consular officer that took the call from the Queensland Police to say that Caroline had been murdered. I remember immediately thinking how sad it was to have lost a young woman with so much to live for and in such awful circumstances. I also remember thinking that my actions, in informing London colleagues who would in turn contact the Yorkshire Police to deliver the sad news, meant that this family's life would be impacted forever.

I have met many families at times when they face unimaginable grief, but it is rare, quite understandably, that families are able to take a dreadful event and put their energies into the positivity of keeping others safe. Yet this is what Richard and Marjorie chose to do with Caroline's Rainbow Foundation. In their description of Caroline in their own thoughts and words I came to have an understanding of the person she was. I never had the privilege of meeting her but having come to know her family over the years, as they continue to honour her memory through travel safety awareness, I feel a sense of just how special she was and through their vision continues to be.

Richard Crinnion
Detective Superintendent, West Yorkshire Police

I remember the day well. I was a uniformed Police Sergeant based in York, and in the early hours of the 11th April 2002, I was contacted by the Force's Family Liaison Coordinator who asked me to contact the Foreign and Commonwealth Office regarding a death of a British student. I had volunteered to become a Family Liaison Officer as an additional role and had been deployed on a number of occasions to support major crime and homicide investigations. Whilst often over-dramatised on TV, it is a role I found both extremely demanding and also very rewarding. The journey of grief experienced by families along with the search for justice was always difficult to manage, there were never any winners! Every deployment being unique and having its own challenges, this one was very unusual.

In the early hours, some uniformed colleagues had delivered one of the worst jobs of a police officer, about the death of Caroline. My initial tasks were to talk the family through what was known, the process of identification, post-mortem, coroner's enquiries, media advice and how they can assist the investigation, these things very few people think about until the worse happens. All my previous deployments were within North Yorkshire so communication with the key individuals was simple.

The time delay, political interests through the FCO and increased media attention made this deployment more difficult and very frustrating for the family. It took a few days to establish contact with the investigators and obtain information about the incident that led to Caroline's death. I soon established a rapport and communication channels with the lead investigators Dave Batt and Megan Hunt and carried out some early investigative enquiries. One task included identifying a bag that was in Caroline's possession that could not be found, this was key to a witness appeal as the offender was believed to be in possession of it. We were able to locate the receipt for this bag Caroline purchased before she left and although the bag had stopped being produced, the manufacturers were able to create another. By this time those that had travelled with Caroline and witnesses to the incident had returned home. I obtained witness statements from them and ensured they were also provided with the necessary information, support and advice.

On the 18th April 2002, I remember taking Richard and Ian (Caroline's boyfriend at the time) over to collect Caroline from Manchester airport. It was essential for the local coroner to have continuity, legal documentation in place with the FCO and the identity confirmed. The next day I took Alan to the hospital to formally identify Caroline, something that all parents should never have to do.

Over the following months and years, I got to know the family well. How Marjorie was determined to set up a Foundation to support young people who wanted to travel like Caroline, how supportive and helpful David was in many small but important ways, how Richard was determined to get justice but ensure the events did not stop him adventuring and making a success of his life and how Alan used his paintings to help him grieve and find solace. I remained in contact with the investigative developments who had worked tirelessly to identify a suspect and made an arrest. In 2004 the case was progressing to a trial at court. It became apparent that the prosecutors were keen to get the UK witnesses to attend, as well as myself. The jury needed to understand the impact this had had on the family thousands of miles away in the UK. I travelled over to Bundaberg with the witnesses and met the local police, prosecutors and people involved in the investigation. As with any murder trial this is a very impactive time for witnesses having to relive the experience. The trial concluded with the guilty verdict and sentencing of Ian Douglas Previte to fifteen years imprisonment. Certain events in my police career will never be

348

forgotten, this is most certainly one of those! Every year on the 10th April I am reminded, not only as this is the anniversary of Caroline's death, but it also happens to be the birthday of my daughter (spooky) who herself is approaching the age of Caroline when she left on her travels. I am also reminded of the excellent work of Caroline's Rainbow Foundation in supporting others to travel safe. Also, I always take a moment when passing the memorial in Castlegate which I took Sgt Dave Batt to when he visited in 2007.'

David Batt
MP for Bundaberg

Bundaberg is a beautiful city located in regional Queensland, about four hours north of the capital Brisbane. Home to approximately 50,000 people, Bundaberg is the Southern Gateway to the Great Barrier Reef and is regarded as the 'food bowl' of Queensland. Our rich volcanic soils and amazing year-round climate make the Bundaberg region the perfect place to grow almost any produce you can think of. Our impressive agricultural and horticultural industry is one of the many reasons Bundaberg is a popular backpacker destination. On any given day, there are more than 3000 people in Bundaberg. They come for the weather, the beaches and the job opportunities — picking small crops to fund their Australian adventure. In April 2002, Caroline Stuttle was one of the thousands of backpackers temporarily calling Bundaberg home.

I was born and raised in Bundaberg and after working away for a few years, I returned in 1994 and continued my work as a detective. Like any city, we have our share of criminals, but crime was not 'rife', and people generally felt safe. However, in June 2000, our region had the international spotlight thrust on us when fifteen backpackers were killed in an arson attack on the Palace Backpackers in the small town of Childers, just a short drive from Bundaberg. I was one of the detectives tasked with investigating the fire, successfully arresting and prosecuting the perpetrator. No one ever imagined something like this happening in the sleepy town of Childers and it's certainly had a lasting impact.

Two years after the Childers' backpacker fire, on the night of April 10th 2002, I received a call from my Officer in Charge. He told me a body had been found under the Burnett River Traffic Bridge, located in the centre of

Bundaberg. I was tasked with being the lead detective on the case, alongside my partner Detective Russell Williams.

When it was identified that British backpacker Caroline Stuttle was the victim of a horrific murder, Bundaberg was once again subjected to public and international media scrutiny. The Police Commissioner gave an assurance that Caroline's murder would be investigated until the killer was found. There were no eyewitnesses, no suspects and no DNA evidence linking a killer to the scene, making for a very difficult investigation.

Homicide Squad detectives assisted in the major incident room and the investigation continued every day for more than ten months. Hundreds of statements and leads were taken and followed until the murderer Ian Douglas Previte, a thirty-year-old homeless drug addict, was finally identified.

After a long, intense investigation involving hundreds of police, various government departments, prison staff and prison inmates, the Supreme Court jury finally brought about a guilty verdict — some eighteen months after the crime was committed.

After working on Caroline's case every day over those eighteen months, the day Previte was found guilty was one of the best in my twenty-three-year career as a copper. No other investigation had ever become personal to me before, but this one really made me think about my two young daughters and how much of their life I had been missing over this time.

Before and during the trial I kept in contact with Caroline's brother Richard and I was over the moon when he told me he and his mum, Marjorie were going to start Caroline's Rainbow Foundation, a charity to assist backpackers to stay safe when travelling abroad.

While in England for a Rotary Study Exchange in 2007, I was honoured to meet Richard and Marjorie in York and learnt more about the Foundation and visited the rainbow mosaic and tree planted in Caroline's memory. As a police officer, who had never been involved with a victim's family before, I was so nervous to meet them. But, since then we have kept in regular contact and I have followed the fantastic work of the Foundation and was honoured to arrange the instillation of a rainbow mosaic in Bundaberg's Buss Park, a location many backpackers visit every day.

Nothing will ever take away the pain of losing Caroline, but the work Richard and Marjorie have done since 2002 is an amazing and wonderful tribute to their sister and daughter.'